Emotional First Aid

Emotional First Aid

IIIIIIIIIIIIIIIIIIIIIIIIIIIII

PRACTICAL STRATEGIES FOR TREATING
FAILURE, REJECTION, GUILT, AND OTHER
EVERYDAY PSYCHOLOGICAL INJURIES

Guy Winch, Ph.D.

HUDSON
STREET
PRESS

HUDSON STREET PRESS
Published by the Penguin Group
Penguin Group (USA) Inc., 375 Hudson Street
New York, New York 10014 USA

USA | Canada | UK | Ireland | Australia | New Zealand | India | South Africa |China
Penguin Books Ltd, Registered Offices: 80 Strand, London WC2R 0RL, England
For more information about the Penguin Group visit penguin.com

First published by Hudson Street Press, a member of Penguin Group (USA) Inc.

First Printing, July 2013

REGISTERED TRADEMARK—MARCA REGISTRADA
HUDSON
STREET
PRESS

LIBRARY OF CONGRESS CATALOGING-IN-PUBLICATION DATA

Winch, Guy.
    Emotional first aid : practical strategies for treating failure, rejection, guilt, and
other everyday psychological injuries / Guy Winch, Ph.D.
        pages cm
    Includes bibliographical references and index.
    ISBN 978-1-59463-120-7
    1. Self-help techniques. 2. Emotions. 3. Mental health. I. Title.
    BF632.W556 2013
    158.1—dc23   2013005852

Set in Minion Pro
Printed in the United States of America
10   9   8   7   6   5   4   3   2   1

PUBLISHER'S NOTE
While the author has made every effort to provide accurate telephone numbers and
Internet addresses at the time of publication, neither the publisher nor the author as-
sumes any responsibility for errors, or for changes that occur after publication. Further,
the publisher does not have any control over and does not assume any responsibility for
author or third-party Web sites or their content.

Contents

Introduction

Ask a ten-year-old what you should do if you catch a cold and the child would immediately recommend getting into bed and drinking chicken soup. Ask what you should do if you get a cut on your knee and the child would advocate cleaning it (or using antibacterial ointment) and bandaging it. Children also know that if you break a bone in your leg you need to get a cast on it so it mends correctly. If you then asked why these steps were necessary they would tell you that treating such injuries helps them heal and prevents them from getting worse, that colds can turn into pneumonia, that cuts can become infected, and that if broken bones heal incorrectly you'll have trouble walking once the cast comes off. We teach our children how to take care of their bodies from a very young age and they usually learn such lessons well.

But ask an adult what you should do to ease the sharp pain of rejection, the devastating ache of loneliness, or the bitter disappointment of failure and the person would know little about how to treat these common psychological injuries. Ask what you should do to recover from low self-esteem or loss and trauma and adults would be equally challenged. Ask how you might deal with intrusive ruminations or nagging guilt and you are likely to be met with sheepish looks, feet shuffling, and a pointed effort to change the subject.

Some might confidently suggest the best remedy is to talk about our feelings with friends or family members, certain that no mental health professional in his or her right mind would object to talking about feelings. But while discussing our feelings might offer relief in some situations, it can actually be damaging in others. Pointing out these dangers usually causes another round of sheepish looks, feet shuffling, and a pointed effort to change the subject.

The reason we take little to no purposeful action to treat the psychological wounds we sustain in daily life is because we lack the tools with which to manage such experiences. True, we could seek the counsel of a mental health professional in such situations, but doing so is often impractical, as most of the psychological wounds we sustain in life are not serious enough to warrant professional intervention. Just as we wouldn't pitch a tent outside our family doctor's waiting room at the first sign of a cough or sniffle, we can't run to a therapist every time we get rejected by a romantic prospect or whenever our boss yells at us.

But while every household has a medicine cabinet full of bandages, ointments, and pain relievers for treating basic *physical* maladies, we have no such medicine cabinet for the minor *psychological* injuries we sustain in daily life. And sustain them we do, just as frequently as we do physical ones. Each of the psychological wounds covered in this book is extremely common and each of them is emotionally painful and potentially psychologically damaging. Yet, until now, we've had no conventional means to ease the pains, soothe the aches, and relieve the distresses of these events despite the regularity with which they occur in our lives.

Applying emotional first aid to such injuries can prevent many of them from affecting our mental health and emotional well-being going forward. Indeed, many of the diagnosable psychological conditions for which we seek professional treatment could be prevented if we applied emotional first aid to our wounds when we first sustained them. For example, a ruminative tendency can quickly grow into anxiety and depression, and experiences of failure and rejection can easily lead to erosions in our self-esteem. Treating such injuries not only accelerates their healing but also helps prevent complications from developing and mitigates the severity of any that do arise.

Of course, when the psychological injury is serious, emotional first aid treatments should not replace seeing a mental health professional any more than having a well-stocked medicine cabinet abolishes the need for physicians and hospitals. But while we know our limitations when it comes to our physical health, the same is not true of our mental health. Most of us can recognize when a cut is deep enough to require stitches, we can usually tell the difference between a swollen bruise and a broken bone, and we tend to know when we're dehydrated to the point of needing an infusion of plasma. But when it comes to our psychological wounds, we lack not only the wherewithal to do anything about them but also the ability to identify when they require professional intervention. As a result, we often neglect our psychological wounds until they become severe enough to impair our functioning. We would never leave a cut on our knee unattended until it compromised our ability to walk, but we leave psychological wounds unattended all the time, often until they literally prevent us from moving forward in life.

This discrepancy between our general competence in treating assaults to our physical health and our complete incompetence where our mental health is concerned is extremely unfortunate. If no such emotional first aid techniques existed, if it were impossible to treat these psychological wounds, this state of affairs might be tolerable. But such is not the case. Recent progress in numerous areas of psychological research has unveiled many treatment options for exactly the kinds of psychological injuries we sustain most often.

Each chapter in this book describes a common and everyday psychological injury and the various emotional first aid techniques we can apply to ease our emotional pain and prevent the problem from becoming worse. These science-based techniques can all be self-administered, much as we self-administer first aid for our physical ailments, and they can also be introduced to our children. The techniques in this book represent the future staples of our psychological medicine cabinets, the mental health medical kits we can carry with us as we go through life.

During my years studying clinical psychology in graduate school I was frequently criticized for giving my patients specific and concrete suggestions for how they might alleviate their emotional pains. "We're here to do deep psychological work," one supervisor used to admonish me, "not to dispense psychological aspirin—it doesn't exist!"

But offering immediate relief and doing deep psychological work are not mutually exclusive. I believe everyone should have access to emotional first aid treatments, just as they should any other treatments for dressing emotional wounds. Over the years, I've made it a practice to distill innovative research findings into practical suggestions, treatments my patients can apply to the emotional hurts of daily living. I've done so for one main reason—they work. For some years now, my patients, friends, and family members have been urging me to collect these emotional first aid treatments into a book. I decided to do so because it's time we took our mental health more seriously. It's time we practiced mental health hygiene just as we do dental and physical hygiene. It's time we all owned a psychological medicine cabinet with the emotional equivalents of bandages, antibacterial ointments, ice packs, and fever suppressants.

After all, once we know psychological aspirins do exist, we'd be foolish not to use them.

How to Use This Book

The chapters in this book cover seven common psychological injuries we sustain in daily life: rejection, loneliness, loss, guilt, rumination, failure, and low self-esteem. Although they were written as stand-alone chapters I advise reading the book in its entirety. Even if some of the chapters have no immediate relevance, knowing the kinds of psychological injuries we might sustain in various situations will help us recognize them when we or our friends and family members encounter them in the future.

Each chapter in this book is divided into two sections. The first describes the specific psychological wounds each injury inflicts—including those we often fail to recognize. For example, we might think it obvious that loneliness causes emotional pain, but we might not be aware that untreated loneliness has such serious implications for our physical health that it can shorten our life expectancy. Also less apparent is the fact that lonely people often develop self-defeating behaviors that lead them to unconsciously push away the very people who could alleviate their suffering.

The second section of each chapter presents the treatments readers can apply to each of the wounds discussed in the first section. I provide general treatment guidelines to clarify how and when each of the recommended techniques should be administered as well as treatment summaries and "dosage" recommendations. Because this book represents a psychological medicine cabinet and is by no means intended to function as a substitute for medical or psychological care by a trained professional, I end each chapter with guidelines for when readers should consult a trained mental health specialist.

The suggestions in this book are based on top-notch scientific studies that have been subjected to peer review procedures and published in first-rate academic journals. References for each of the studies and treatments can be found in the endnotes.

Emotional First Aid

||||||||||||||||||||||

CHAPTER 1

||||||||||||||||||||

REJECTION

The Emotional Cuts and
Scrapes of Daily Life

O f all the emotional wounds we suffer in life, rejection is perhaps the most common. By the time we reach middle school we've already been turned down for play dates, picked last for teams, not invited to birthday parties, dropped by old friends who joined new cliques, and teased or bullied by classmates. We finally get through the gauntlet of childhood rejections only to discover that an entirely new array of rejection experiences awaits us as adults. We get turned down by potential dates, refused by potential employers, and snubbed by potential friends. Our spouses rebuff our sexual advances, our neighbors give us the cold shoulder, and family members shut us out of their lives.

Rejections are the psychological cuts and scrapes that tear our emotional skin and penetrate our flesh. Some rejections are so severe they create deep psychological gashes that "bleed" profusely and require urgent attention. Others are like emotional paper cuts that sting quite a bit but bleed only a little. One might expect that, given the frequency with which we encounter rejection in one form or another, we'd have a clear understanding and appreciation of its impact on our emotions, thoughts, and behaviors. But such is not the case. We drastically underestimate the pain rejections elicit and the psychological wounds they create.

The Psychological Wounds Rejection Inflicts

Rejections can cause four distinct psychological wounds, the severity of which depends on the situation and our emotional health at the time. Specifically, rejections elicit emotional pain so sharp it affects our thinking, floods us with anger, erodes our confidence and self-esteem, and destabilizes our fundamental feeling of belonging.

Many of the rejections we experience are comparatively mild and our injuries heal with time. But when left untreated, even the wounds created by mild rejections can become "infected" and cause psychological complications that seriously impact our mental well-being. When the rejections we experience are substantial, the urgency of treating our wounds with emotional first aid is far greater. This not only minimizes the risk of "infections" or complications but also accelerates our emotional healing process. In order to administer emotional first aid and successfully treat the four wounds rejection causes, we need a clear understanding of each of them and a full appreciation of how our emotions, thought processes, and behaviors are damaged when we experience rejections.

1. Emotional Pain: Why Even Stupid Rejections Smart a Lot

Imagine you're sitting in a waiting room with two other strangers. One of them spots a ball on the table, picks it up, and tosses it to the other. That person then smiles, looks over, and tosses the ball to you. Let's assume your tossing and catching abilities are up to the task. You toss the ball back to the first person, who quickly tosses it to the second. But then instead of tossing the ball to you, the second person tosses it back to the first person, cutting you out of the game. How would you feel in that situation? Would your feelings be hurt? Would it affect your mood? What about your self-esteem?

Most of us would scoff at the idea. *Two strangers didn't pass me a stupid ball in a waiting room, big deal! Who cares?* But when psychologists investigated this very situation, they found something quite remarkable. We do care, far more than we realize. The ball-tossing scenario is a well-researched psychology experiment in which the two "strangers" are actually research confederates. The "subject" (who thinks they are all waiting to be called for an entirely different experiment) always gets excluded after the first or second round of ball tossing. Dozens of studies have demonstrated that people consistently report feeling *significant emotional pain* as a result of being excluded from the ball-tossing game.

What makes these findings remarkable is that compared to most of the rejections we experience in life, being excluded by two strangers tossing a ball is about as mild as rejection gets. If such a trivial experience can elicit sharp emotional pain (as well as drops in mood and even self-esteem) we can begin to appreciate how painful truly meaningful rejections often are. That is why getting dumped by someone we're dating, getting fired from our job, or discovering that our friends have been meeting up without us can have such a huge impact on our emotional well-being.

Indeed, what separates rejection from almost every other negative emotion we encounter in life is the magnitude of the pain it elicits. We often describe the emotional pain we experience after a significant rejection as analogous to being punched in the stomach or stabbed in the chest. True, few of us have actually been stabbed in the chest, but when psychologists asked people to compare the pain of rejection to physical pains they had experienced, they rated their emotional pain as equal in severity to that associated with natural childbirth and cancer treatments! As a counterpoint, consider that other emotionally painful experiences, such as intense disappointment, frustration, or fear, while highly unpleasant, pale in comparison to rejection when it comes to the sheer visceral pain they cause.

But why do rejections hurt so much more than other emotional wounds?

The answer lies in our evolutionary past. Humans are social animals; being rejected from our tribe or social group in our pre-civilized past would have meant losing access to food, protection, and mating partners, making it extremely difficult to survive. Being ostracized would have been akin to receiving a death sentence. Because the consequences of ostracism were so extreme, our brains developed an early-warning system to alert us when we were at risk for being "voted off the island" by triggering sharp pain whenever we experienced even a hint of social rejection.

In fact, brain scans show that the very same brain regions get activated when we experience rejection as when we experience physical pain. Remarkably, the two systems are so tightly linked that when scientists gave people acetaminophen (Tylenol) before putting them through the dastardly ball-tossing rejection experiment, they reported significantly less emotional pain than people who were not given a pain reliever. Sadly, other negative emotions like embarrassment do not share these characteristics, rendering Tylenol ineffective when we get the date wrong for our office Halloween party and show up to work dressed like Marge Simpson.

Rejection Rejects Reason

Martha and Angelo came to couples therapy to deal with frequent arguments about Angelo's inability to seek new employment after he had been downsized by his company six months earlier. "I'd been with that shipping company twenty years," Angelo explained. The hurt was still apparent on his face. "Those people were my friends! How could they do this to me?"

While Martha had been sympathetic initially, she was becoming increasingly frustrated about Angelo's inability to recover from the emotional blow and start looking for a new job. It quickly became apparent that Angelo was as frustrated with himself as Martha was. He tried to motivate himself and talk himself into making efforts, but he simply felt too consumed by emotional pain. He tried reasoning with himself to let go of the hurt and "get over it," but nothing worked.

Many of us find it difficult to talk ourselves out of the hurt we feel when we experience rejection. One of the reasons rejection is often so devastating is that our reason, logic, and common sense are usually ineffective when it comes to mitigating the pain we feel. For example, when scientists told participants who had been excluded in a computerized version of the ball-tossing experiment (called Cyberball) that their exclusion had been rigged, finding out the rejection wasn't even "real" did little to ease the pain they felt. Scientists are a tenacious bunch, so they told a different set of participants that the people who'd excluded them were members of the Ku Klux Klan. Surely rejection would hurt less if we despised the people who rejected us. But nope, it still hurt just as much. They even tried replacing the cyber*ball* with an animated cyber-*bomb* that was programmed to explode at random, "killing" whoever had possession of it at the time. But subjects felt just as much rejection pain when they were not passed a cyberbomb as they were when they were not passed a cyberball.

Rejections impact our ability to use sound logic and think clearly in other ways as well. For example, merely being asked to recall episodes of acute rejection was sufficient for people to score substantially lower on subsequent IQ tests, tests of short-term memory, and measures of reasoning ability and decision making.

Romantic rejections are especially potent when it comes to scrambling our brains and tampering with our good judgment, even when they occur extremely early in a relationship or, indeed, before a "relationship" even exists (breakups after long or serious relationships are covered in chapter 3). One young man I worked with flew to Europe to "surprise" a woman he had met on a week-long summer vacation despite her clearly telling him she was not interested in pursuing a relationship. Still smarting from that rejection, the young man convinced himself that his impromptu "romantic gesture" would "melt her heart and change her mind for sure!" The woman was so startled when he showed up at her front door at an indecent hour of the morning the only thing she changed was the locks. The desperation we feel in the wake of certain rejections can drive many of us to confuse a romantic gesture with a creepy one.

2. Anger and Aggression: Why Doors Get Broken and Walls Get Punched

Rejections often trigger anger and aggressive impulses that cause us to feel a powerful urge to lash out, especially at those who rejected us, but in a pinch, innocent bystanders will do. One group of innocent bystanders that know this all too well are the countless doors and walls that have had fists punched through them by freshly rejected men, and at times women (although those made of brick and solid wood usually get the last laugh). Keeping such dangers in mind is equally important when we're the ones doing the rejecting. Even if the person we plan to reject is a model of kind-heartedness, our Hummel figurine collection might still be in grave danger.

Lest we judge the wall punchers and figurine breakers too harshly, we should consider that even the most inconsequential rejections stir up highly aggressive tendencies in the best of us. For example, after a game of Cyberball, people were given the option to blast an *innocent* participant with unpleasant white noise (someone they were explicitly told had not been part of the ball-tossing situation). Rejected subjects blasted innocent participants with much louder and much lengthier durations of noise than nonrejected subjects did. In different series of studies, rejected subjects forced innocent participants to eat four times as much hot sauce as nonrejected subjects did, to consume terrible-tasting beverages, and to listen to extremely aversive audiotapes. In case you're wondering how often the scientists behind such experiments get recruited by reality TV executives to devise disgusting challenges for their game show contestants, your guess is as good as mine.

Unfortunately, our tendency to respond to rejection with anger has far darker and more serious manifestations as well. Severe and repeated experiences of rejection can elicit the kind of aggression that goes far beyond the realm of white noise or hot sauce. When psychological wounds of this nature are left untreated they quickly become "infected" and threaten serious damage to a person's mental health. Stories of injurious and self-injurious aggressive behaviors following rejections are frequently in the news. Jilted lovers who seek revenge, fired postal workers who . . . "go postal," and the terrible epidemic of bullied children who take their own lives are just a few such examples of what happens when the psychological wounds caused by chronic and severe rejections remain untreated.

In 2001 the office of the surgeon general of the United States issued a report that found social rejection to be a greater risk factor for adolescent violence than gang membership, poverty, or drug use. Feelings of rejection also play a huge role in violence between romantic partners. Many incidents of violence are triggered by jealousy and suspicions of infidelity, which are tightly related to feelings of rejection. When scientists examined 551 cases in which men killed their wives, they found that almost half occurred in response to real or imminent separations. Indeed, men who murder their wives often later admit to being unable to deal with the rejection they felt.

Studies of school shootings, including the 1999 Columbine tragedy, found that thirteen of fifteen incidents involved perpetrators who had experienced significant interpersonal rejection and ostracism from schoolmates. In many cases, shooters specifically targeted students who had bullied, teased, or rejected them in the past, often seeking them out first.

We all experience rejection to some degree and thankfully only a tiny minority of us end up in the headlines as a result. However, the link between rejection and aggression is strong, and it is extremely important to recognize that the pain rejections cause can spur some of us to behave in ways we never would otherwise.

3. Damaged Self-Esteem: Kicking Ourselves When We're Already Down

Experiencing profound or repeated rejection is extremely harmful to our self-esteem. In fact, the mere act of recalling a previous rejection is sufficient to cause a temporary drop in feelings of self-worth. Unfortunately, the pounding our self-esteem takes rarely stops there. We often compound our rejection experiences by becoming extremely self-critical—essentially kicking ourselves when we're already down. Responding this way is common but it can easily cause the psychological cuts and scrapes of the original rejection to become "infected" and consequently to have a truly debilitating effect on our mental health.

Angelo lost his job at the shipping company because his entire department got eliminated in a cost-cutting measure, yet he perceived the rejection as highly personal ("Those people were my friends! How could they do this to me?"). Personalizing the rejection made Angelo feel as though he was unwanted by his friends and abandoned by his long-time colleagues. He avoided contact with anyone from his former company, as he was convinced that communicating with them would only expose him to the disapproval, disappointment, or disrespect they felt toward him, despite such fears being utterly unfounded. When friends and coworkers did reach out to him (which of course they did), he avoided responding to their e-mails and voice messages even when they contained leads for other jobs. After several months, his friends stopped reaching out entirely. In Angelo's mind, their eventual silence only justified his fear that they'd never cared for him in the first place.

Angelo is not alone. We all have a tendency to take rejections too personally and to draw conclusions about our shortcomings when there is little evidence that such assumptions are warranted. Think back (even if way back) to when you were rejected by someone romantically. Did you find yourself listing everything that might be wrong with you? Did you fault yourself for not being attractive enough or sophisticated enough or smart enough or rich enough or young enough, or all of the above? Did you think, "This always happens to me!" or "No one will ever love me!" or "I'm never going to find someone!" Personal rejections are rarely as personal as we experience them to be, and even when they are, they rarely involve such a sweeping indictment of our flaws.

In addition to unnecessarily personalizing rejection, we also tend to overgeneralize it even when we have no grounds to do so (for example, by thinking, "This always happens to me" or "I'm never going to find someone") or to engage in needless self-criticism by assuming we could have prevented the rejection had we done something differently. Self-criticism is especially problematic following romantic rejections, as many of us spend hours analyzing everything we said or did in a desperate search for our elusive "critical wrong move" (e.g., "Why did I wait so long before calling her?" "I should never have had that last drink!" or "Maybe it was too soon to show her my Elmer Fudd underwear collection").

In reality, critical wrong moves are exceedingly rare (although, granted, there's probably never a *right* time to show a woman one's Elmer Fudd underwear collection). The most frequent reasons we get turned down as romantic prospects (or as job applicants) are because of a lack of general chemistry, because we don't match the person's or company's specific needs at that time, or because we don't fit the narrow definition of who they're looking for—not because of any critical missteps we might have made nor because we have any fatal character flaws.

These errors in thinking serve little useful purpose and they only deepen the pain we already feel by adding unnecessary and highly inaccurate self-recriminations that further damage our already battered self-esteem. Rejections hurt enough—we certainly don't need to add salt to our own wounds or kick ourselves once we're already down.

4. Threatening Our Need to Belong: People Who Need People Are *Not* the Luckiest People

One of the reasons our self-esteem is so vulnerable to rejection is that we are wired with a fundamental need to feel accepted by others. When our need to belong remains unsatisfied for extended periods of time, either because of the rejections we've experienced or because we lack opportunities to create supportive relationships, it can have a powerful and detrimental effect on our physical and psychological health.

Some of us have such challenging life circumstances that satisfying our need to belong can present a real challenge. David, a young man I worked with some years ago, faced far greater hurdles than most in this regard. His story taught me that once we've suffered profound and repeated rejection over our lifetimes, finding our place in the world and feeling as though we belong can be the hardest struggle of all.

David was born with a rare genetic illness that typically affects multiple bodily systems and causes a significantly shortened life span (at the time, most children born with the illness died before reaching the age of twenty). Although David had a relatively mild form of the disorder, he still required numerous surgeries and hospitalizations throughout his childhood. David's illness affected not just his health but his appearance as well. Musculoskeletal problems made his gait unsteady and he had noticeable irregular facial characteristics, such as a flattened upper lip, a prominent lower jaw, and significant dental trauma. Further, problems regulating saliva meant he was prone to drooling.

Children born with more severe forms of David's illness often have significant physical disabilities and life-threatening medical problems that prevent them from attending regular schools. David's milder condition (and the fact that intelligence is not affected) meant he was one of the few children with the disorder who was able to attend a local elementary and high school. But for David, this "blessing" came at a terrible price. His appearance, his lack of coordination, and his tendency to drool when he concentrated led him to experience cruel and daily rejections from his peers throughout his school years.

David was never invited to parties, he had virtually no friends, and he spent every lunch hour and recess sitting alone. His lack of coordination and muscle weakness prevented him from participating in after-school or extracurricular sport activities with the other neighborhood boys. His few attempts to explore after-school activities for children with disabilities ended poorly because his comparative "health" made him stand out (at times, literally) and rendered him a poor fit for such programs as well. As a result, David's basic need to belong remained entirely unmet throughout his childhood and teen years and the regular (and often harsh) rejections he suffered caused him tremendous emotional pain.

I met David soon after he graduated from high school and a few months before he was to start classes at a local community college. Although David was excited to attend college he was terrified at the prospect of facing a novel round of painful rejections from a new cadre of peers. His well-meaning parents assured David that college students were more "mature" and more accepting than high school kids were and that he would have a far easier time "fitting in" than he did in high school. But a lifetime of rejection had devastated David's self-esteem and he feared otherwise. "They're going to take one look at me and turn away," he said in our first session. "And those will be the nice ones. The mean ones will turn away and laugh behind my back."

I agreed with David that first impressions might be problematic for him (I saw no point in denying what a lifetime of experi-ence had already demonstrated), so I asked him whether he had a plan to correct those first impressions when opportunities arose to do so. We started discussing how he might handle potential social interactions and it quickly became clear that David's social skills were severely underdeveloped. Years of alienation and a dearth of social experiences meant David often struggled to come up with the right thing to say or do in common situations, something he readily acknowledged.

We decided to spend the summer working on his social skills. We identified potential social situations and role-played how he might handle them. David was also willing to accept that any ini-tial harsh or rejecting reactions he received from college class-mates would likely not be strictly personal, but rather a result of their unfamiliarity with his medical problems and their own feel-ings of discomfort around people with disabilities. Consequently, we decided to brainstorm possible ways for him to relieve any awkwardness or tension his unsteady gait and his drooling might evoke in his classmates (for example, by joking about them when it was appropriate to do so). By the time September rolled around, David felt ready to begin his college career. He was still apprehen-sive about the prospect of being rejected, but he also felt as though he had much better tools with which he could approach social situations. We scheduled his next session for after his first week of classes.

The anguish on David's face was evident from the second he walked into my office. He dropped onto the couch and sighed deeply. "I arrived early for my first class and sat in the front row," he said. "No one else sat there. So when I arrived early for my sec-ond class I sat in a middle row. The row in front of me filled up, as did the row behind me, but no one sat in my row. I arrived early to my third class as well but this time I waited until class was about to begin and went and sat between two people. I said hello. They nodded. One of them moved two seats away from me a few minutes into the class. The other never glanced at me again and bolted as soon as the class was over. As for everyone else, it was the same story. People stared if they thought I couldn't see them or they looked away. No one talked to me. No one made eye contact, not even the professors."

I was extremely disappointed to hear David's news. After dealing with so much physical and emotional hardship and after suffering such extreme social rejection, I truly wanted for him to have a positive experience. My hopes had not been unreasonably high, as I believed that even a small taste of social acceptance would have done so much for his self-esteem and his quality of life. We had spent months working on how David might correct any negative first impressions he evoked, but if his classmates continued to avoid him, if no one would sit next to him or meet his eye, if no one was willing to talk with him, it would be extremely difficult for him to do so.

David's morale was at a low point and I was afraid he might slip into despair. The psychological wounds inflicted by lifelong rejection ran deep and David had already been exposed to more emotional pain than most people experience in their lifetime. I was determined to help David turn things around. Disappointing as his first week had been, I believed it was too soon for him to lose hope. But if he was to have any chance of succeeding, he would first need to treat the fresh wounds inflicted by the rejections he had just suffered.

How to Treat the Psychological Wounds Rejection Inflicts

Many of the rejections we face are significant (like Angelo's), reoccurring (like school or workplace bullying), or both (like David's repeated rejections by his peers and classmates). In such situations, the risk of leaving our emotional wounds unattended can be profound. But not all rejections require emotional first aid. For example, the "survivors" of the ball-tossing experiments would probably have recovered fully from their experiences even if they hadn't been thoroughly debriefed about the real purpose of the studies (which they all were). Let's open our psychological medicine cabinet and review our treatment options.

General Treatment Guidelines

Rejections can inflict four distinct emotional wounds, each of which might require some form of emotional first aid: lingering visceral pain, anger and aggressive urges, harm to our self-esteem, and damage to our feeling that we belong. As with any kind of wound, it is best to treat the emotional wounds of rejection as soon as possible to avoid the risk of "infection" and psychological complications. Remember, these are first aid treatments only and might be inappropriate or insufficient for more profound rejection experiences or ones that have a substantial impact on our mental health. At the end of the chapter I present guidelines for when one should consult a mental health professional.

Some of the treatments that follow are effective for soothing more than one type of wound while others are more specialized. The treatments are listed in the order in which they should be administered. Treatments A (managing self-criticism) and B (reviving self-worth) primarily target emotional pain and damaged self-esteem, while Treatment C (replenishing social connections) targets threatened feelings of belonging. Each of these three treatments is also beneficial for reducing anger and aggressive impulses. Treatment D (lowering sensitivity) is optional as it can have uncomfortable emotional side effects.

Treatment A: Argue with Self-Criticism

Although it is important to question our part in a rejection so we might rectify any obvious mistakes we made and avoid such experiences in the future, doing so requires a delicate touch. Too often our quest to understand "what went wrong" leads to overpersonalizing or overgeneralizing the rejection or becoming too self-critical in its wake. Needlessly finding all kinds of faults in our character, our physical appearance, or our behavior will only deepen the pain we feel in the moment, provoke further emotional bleeding, and significantly delay our healing. Therefore, it is far more useful to err on the side of self-kindness when evaluating our role in a rejection experience than it is to criticize ourselves for any mistakes or shortcomings.

Nonetheless, the urge to be self-critical in such situations can be extremely powerful. In order to avoid kicking ourselves when we're down, we have to be able to "argue" with our self-critical voice and adopt a kinder perspective. To win this internal debate we need talking points, arguments we can use to formulate a more balanced understanding of why the rejection occurred.

EXERCISE FOR ARGUING WITH SELF-CRITICISM

1. List (in writing) any negative or self-critical thoughts you have about the rejection.

2. Use the following self-criticism "counterarguments" from a variety of rejection scenarios to formulate personalized rebuttals to each of the self-criticisms you listed. Feel free to list more than one counterargument per self-critical thought when it is relevant to do so.

3. Whenever you have a self-critical thought, make sure to immediately articulate the relevant counterargument(s) fully and clearly in your mind.

Counterarguments for Romantic Rejections

After twenty years as a psychologist in private practice, I've heard countless tales of romantic rejection both from those doing the rejecting and those getting the heave-ho. People reject romantic partners and prospects for many different reasons, most of which have nothing to do with anyone's shortcomings. Most often it is a simple matter of chemistry—either there is a spark or there isn't. Rather than reaching unnecessary and inaccurate conclusions about your faults, consider these alternative explanations: Perhaps the person prefers a specific type that you do not fit (e.g., she's into blonds and you have brown hair or she has a thing for guys with shaved heads and you have an unruly mop). It's also possible the person's ex reentered the picture, or she might be going through a crisis at home or in her personal life. Or you might simply be a poor lifestyle match (e.g., she's a creature-comfort homebody and you love camping and urinating in the woods).

It's also possible you're "too good" for the person in some way. You take a hard line on vices and unbeknownst to you he parties so hard he has regular blackouts, or your professional success might shine a spotlight on his floundering career, or you're a police officer and his best friend is the neighborhood pot dealer, or you're a talented pastry chef and he's struggling with weight loss and a weakness for Bavarian strudel. The person might have commitment issues and tend to run the moment he feels another person getting too close, he might have self-esteem issues and worry that if you're that interested in him there must be something wrong with you, or he might not be an especially nice, kind, or sensitive person to begin with.

Timing can be a crucial issue as well. You might be looking to settle down and the other person is not, or vice versa, one of you likes to proceed slowly and the other prefers intense courtships and more "instant" relationships, or you're just out of a long-term partnership and the person you're interested in had a bad experience with being someone's rebound romance.

In each of the above situations the person getting rejected did nothing wrong and the rejection had nothing to do with any inadequacies on his or her part. The bottom line is, if people give you the "It's not you, it's me" speech—believe them! And when they don't, assume it's them anyway. The rejection will still hurt, but much less so than if you insist on spreading the salt of self-blame on an already painful wound.

Counterarguments for Workplace Rejections

Similarly to dating, getting rejected by prospective employers has usually much less to do with any mistakes or inadequacies you displayed and more to do with your fit with the company or the job description. Some jobs listings are required to be publicized but were always meant to be filled internally, other times employers are looking for a specific skill set or background, and yet others might be required to come up with several candidates even though they already know who they plan to hire. I've heard some employers confess to rejecting candidates solely because they've had bad experiences with other graduates of their academic institutions, their former companies, or their home states.

One aspect receiving increased attention from scientists is the impact of being rejected in the workplace by members of our workgroup, our superiors, or both (e.g., you're never informed of group lunches or after-work get-togethers, you don't get e-mails about certain meetings, or you repeatedly get criticized and singled out by your colleagues and/or your boss). In most situations, the rejection or exclusion is motivated by dynamics related to the organization and its culture, not to your character or job performance. For example, whistle-blowers are frequently given the silent treatment and shunned by their fellow employees (shunning is an extremely painful form of social rejection) even when the whistle-blower's actions were beneficial to them.

One young man I worked with was extremely outspoken about how poor the work conditions and compensation were in his company (which they were) and he quickly became the target of mistreatment by his supervisor as a result. Even though his colleagues cheered his efforts at first, the culture of bullying in the company soon led them to treat him just as poorly in hopes that doing so would curry favor with their supervisor. Fortunately he was able to recognize that the rejections he suffered at work were not a reflection on his performance (he was an outstanding employee) or his character. Indeed, his initiative and courage were admirable.

When we encounter rejection in the workplace we should

consider the extent to which it is motivated by conforming to a negative or bullying corporate culture, acting out of ambition and rivalry, or making efforts to appeal to higher-ups and superiors. Doing so will help us avoid unfounded assumptions about our abilities or character and prevent us from making the experience even more painful and damaging than it already is.

Counterarguments for Social Rejections

Our friendships and social circles usually nourish our belonging needs but they can also be the source of extremely painful rejections. One of the situations I hear about most is when individuals discover their friends have been meeting up without them. Although it might seem impossible not to take such exclusions personally, these things often happen for entirely other reasons. For example, an established group of friends might have an unspoken requirement of exclusivity of the kind you are not willing to give. Sure, you hang out with them but you also want to be able to hang out with other groups and they do not (a trend that is extremely common in middle school and high school but also occurs among adults).

The same situation might be true of individual friends. Someone might be looking for a best friend scenario that requires the kind of time and emotional commitment you are unable or unwilling to give (because of family, work, or other constraints or because it would take away from other friendships you value). This friend then intensifies his relationship with a different friend who is willing to give him the time and attention you were not, and your friendship with each of them gets marginalized as a result. Hurtful as it is to discover two of your friends are now spending more time with one another than they are with you, it is usually not your fault, nor in essence is it theirs. Certainly it says nothing about your desirability as a friend.

In other instances, you might find yourself being excluded from a group that shares a passion you feel less fanatical about than they do. Some social groups love to get together and discuss the same issues over and over again, whether sports, politics, parenting, or celebrities. In one case, a mother of a toddler was "dropped" by her "mommy group" because she had made repeated efforts to expand the topics of conversation beyond diaper changing, breastfeeding, and developmental milestones. Doing so threatened the integrity of the group and so she was slowly marginalized. Once she understood why this occurred she was actually relieved. She told me, "If I had to listen to one more story about cleaning vomit out of car seats I would have screamed."

Sometimes our social groups recognize we've outgrown them even before we do.

Treatment Summary: Argue with Self-Criticism

Dosage: Administer whenever you experience a rejection and repeat as necessary whenever you have self-critical thoughts related to the rejection experience.

Effective for: Soothing hurt feelings and emotional pain and minimizing damage to self-esteem.

Secondary benefits: Reduces anger and aggressive impulses.

Treatment B: Revive Your Self-Worth

One of the best ways to mitigate the hurt rejection causes and replenish our confidence and self-worth is to remind ourselves of important aspects of our character that others find valuable and desirable (even if those who rejected us did not). As an example, one attractive young woman I worked with dealt with any rejections from men by examining herself in a full-length mirror and saying aloud to her reflection, "Nope, it's not you. You look great!"

A similar albeit more complex process of self-validation played a critical role for David, the young man with a rare genetic illness, when it came to his recovery from the rejections he experienced during his first week in college. David's classmates seemed to reject him outright, much as his high school peers had, and David's self-esteem suffered accordingly. I knew that unless David's sense of self-worth recovered, even a little, he would lack the strength to make any efforts to connect with his classmates and correct their first impressions of him. Fortunately, there was one area in which David excelled and although it had nothing to do with academia, I was certain it could bridge the gulf that separated him from his fellow students.

David had the habit of arriving early both to his appointments with me and to his classes. Armed with several local newspapers, he would then proceed to scour each of their sports sections, reading every word and examining every statistic. He also spent hours listening to sports radio. As a result, David was extremely knowledgeable about sports, none more so than baseball. David was a huge Yankees fan and discussing them always caused a huge shift in his demeanor. He would sit up straighter, state his opinions fluidly and with confidence, and come across as enthusiastic, smart, and insightful about his team, the league, and the sport at large.

After his second week of college, David observed that he was not the only person who tended to arrive early to class. Several male classmates also came early and they too read the sports sections while waiting for class to begin. Given their attire and paraphernalia, David concluded that most of them were Yankees fans as well. I suggested that David choose one of them and start a conversation about the Yankees. David's first reaction was to refuse. He was convinced any such move on his part would be rebuffed or ignored. But a few days later the Yankees secured their place in the playoffs and David discussed the team's prospects in our session. His analysis was impressive.

"I feel like taking notes," I joked, "so I could pass off some of your opinions as my own."

"Feel free," he said. "Trust me! That's exactly what's going to happen in the playoffs."

"You're that certain?"

"No one knows the Yankees like me!" he said proudly.

"Not even those other guys who come to class early?" I challenged him.

"No way!" David insisted.

"That would make for an interesting discussion then," I pointed out. David didn't answer. His fear of rejection was still too strong to allow him to commit to a course of action. But after the Yankees won their first playoff game, his excitement got the better of him and he found himself throwing out a comment to a classmate about the team's prospects of winning the World Series. Much to his surprise, the young man responded by agreeing heartily and raising his hand for a high-five. David was stunned. He offered another comment and was soon shocked to find himself in the midst of a three-way discussion with two of his classmates.

This one preclass interaction had a huge impact on David's feelings of self-worth and he agreed to instigate further discussions about the Yankees. He was thrilled to discover that his classmates were just as eager to discuss their team's success as David was. The more David spoke up, the more interest his classmates took in his opinions. Their preclass discussions soon became a ritual. David and several other classmates gathered before each class to dissect the Yankees' latest game and discuss the team's prospects for winning the World Series.

The impact these unofficial gatherings had on David's demeanor and mood was profound. For the first time in his life, he felt respected by his peers. The more the Yankees succeeded, the more eager David was to get to class and discuss the games with his classmates. And the more he exhibited his knowledge and insights, the more acceptance and validation he received from them.

A key moment occurred when during one of their discussions, David was so focused on what he was saying he forgot to swallow and drool dripped down his chin. Despite a moment of panic, David was able to keep his composure well enough to use one of the lines we had come up with to address exactly such a situation. He wiped his chin and said, "You're not a real Yankees fan unless their success makes you drool." His classmates laughed and continued their discussion as though nothing had happened. David's ability to avert a potentially awkward moment served to fuel his confidence even further.

Fortunately, the Yankees had a great postseason that year and they provided ample opportunity for David and his classmates to get to know each other. His proudest moment came when he arrived later than usual and just in time to hear one student ask another, "Where's David, the Yankees guy?" He walked in a second later and was received with warm hellos.

"I've overheard people talking about me all my life," David confessed in our next session. "I was always *the weirdo, the retard, the spaz*." He paused, a big smile breaking onto his face. "Now I'm *David, the Yankees guy*!" David beamed with pride. "It feels like I finally found a way in, like I'm one of them. They look at me and see me as a real person. I can't tell you how good that feels!"

Connecting to a sense of self-worth played a vital role in David's recovery from the wounds inflicted by the rejections he suffered. Although he still had a long path of emotional healing ahead of him, David's first semester at college allowed him to experience social acceptance, and for the first time in his life, he felt like he belonged.

EXERCISE FOR REVIVING YOUR SELF-WORTH

The following exercise will help you get in touch with meaningful aspects of your character and revitalize feelings of self-worth.

1. Make a written list of five characteristics, attributes, or traits you value highly that you possess within yourself. Try to keep your list relevant to the domain in which the rejection occurred. It is important to take the time to think about qualities that really matter to you (for example, if you've been rejected by a romantic partner and you know the following qualities to be true you might list items such as caring, loyal, good listener, considerate, and emotionally available).

2. Rank your list of characteristics according to their order of importance to you.

3. Choose two of the top three attributes you listed and write a short essay (one or two paragraphs) about each one, covering the following points:

   - Why the specific quality is important to you

   - How this attribute influences your life

   - Why this attribute is an important part of your self-image

Treatment Summary: Revive Your Self-Worth

Dosage: Administer whenever you experience a rejection and repeat as necessary.

Effective for: Soothing hurt feelings and emotional pain and rebuilding damaged self-esteem.

Treatment C: Replenish Feelings of Social Connection

Although the sting of rejection can make us hesitant to engage others, we should make efforts to overcome these fears and turn to our social networks for support or find other ways to refuel our feelings of social connection. Social support mitigates stress of all kinds but it is especially valuable in the wake of rejection. It creates an immediate reminder of our significant relationships, which in turn can help restore depleted feelings of belonging. In one study, even a brief exchange with a friendly experimenter was sufficient to reduce subjects' aggression following a social rejection. In another, instant messaging online with an unfamiliar peer after a rejection restored adolescents' and young adults' self-esteem.

Getting social support from our close friends and confidants following a rejection can sometimes be challenging because they are likely to underestimate the pain the rejection in question caused us. Estimating visceral and physical pain, whether our own or that of others, is something we're all bad at (unless we happen to be experiencing the same kind of pain in the moment). For example, the majority of women who plan to forgo pain medication during childbirth reverse their decision once they go into labor.

Family members, friends, and teachers of bullied students

who've resorted to desperate measures (such as suicide) are often stunned because they had not appreciated the magnitude of the distress the person was feeling. A recent and compelling study found that teachers who were first put through the ball-tossing exclusion experiment had a far greater appreciation for the emotional pain a bullied student felt than teachers who were not made to feel rejected. They also recommended the bully get a more severe punishment as a result.

Social support can be even more crucial when the rejection we experience involves discrimination. Much as we would like to believe we are an enlightened society, our track record when it comes to accepting those who are different from ourselves argues otherwise. Race, nationality, sexual orientation, religious beliefs, disability, gender, and age are all factors that cause millions of people to face extremely painful rejections by their friends, family, employers, neighbors, and strangers. Seeking support from members of our group after being the target of discrimination has been shown to reduce feelings of anger and depression, strengthen our group identity, and counterbalance the harmful effects of being devalued by a dominant culture.

Find New Affiliations with a Better Fit

Our need to belong has some *substitutability*, meaning that new relationships and memberships can psychologically replace those that have ended, especially if they provide a better fit for our personality and interests. Painful as rejections are, we can always view them as opportunities to evaluate whether the romantic partner, social circle, friend, or employer in question was a good fit for our personalities, interests, lifestyles, or careers.

Our choice of social group is often motivated by circumstance.

We get close to randomly assigned college roommates, colleagues we meet at work, or the parents of our children's playmates. While many such friendships succeed, others dissolve when we or they outgrow them. This is especially common when the circumstances that brought us together change: when we graduate from college, move to new jobs, or our children stop playing with theirs. Despite the initial sting of rejection we feel, we might later realize we're far less upset about losing the relationship or friendship than we initially thought.

Sometimes merely spending time with a group with whom we feel a strong connection can help replenish feelings of social connectedness even if few words are spoken (such as shooting hoops with our buddies or seeing a show or a movie with friends). When seeking one-on-one social support we should be thoughtful about our choices, especially if we're still hurting from the wounds of a fresh rejection. Dear friends might care for us deeply, but if they are limited in their capacity to express empathy and support they might not be our best choice.

Anyone who has suffered a serious illness or physical injury or struggled with a disability (like David) has probably experienced people feeling uncomfortable and looking away, avoiding contact, "forgetting" to call or visit, and even losing touch entirely. Cancer patients and those with other illnesses often join support groups to help manage the stress of the illness and their treatments while gaining support from others who've faced similar struggles and rejections.

Have a "Social Snack"

Although it is best to connect with those who can provide social support and feelings of connection it might not always be possible for us to do so. In the film *Cast Away*, Chuck Noland (Tom Hanks) is stranded alone on an island for four years, during which he copes with social starvation by looking at a photograph of his girlfriend, Kelly, and by talking aloud to a volleyball he names "Wilson" and who becomes his much-beloved companion. Much like having a snack eases our hunger when we don't have the opportunity to eat a full meal, "snacking" on reminders of our significant emotional connections eases our "social hunger" when we feel rejected, excluded, or alone.

Social snacking can take many forms, but scientists have found that photographs of loved ones are one of the most emotionally nutritious snacks we can consume after being rejected. In one study, subjects placed photographs on their desks of either loved ones or celebrities and were asked to vividly relive a significant rejection experience from their own past. Subjects with pictures of celebrities on their desks suffered a large drop in mood as a result of recalling the rejection while those with pictures of loved ones registered almost no change in mood at all. Such findings imply that teens and tweens entering the gauntlet of middle school might be well advised to replace posters of musicians and actors with glossy eight-by-tens of Grandpa Dwight and beloved Aunt Flossie.

Photographs are not the only social snacks with nutritional value. Other experiments found that merely recalling positive relationships or warm interactions we've had with our nearest and dearest was sufficient to reduce the amount of aggression people felt after being rejected. Reading meaningful e-mails or letters, watching videos of loved ones, or using valued mementos of those to whom we feel most connected also have nutritional value as social snacks. Mementos and inanimate objects can also have significant "caloric value," especially when a rejection is compounded by general loneliness, as was the case for Chuck Noland with "Wilson." The next time we ask someone on a date or apply for a new job we might want to have pictures of our friends and loved ones available in our pocket just in case, or, if we must, a volleyball.

Treatment Summary: Replenish Feelings of Social Connection

Dosage: Make sure to administer whenever you experience a rejection. Since there are numerous ways in which you might be able to replenish feelings of social connection, you may wish to apply several forms of this treatment as necessary (e.g., spending an afternoon with family members who appreciate and love you and social snacking on pictures of them later on).

Effective for: Replenishing your need to belong and reducing anger and aggressive urges.

Secondary benefits: Soothing hurt feelings and emotional pain and rebuilding damaged self-esteem.

Treatment D: Desensitize Yourself

Anyone who has ever made cold calls (for example, to prospective employers or to ask people to donate to a charity) knows how difficult it is to make the first few calls. It's extremely unpleasant to hear "No, thanks" and have the phone slammed in your ear. But something interesting happens around the fifth or sixth call—we begin to take "no" much less personally. We shrug it off, strike a line through the entry, and move on to the next person on our list. Actors, musicians, and performers have the same experience. If an actor rarely auditions, getting rejected is likely to feel painful, but those who audition several times a week find it much easier to let such rejections go.

The reason this happens is because of a psychological process called *desensitization*. The more we're exposed to situations we find uncomfortable or unpleasant, the more used to them we become and the less they disturb us. Of course, this isn't true for all situations and it certainly isn't true for some of the more significant or profound rejections we might encounter. Some life experiences are acutely painful and emotionally damaging no matter how repetitive they become. But when it comes to situations such as asking people out on dates, calling prospective employers for jobs, applying to internships or other educational programs, or initiating new friendships, trying to desensitize ourselves can be beneficial.

I once had a male patient in his twenties whose fear of rejection made him hesitant to approach women, and I gave him the task of asking out nine women in one weekend. He had plans to attend three different social events, and I promised him that if he approached three women per event, by the time he got to the third (a birthday party for a work colleague) he would feel very differently about the prospect of getting turned down. Interestingly, merely agreeing to the challenge had an immediate impact on him. "The thought of approaching so many women made me feel kind of confident before I even began. Once I accepted that I'd be getting rejected *a lot*, it made the idea of any one woman rejecting me seem more manageable for some strange reason."

As we now know, that "strange reason" is actually desensitization. My patient never made it to the third social event. He struck out three times at the first event of the weekend, but was shocked when two women gave him their number at the second, "and one of them wasn't even fake!" he reported happily. The young man ended up skipping the third event in order to go on a date with the woman who had given him her nonfake number.

Desensitization can be an effective technique for reducing the emotional impact of rejections but it should be used both sparingly and wisely. It is one of those treatments that should come with clear warning signs on the label. Readers should be advised to treat themselves with desensitization only if they feel their self-esteem is up for the challenge and only after giving careful thought to how they could implement the treatment in ways they would find beneficial. The most important aspect is to concentrate our efforts into a limited time frame, as spreading out the task over time dilutes it and renders it ineffective. For example, if my patient hadn't had several social events planned, it would have been harder for him to find the right circumstances in which to ask out nine women within three days.

TREATMENT SUMMARY: DESENSITIZE YOURSELF

Dosage: Administer for specific tasks only: when seeking to initiate dates or friendships, when applying to jobs, internships, or other programs, or when making cold calls.

Caution: Use sparingly and wisely, as this treatment involves significant discomfort. Use only if you feel your self-esteem can tolerate being exposed to numerous "minor" rejections.

Effective for: Creating a layer of resilience to future rejections so as to reduce the hurt feelings and emotional pain they evoke and the damage to self-esteem they cause.

When to Consult a Mental Health Professional

Applying emotional first aid following rejections should soothe each of the four wounds we typically suffer as a result of such experiences and reduce our risk of long-term psychological complications. Treating older rejections might also be beneficial as it can help nudge us toward a path of healing and recovery. However, some rejections are so painful and the wounds they create are so deep, emotional first aid alone is not sufficient to correct the psychological damage they cause.

If the rejection you've experienced is profound (e.g., you've been rejected by your entire family or community because of your sexual orientation or religious beliefs) or if you've experienced chronic rejection over a period of time, you might benefit from seeking the advice of a mental health professional. If you've applied the treatments in this chapter and your emotional pain did not subside, your self-esteem remains too damaged, and engaging with people feels too risky, you should consult a mental health professional. If your anger and aggressive impulses have become too powerful for you to control, or if you have any thoughts of harming yourself or others, seek the immediate help of a mental health professional or go to your nearest emergency room.

CHAPTER 2

||||||||||||||||||

LONELINESS

Relationship Muscle Weakness

Our world is shrinking. Social media platforms allow us to stay in touch with dozens if not hundreds of friends at once, dating websites offer us lavish smorgasbords of potential mates we can peruse from the comfort of our homes, and a simple click of a computer key allows us to forge new connections with strangers from across the globe who share our interests and passions. Yet, despite this era of unprecedented global human connection, more people than ever are suffering from severe loneliness.

The 2010 U.S. Census found that 27 percent of households in America are single-person households, now outnumbering all other groups (such as one- or two-parent households with children). Of course, not everyone who lives alone is lonely and not everyone who is lonely lives alone. Many of us suffer from loneliness despite living with a spouse or being in a committed relationship. In fact, cohabitating with someone with whom we share a physical proximity but little else often highlights the immense emotional distance and profound disconnection we feel, leading to powerful feelings of isolation.

What determines our loneliness is not the quantity of our relationships but rather their subjective quality, the extent to which we perceive ourselves to be socially or emotionally isolated. Indeed, many of us have address books full of casual acquaintances yet still ache from a lack of deep friendships. Some of us have a tight network of supportive friends yet feel the acute absence of a romantic partner. We might spend our days surrounded by work colleagues yet feel removed and isolated from all of them. We might be blessed with strong familial relationships but find ourselves geographically distant from those who care for us most. Those of us who are fortunate enough to grow into old age with our health and faculties intact might experience a rising tide of loneliness as we witness friends and partners succumb to illness and die one after the other.

What Loneliness and Cigarette Smoking Have in Common

Having meaningful relationships is essential for leading a happy and self-fulfilled life, but chronic loneliness can damage us in ways that go far beyond limiting our basic happiness. In addition to the emotional pain and longing loneliness causes, it is also associated with clinical depression, suicidal thoughts and behaviors, hostility, and sleep disturbances.

More important, loneliness has an alarming effect on our general health. It alters the functioning of our cardiovascular systems (leading to high blood pressure, increased body mass index, and higher cholesterol), our endocrine systems (increasing stress hormones), and even our immune systems. As an illustration of how directly loneliness impacts our physical health, one study found that in otherwise healthy college students, lonely students had a significantly poorer response to flu shots than nonlonely students did. Loneliness also causes a decline in our mental abilities, including poor decision making, decreased attention and concentration, impaired judgment, and a more rapid progression of Alzheimer's disease.

Shocking as it may seem, loneliness poses just as large a risk factor for our long-term physical health as cigarette smoking does, as it literally shaves years off our life expectancy. While cigarette packs come with health advisories, few of us are aware of the dangers of inhaling two packs a day of social isolation. As a result, feeling lonely rarely triggers a sense of urgency and we rarely prioritize the need to break free of its clutches and treat our psychological wounds.

Loneliness Is Contagious

Another factor that adds urgency to our need to treat the psychological wounds loneliness inflicts is that recent studies have demonstrated something rather stunning—loneliness is contagious! One study tracked the spread of loneliness within social networks over time and found that loneliness spreads through a clear contagion process: individuals who had contact with lonely people at the start of the study were more likely to become lonely themselves by the end of it. Further, the virulence of the contagion depended on the degree of closeness between the lonely and nonlonely person. The closer nonlonely individuals were to a lonely person the more virulent the effect of the contagion and the lonelier they became later on.

Specifically, scientists found that lonely individuals were continually pushed toward the periphery of their social networks and into positions that were increasingly more isolated. Once people were in close contact with lonely people they became affected and were pushed toward the periphery as well. Alarmingly, this contagion was "transmitted" from one person to another even beyond the immediate circle of the lonely person, such that it spread throughout the entire social network. Such studies help demonstrate both why and how loneliness is at epidemic proportions in today's society.

Unfortunately, despite its contagiousness and despite the severity of the health risks it poses, loneliness remains one of the most neglected psychological injuries we sustain in daily life. Few of us realize how crucial it is to treat the psychological wounds loneliness inflicts and fewer still know how to do so effectively.

The Psychological Wounds Loneliness Inflicts

Given the severity of the risk loneliness poses to our physical and mental health, we should make every effort to escape its impact as soon as possible. However, two factors are likely to make it challenging for us to do so. First, loneliness causes us to become overly critical about ourselves and those around us, and it makes us judge our existing relationships too negatively, all of which impact our interactions with others. Second, one of the more insidious effects of loneliness is that it leads us to behave in self-defeating ways that diminish the quality and quantity of our social connections even further. As a result, the very fibers that comprise our "relationship muscles"—our social and communication skills, our ability to see things from another person's perspective, and our ability to empathize and understand how others feel—become weak and are likely to function poorly when we need them most.

To be clear, it is not our fault that we are lonely, nor is it usually a reflection on our social desirability. But regardless of the circumstances that cause it, once loneliness sets in, it triggers a set of psychological reactions that can lead us to inadvertently perpetuate our situation and even to make it worse. Because such dynamics usually operate outside our awareness, the most important tool we can carry with us going forward is an open mind. We might strongly believe we've done everything in our power to change our situation and that we're certainly doing nothing to make matters worse. But by being open to the possibility that our behaviors might be contributing to our predicament, we can be open to discovering ways to change them. Difficult as it is to open our hearts and minds, to challenge our established perspectives, and to take emotional risks, we must be brave enough to do so if we wish to treat our loneliness.

1. Painful Misperceptions: Why We Feel Invisible but Our Loneliness Isn't

People confide many negative things about themselves to their therapists, but one of the things people rarely have the courage to admit is how lonely they feel. Loneliness carries a stigma of shame and self-blame that operates in all our minds to some extent. Over 40 percent of adults will suffer from loneliness in their lifetime and virtually all of them will think poorly of themselves because of it. Indeed, one of the more significant emotional wounds loneliness creates is that it leads us to develop inaccurate perceptions of ourselves as well as of others and to take too harsh a view of our existing relationships and social interactions.

Lionel, a former World War II officer who received numerous medals for valor, was referred to me for psychotherapy some years ago by his daughter, a social worker who lived out of town and was concerned about her father's increasing social isolation. Lionel lived alone (his wife had died some years before), and although his daughter called him every day, their conversations were usually quite brief as Lionel believed that "phones are for making appointments, not for idle chitchat!" I quickly learned that Lionel was not a fan of any kind of chitchat, idle or otherwise, something that made our sessions somewhat challenging at first. For example, my efforts to assess the extent of Lionel's social isolation went something like this.

"Who else do you speak with regularly other than your daughter?"

"Housekeeper. Comes twice a week. Cooks and cleans."

"Tell me about the conversations you have with her."

"She tells me what she made. I leave her money on the counter."

"What about other family members?"

"No relatives other than my daughter."

"What about friends from the service or even former colleagues, are you in touch with any of them?"

"No."

"Why do you think that is?"

"Because they're dead."

I resisted the urge to sigh and gave Lionel a sympathetic nod. I kept probing and eventually discovered that Lionel did engage in one regular social activity—he belonged to a chess club. Every Tuesday Lionel would put on a jacket and tie and go down to the seniors' center to play a couple of games. Unfortunately, as far as games go, chess is about as conducive to social interaction as solitaire is, if not less so. True, chess does require two people to play, but any talking during the game is strictly discouraged as it can interfere with the concentration of the other player.

"Do you play with the same people?" I inquired. I was curious about whether any of the regulars tended to meet outside of chess club hours.

"Mostly."

"Have you ever socialized with any of them?"

"They're not interested."

"How do you know?"

"Why would they want to socialize with me? I'm eighty!" I doubted that age was the real issue. The club was for seniors, after all; how much younger could the other players be?

"You're eighty and they are . . . ?"

"Not interested."

"Do they socialize with one another?"

"Sometimes."

"And they've never invited you to join them?"

"They're not interested!"

Lionel was convinced the other, "younger" members of the chess club would rebuff any attempt he made to forge friendships with them, despite the fact that he had no evidence whatsoever that his age or anything about him would cause them to snub him. But he was determined to avoid disappointment and rejection at all costs. He arrived right before game time and left immediately following the last round. He approached no one and spent coffee breaks sitting in a corner reading a book. In other words, he gave the other chess club members no opportunity whatsoever to get to know him.

Lionel had already been suffering from loneliness for some years when we first met and his self-defeating strategies were already well entrenched. However, the damage loneliness inflicts on our perceptions of social situations can happen extremely quickly. For example, scientists found that simply asking college students to recall a time in their life when they felt lonely or socially isolated was sufficient to elicit from them a more negative assessment of their current social support systems as well as to boost their shyness, increase their social anxiety, cause a drop in their mood and self-esteem, and impair their optimism.

Loneliness also causes us to evaluate others more harshly and to perceive our interactions with friends and loved ones more negatively than we would if we were not lonely. Another study videotaped students as they interacted with a friend and then asked them to rate the quality of the interaction and that of the friendship. Lonely individuals rated both their interactions and their friendships far more negatively than nonlonely people did. The participants were then shown the videotapes again one week later. While there was no change in the assessments of nonlonely people, lonely people rated their friendships even more negatively the second time around.

Lionel believed the members of the chess club ignored him and marginalized him because he was essentially invisible to them. However, the tragic irony of loneliness is that while we often feel invisible to others, our loneliness is usually very visible to them indeed. Numerous studies have found that lonely people are easily recognizable to others and that once we're judged as being lonely we're likely to be viewed negatively as a result. Lonely people are often seen as less attractive and even less intelligent than nonlonely people (physical attractiveness provides no immunity from loneliness whatsoever; attractive individuals might draw a greater quantity of people initially but the quality of their relationships are no different and they are just as likely to experience loneliness).

The bottom line is that loneliness affects perceptions in numerous ways. It impacts how we perceive ourselves and others, as well as how we perceive the quality of our interactions and our relationships. Loneliness also impacts how others perceive us, making us appear less interesting and less appealing as social prospects. The combination of these factors makes it extremely difficult to shed our cloaks of invisibility and engage in successful efforts to forge new social connections or deepen existing ones.

2. Self-Defeating Prophecies: Why Trying Harder Leads to Failure

Many journeys into loneliness begin during periods of transition and change. College freshmen often feel extremely lonely when they first arrive at college, surrounded by unfamiliar faces, far from home, and removed from the comfort of their friendships. Divorce, separation, and bereavement, especially when they befall us unexpectedly, can leave us entirely unprepared for the palpable loneliness that accompanies such losses. When work and colleagues provide our primary source of social interaction and engagement, losing our job can mean losing our entire social support system when we most need it. Relocations and emigrations are often characterized by extended periods of loneliness as we labor to build new social and support networks from scratch.

In each of these cases, we typically emerge from loneliness once we adjust to our new realities and rebuild our social infrastructures. Most college freshmen eventually make new friends, divorced people typically begin to date within a year following their separation (although it takes longer in cases of bereavement), looking for a new job often requires us to network and to contact people with whom we lost touch, and most of us eventually forge social and intimate connections in our new towns and communities.

Yet, at times, the cold grip of loneliness extends far beyond the normative adjustment period. We become trapped in it, paralyzed by waves of emotional pain, defeated by feelings of worthlessness and hopelessness, and overcome by the devastating emptiness of our profound social and emotional isolation.

Why does this happen? What is it that prevents some of us from breaking free of the bonds of loneliness and getting our lives back on track?

The answer is that in addition to painful misperceptions, loneliness also drives us into cycles of self-protection and avoidance that cause us to create self-fulfilling prophecies and to inadvertently push away the very people we hope to engage.

Serena, a high school teacher I worked with recently, found herself in exactly such a vicious cycle and she too was entirely unaware of it. What brought her to psychotherapy was her "nonexistent dating life." At first I was at a loss to understand why she had never been in a serious relationship. She was in her midthirties and, furthermore, she was simply stunning. I had no doubt that she received plenty of attention from men. I soon learned that Serena's appearance had gone through a radical transformation four years earlier, when she lost eighty pounds.

"I was heavy my whole life. Men would look right past me as if I wasn't even in the room. And trust me," Serena added with a wistful smile, "I was hard to miss. Now they stare, they smile, they wink, and somehow it still feels the same. Like they're responding to my appearance, but when it comes to who I am as a person, they're still looking right past me."

Serena was desperate to find a husband, but she was equally desperate to avoid getting hurt. While her hesitancy and mistrust were certainly justified after the years of rejection and loneliness she'd experienced, her fears caused her to come across as withdrawn, defensive, and suspicious. As a result, her dates with men were often tense and awkward, and few of the men expressed an interest in seeing her again. Their failure to follow up only confirmed Serena's suspicions that they were never interested in the "real her" to begin with. The fact that the "real Serena" spent every moment of her dates hiding behind a psychological wall and was never truly present in the first place was something she never considered.

The reason we get trapped in such cycles is that loneliness tips the balance of our social motivations. Once we feel vulnerable and socially disconnected we become intensely self-protective and we seek to minimize any potential negative responses or rejection from others. As a result we approach people with distrust, suspicion, cynicism, and anxiety or we make efforts to avoid them altogether. Because we don't expect our social interactions to be positive, we make fewer efforts to seek them out and we are less responsive to them when they occur.

Unfortunately, the longer our loneliness lasts, the harder it can become to change our perceptions and behaviors and to break the cycle of self-defeating thoughts and behaviors that perpetuate it. We end up behaving in ways that push away the very people who could alleviate our loneliness and we then view their distance as further evidence of our basic undesirability. As a result we feel like passive victims in a harsh world and fail to realize the extent to which we are active contributors to our own predicament.

3. Atrophied Relationship Muscles: We Use Them or We Lose Them

Alban, a successful sales executive, came to couples therapy with his wife, Blanca, after months of urging on her part. "Blanca accuses me of being married to my job and I guess I am. It's not that

I want to be, but my job demands it. Blanca gets frustrated that I have to work even when I'm home and I totally understand how she feels." Alban put his arm around his wife and gave her a wink. "I keep telling her it's natural for the 'other woman' to feel jealous."

Blanca quickly pulled away. "You know I don't think that's funny!" Blanca turned to me and said, "He keeps telling people that joke and I hate it." She turned back to Alban and her eyes welled with tears. "It's not that you're away so much that bothers me, it's that there's a real disconnect between us when you are home. There's no affection, no romance, no intimacy. I'm lonely and miserable . . . and you don't care."

Alban's eyes also welled up. "Of course I care! And I feel lonely too. But it's hard to connect when you're angry all the time. Last week I brought you flowers and a card for Valentine's Day and all you did was yell at me."

"Because you never even gave them to me! You were in such a rush to check e-mails from work you just left them on the kitchen counter. I only discovered them two hours later and by then you were already asleep!"

"But I got them for you! You keep telling me it's the thought that counts, except it doesn't!"

"You got them *for* me but you didn't think to give them *to* me. Your *thought* was to leave them on the kitchen counter in the same spot you leave money for the cleaning lady!"

As their discussion progressed it became evident that leaving the flowers on the kitchen counter was not the only instance of Alban's good intentions going awry. He clearly cared about Blanca, but something went consistently wrong when it came to translating his feelings into actions. Given how angry Blanca felt and the level of disconnection between them, it had clearly been going wrong for some time.

When we lack meaningful and deep connections with others or when we fail to invest in the relationships we have, we stop exercising the skill sets required to maintain such relationships. Our "relationship muscles" function in much the same way regular muscles do. When we fail to use relationship muscles regularly (such as our ability to empathize or see things from the other person's perspective) or when we use them incorrectly, they atrophy and become less functional.

The problem is we're often unaware of just how weak our relationship muscles have already become. Alban believed his relationship muscles were functioning properly, but they were not. True, he'd invested thought and effort in getting Blanca flowers and a card, but leaving his gifts on the kitchen counter and forgetting about them undid any positive impact his efforts might have had.

When we try to walk after spending a week in bed with the flu we are often surprised by how our legs buckle under us and leave us in a heap on the floor. While we are quick to realize our muscles have weakened in such situations, we rarely have the same insight when it comes to poorly functioning relationship muscles, no matter how many times we find ourselves in a metaphorical "heap on the floor." Indeed, rather than concluding that his relationship muscles were faulty, Alban was convinced Blanca was simply being unappreciative.

As another example, when we falter in our first dating efforts after a long dry spell of being alone, we rarely attribute the result to our having rusty dating skills and weak relationship muscles. Instead we take the rejection extremely personally and assume it is merely a reflection of our fundamental undesirability.

Even once we're aware of the need to strengthen our relationship muscles, we often fail to anticipate how uneven our efforts are likely to be. For example, once I made Serena aware that she might be contributing to her lackluster dating experiences, she was determined to change how she was coming across to her dates. However, her first few efforts were just as unsuccessful, this time because she was trying too hard and appearing too desperate.

While improving our social skills is certainly doable, many who experience loneliness face the far more daunting task of developing relationship muscles we've never used before. Serena had no experience with serious dating and Lionel had little to no experience and a very limited tolerance for casual socializing and small talk. Alban, on the other hand, lacked the ability to empathize, to understand Blanca's needs and feelings well enough to make his efforts meaningful to her. In all of these cases, they needed to learn new skills and find the courage to practice them, despite the emotional risks involved.

Lionel was a good example of someone who regularly overlooked vital information of this sort. I was eventually able to persuade him to approach Stanley, the chess club member whom he enjoyed playing against most, and suggest they grab coffee. We discussed how important it was to precede the actual request with a comment or two about the game, so as not to come across as too abrupt. Lionel came into our next session and immediately informed me that he had taken the plunge and asked Stanley to have coffee with him.

"Great!" I responded. "So he said yes?"

"He declined."

I tried to hide my disappointment. "I'm sorry to hear that. Did he say why?"

"He didn't have to. It's because he's a sore loser." Lionel went on to explain that Stanley used to be the best player in the club until Lionel joined and that he'd lost to Lionel regularly ever since. I was dismayed that Lionel had not thought this information important enough to mention earlier. Had he considered things from Stanley's perspective, he might have realized that winning all his games, refusing to interact with the other members, and reading in the corner during breaks made Lionel appear aloof if not actually disdainful of the others, Stanley most of all.

Understanding a person's needs and feelings from his or her perspective is vital for creating and sustaining close friendships and emotional intimacy. When these relationship muscles are weak, we overlook crucial information about how the other person thinks and feels and our efforts often fail.

How to Treat the Psychological Wounds Loneliness Inflicts

Many of the circumstances that lead to being lonely are temporary and allow us to recover in a relatively short amount of time. For example, kids usually forge new friendships within hours or days of starting summer camp, and people whose relationships make them feel lonely might actually feel relieved after a separation if they take steps to reconnect with friends and loved ones with whom they had lost touch. Treating the wounds of loneliness becomes much more urgent when we've been in its grips for extended durations and when we feel discouraged about being able to change our social and emotional isolation. Let's open our psychological medicine cabinet and review our treatment options.

General Treatment Guidelines

In addition to the pain and suffering loneliness causes, three other psychological wounds require emotional first aid. First, we must identify and change the misperceptions that lead to self-defeating behaviors. Although we might struggle to see such patterns, if we've been lonely for some time, they are definitely there. Second, we need to strengthen and enhance our relationship muscles so that our efforts to forge new connections and deepen existing relationships will be more successful, meaningful, and satisfying. Third, we need to minimize the ongoing emotional distress loneliness causes, especially in cases in which the options for improving existing social connections and creating new ones are limited.

The treatments that follow are listed in the order in which they should be administered. Treatments A (challenging negative perceptions) and B (identifying self-defeating behaviors) are effective primarily for correcting the misperceptions loneliness causes and the self-defeating behaviors that result. Treatments C (taking the other person's perspective) and D (deepening emotional bonds) will help strengthen relationship muscles crucial for forming new connections or deepening existing ones. Treatment E (creating opportunities for social connection) will help identify new avenues for social engagement; and Treatment F (adopting animals) discusses ways to reduce the emotional suffering loneliness inflicts and is especially suited for people with limited options to expand or improve the quality of their social connections (because of geographic isolation, health or mobility limitations, or other special circumstances).

As with all emotional injuries, it is best to treat the wounds loneliness inflicts as soon as possible. The longer we go without exercising the full range of our relationship muscles, the more they will atrophy and the longer it will take for us to regain their full functionality. Further, rehabilitating muscles of any kind requires repetition, practice, and patience. If we try to rush our recovery we are likely to reinjure ourselves and encounter setbacks and disappointment. And remember, not all forms of loneliness can be remedied by first aid techniques alone. At the end of the chapter, I discuss when it is recommended to consult a mental health professional.

Treatment A: Remove Your Negatively Tinted Glasses

Loneliness makes us constantly on guard, prepared for the disappointment and rejection we are sure will come. As a result, we miss opportunities to make social connections and we behave in ways that push others away. In order to challenge these distorted perceptions and avoid acting in self-defeating ways we need to do three things.

1. Fight the Pessimism!

Loneliness makes our minds generate instant negative thoughts as soon as we contemplate engaging in social interaction. We get invited to a party and vivid scenes of awkwardness, rejection, and disappointment pop into our heads entirely unbidden. We become convinced we won't know anyone there. We envision ourselves standing alone by the hummus and vegetable dip, feeling conspicuous and embarrassed. The thought of approaching a stranger or, worse, a group of strangers, and initiating a conversation is enough to cause a sense of panic, and we anticipate any such efforts ending disastrously.

Although we are unlikely to prevent pessimistic scenarios from elbowing their way into our thoughts, the best way to fight our fears and pessimism is to purposefully visualize scenarios of success that are both reasonable and realistic. By picturing successful outcomes in our minds we are more likely to recognize such opportunities when they arise and to take advantage of them. For example, we could acknowledge that it is just as likely for people at the party to be friendly, welcoming, and happy to meet and chat with us. Even if we don't meet new people, it's just as possible we'd have a perfectly nice time catching up with the one or two folks we do know. We might even end the night by making plans to see them again in the near future.

Lionel had to overcome the belief that none of the other players in the chess club were interested in socializing with him ("Why would they want to socialize with me? I'm eighty!"). Once Stanley turned him down he was extremely reluctant to approach anyone else. The first order of business was to help Lionel see his part in creating the situation.

"You've been seeing things too negatively, Lionel," I explained. "True, they haven't asked you to hang out but you also haven't given them any reason to do so. They know nothing about you, nothing about your life, and nothing about your thoughts or feelings."

"So you also think it's pointless." Lionel nodded.

"No, I'm saying the opposite. I'm saying it's not as bleak as it seems and that you can do something about it. Let them get to know you. Chat a little, exchange pleasantries, kvetch about the weather, or ask about their weekend. Make the effort for a couple of weeks and I assure you they will be far more open to hanging out, even Stanley."

Lionel was extremely hesitant to initiate conversation with the chess club members, but when I appealed to his military experience and presented the challenge as a mission he had yet to accomplish, he finally agreed. After a few weeks of occasional chatting, he mustered the courage to ask another member to coffee. They met at a diner several weeks later. I told Lionel how impressed I was with his efforts. "I know it was difficult to open up and start chatting but I'm so glad you did. I'm sure it made a difference with other club members as well. Who knows," I added, "maybe you and Stanley will have coffee one day after all."

"That'll never happen," Lionel said immediately.

"Here's that negativity again," I cautioned him.

"It just won't happen," Lionel insisted.

"Really?" I demanded. "Why not?"

"Because Stanley's dead."

Lionel told me Stanley had died two weeks earlier. His death led to the other members talking more among themselves and getting closer. They decided to attend Stanley's memorial service later in the month and when they did, Lionel went with them.

2. Give the Benefit of the Doubt!

Another misperception loneliness burdens us with is that we tend to assume the worst about how others feel about us. Toby, a young man who had recently lost his job, was devastated when the holiday season approached and he failed to receive an invitation to his good friend's annual Christmas party (the friend still worked for the same company). Toby was convinced his friend no longer wanted to be associated with him because he had been fired. Since I knew Toby's e-mail had recently changed (he had used his work e-mail for personal communications) I suggested he check his spam folder. Lo and behold, there was the invitation, where it had been all along. Toby had spent the better part of two weeks feeling betrayed and mourning the loss of a friendship that was still perfectly intact (although, if he had missed his friend's party with no explanation, it might not have been intact for long).

Loneliness might make us question how our friends feel about us, but we should always balance our doubts with reminders of our mutual history and the shared experiences that created and sustained the friendship over time. Doing so will help reassure us that our friendships are probably a lot more stable than our loneliness-fueled fears might lead us to believe.

Serena, the high school teacher who had gone from heavy to bombshell, was also quick to judge others and their intentions toward her. She was certain any man who expressed an interest in her did so solely because of her appearance and had no intention of getting to know the "real" her. Although men were unquestionably drawn to her appearance, they definitely cared about her personality. Indeed, it was her closed and guarded behavior that made most of them reluctant to ask her out again.

A couple of years later, at a social event, Serena bumped into one of the men she thought had rejected her. She was extremely surprised when he introduced her to his friends as "Serena, the beauty who dumped me after one date." Clearly, he had mistaken her guardedness for disinterest. Had Serena given him the benefit of the doubt and expressed interest he would have happily initiated a second date.

Understandable as our fears are when we already feel lonely and leery of rejection, indulging them will only bring about the very thing we seek to avoid. Instead, we must battle the internal tide of skepticism we feel and give the new people in our lives and the ones with whom we have existing relationships the benefit of the doubt.

3. Take Action!

Chronic loneliness causes us to perceive ourselves as passive victims of our harsh circumstances and we feel helpless to change our
social, emotional, or intimate isolation. Such feelings, powerful as
they might be, are nonetheless founded on perceptions that are too
negative and pessimistic. There are always steps we can take to improve our situation. It is important to do so because taking action
of any kind will make us feel better about ourselves as well as about
our prospects. Lionel had a room full of chess players from which
to choose when it came to making new friends, Serena had numerous men clamoring for her attention, and Toby had plenty of people from his former job who were interested in continuing a
friendship with him. Yet loneliness made all of them perceive their
situation as one in which their options were severely limited.

EXERCISE FOR IDENTIFYING AVENUES FOR SOCIAL CONNECTION

The following writing exercise will help identify potential actions
you can take to expand and deepen your social connections and,
by doing so, counter feelings of helplessness.

1. Go through your phone numbers, e-mail addresses, and
    social media contacts and make a list of people you con-
    sider friends or good acquaintances.

2. For each person, note when you last saw or communi-
    cated with him or her and create a master list of people
    you haven't been in touch with for a while.

3. Prioritize your list by ranking all the people on it accord-
    ing to who in the past has made you feel best about being

you. Your final ranking represents the order in which you should contact the people on your list. Reach out to at least one or two people a week and, when possible, initiate plans to meet.

4. Go to websites that list meetings or activities and scroll through their categories. For example, Meetup (meetup .com) is a website that lists meetings for people with mutual interests, hobbies, passions, or careers. Even if you don't find a specific meet-up that fits your interests, such sites are good places to get ideas for activities or hobbies that might intrigue you.

5. Identify at least three activities or topics you might want to pursue (e.g., book clubs, adult education classes, hiking or biking groups). Search online for meetings in your area.

Use your lists to recharge your old friendships and to explore venues for creating new ones.

Treatment Summary: Remove Your Negatively Tinted Glasses

Dosage: Administer full treatment and repeat as necessary until you've revitalized your social or dating life.

Effective for: Correcting painful misperceptions and avoiding self-fulfilling prophecies.

Secondary benefits: Reduces emotional suffering.

Treatment B: Identify Your Self-Defeating Behaviors

Loneliness makes us approach people with caution and suspicion, and our hesitancy usually comes across loud and clear to others, prompting them to retreat from our bad vibe. We then feel crushed and conclude we were right to be suspicious and cautious in the first place. The fact that our own actions created a self-fulfilling prophecy often eludes us entirely. As is often true in life, when we act out of fear we risk inviting the very thing we hope to avoid.

But if our self-defeating judgments and behaviors seem completely justified in our own minds, how are we to identify those that are self-sabotaging?

The truth is that while we're often blind to our self-defeating behaviors in the moment, we're much better at identifying them in hindsight. For example, we might feel justified in keeping to ourselves at a social event if the few people we know are already engaged in other conversations. But once our social anxiety has diminished the next day, we would probably recognize that we could have simply joined their conversations or introduced ourselves to at least one or two people we didn't know.

More important, we tend to repeat the same self-defeating behaviors in a variety of situations, which should make identifying them easier once we're alerted to their existence. Once we recognize what these tendencies are we can become more mindful of them and catch them in action going forward.

So consider yourself alerted.

While the notion of analyzing our own behavior accurately might seem daunting at first, when I ask patients to reflect on their social encounters and identify their errors, they typically do so quite successfully. Once we accept the basic premise that at least some of our actions are not serving us well, we should be able to start identifying things we've said and done that might have had unintended consequences. For example, Serena was quick to recognize that she asked her dates very few questions about themselves and that such omissions probably led her dates to conclude she had little interest in them. In addition, her anxiety was such that she rarely smiled when she was on a date and she was certainly too tense to laugh. Once she realized this, she thought back on her dates with dismay but with insight.

"They must have thought I really wasn't enjoying their company. Geez, I'm one heck of a lousy date!"

"Lousy!" I agreed, which made Serena laugh. "But whether you continue to be is up to you."

Serena's self-sabotaging behaviors are by no means unusual. Other common forms of self-defeating behaviors are finding poor excuses to turn down invitations to social events, skipping spontaneous get-togethers because you're "unprepared" either emotionally or otherwise, neglecting to convey birthday wishes or other celebratory messages to friends and colleagues, taking friendly ribbings too personally, using defensive body language (e.g., folding your arms over your chest, standing with your hands in your pockets, exaggerated rummaging through your purse, or faking intense interest in nonexistent text messages), responding with curt or monosyllabic sentences or overtalking and hogging the conversation, neglecting to ask others about their lives and opinions, and confessing your faults and insecurities to people you've just met.

Exercise to Identify Self-Defeating Behaviors

Take time to reflect on how you might come across to your friends, colleagues, and loved ones or when you are on a date or any other type of social engagement. Try to identify at least three behaviors (including omissions, such as not conveying interest), even if they seem entirely justified and even if they seem relatively minor, that might be pushing other people away.

1.   My self-defeating behaviors are:

2.   Once you've identified what you might be doing incorrectly, be extremely mindful of avoiding such behaviors in the future. Keep your list handy and read it before you attend social engagements. Self-defeating mechanisms can be changed once you've identified them correctly but don't expect to eliminate them all at once. As we will see in the next section, all social skills require practice.

Treatment Summary: Identify Behaviors That Work Against You

Dosage: Administer full treatment as soon as possible after unsuccessful social interactions. Make sure to go over your list before attending any forthcoming social interactions so you can be as mindful as possible to minimize self-defeating behaviors.

Effective for: Improving social and romantic interactions, avoiding self-defeating behaviors, and correcting painful misperceptions.

Secondary benefits: Reduces emotional suffering.

Treatment C: Take the Other Person's Perspective

Relationships of any kind are always about give-and-take. But to "give" successfully we have to be able to "take" the other person's point of view. Known as *perspective taking*, accurately reading another person's point of view is a vital relationship muscle. It allows us to understand their priorities and their motivations, to anticipate their behavior, and even to predict their reactions. It enhances our ability to negotiate and cooperate successfully, to strategize and problem-solve, to communicate effectively, and to access our compassion, altruism, and empathy.

Loneliness and social isolation weaken our perspective-taking muscles and make us far more likely to commit social gaffes or to come across as inappropriate, too eager, or too detached. The fastest way to rehabilitate this relationship muscle is to identify our perspective-taking blunders and to correct them. The following three errors are the most important to keep in mind, as they represent our most frequent oversights.

1. Failing to Engage Our Perspective-Taking Muscles When We Should

As simplistic as it may sound, the reason we usually don't understand the other person's perspective is we never tried to in the first place. Perspective taking is a mental exercise, not a mind-reading trick. If we don't make the effort to think through how other people might see things, how they might react, or how their agenda might be different from our own, we are unlikely to take such considerations into account when interacting with them. One common manifestation of this omission involves our use of humor. When we're considering whether to tell a joke, we typically give almost exclusive priority to whether *we* find the joke funny and fail to consider whether it will be funny to others. Alban thought referring to his wife as "the other woman" (relative to his job) was hilarious, while Blanca obviously did not. Had Alban given even a moment's thought to how she reacted to the joke in the past, her feelings about it would have been immediately obvious to him.

2. We Favor Our Own Point of View

Our own perspective is so apparent to us that we often fail to give the other person's point of view sufficient weight. For example, scientists studied how people interpret sincere versus sarcastic phone messages (where tone of voice is helpful in detecting sarcasm) and those communicated by e-mail. We are all aware that written messages lack tonal cues that help the recipient understand our intended meaning. Yet time and again we anticipate readers will be able to distinguish between our sincere and sarcastic e-mail messages with the same accuracy as they would a phone message. And time and again we are surprised to discover that our messages are taken the wrong way.

The reason this happens is that although we're aware electronic communications can easily be misinterpreted, we tend to assume such errors are the reader's fault; but research clearly demonstrates it is the person who sends the message whose assumptions are faulty. To correct this specific error we must give sufficient weight to how the other person might interpret our electronic communications (and, no—emoticons are not the answer).

3. We Consider the Wrong Information

We often fail to consider *accurate* information that could potentially provide insight into another person's point of view (such as
his or her facial expressions) but happily consider *inaccurate* information (such as broad stereotypes or gossip). For example, when
evaluating the preferences of people we perceive as similar to us,
we tend to use ourselves as reference points. But when we perceive
others as being less similar, we are more likely to resort to stereotypes to assess their preferences. Once we consider how this dynamic might play out in gift-giving scenarios, it becomes clear why
Grandpa ended up with twenty-three pairs of woolen socks for
Christmas but without the Kindle he'd been hinting at since
Thanksgiving.

Perspective-Taking Errors in
Intimate Relationships

The more familiar we are with another person, the more accurate
our efforts to understand their point of view should be. As such,
we might assume that the longer a couple has been together, the
fewer perspective-taking errors they make with one another. But,
as most couple therapists can attest, couples who've been together
longest are often those who exhibit the most perspective-taking
flubs.

Why does this happen?

Unfortunately, it is the couple's very familiarity with one another that trips them up. The more time we've spent with our partner the more confident we feel in our ability to assess his or her
point of view without giving it much thought (perspective-taking
error #1 in action). However, since familiarity with a person rarely

bestows the ability to read the person's mind, such confidence is likely to land us in the doghouse more often than not.

This blind spot can be extremely troublesome for intimate relationships. For example, partners often dread birthdays and Valentine's Day for this exact reason. One thinks, "Why can't my spouse ever get it right?" and the other, "No matter how much trouble I go to, nothing is ever good enough." In reality, neither person is taking the time to examine things from the partner's point of view. If they did they would communicate with one another and clarify their expectations ahead of time, rather than just playing out the same gift-giving debacle year after year.

Of course, having such "relationship discussions" is not always easy. One of the reasons Blanca initiated couples therapy with Alban was that he tended to clam up whenever she tried discussing relationship issues with him. Indeed, women are often more proficient than their husbands at discussing their feelings and expectations, which can make men feel they're fighting a losing battle. Rather than saying the wrong thing, they prefer to say nothing and get their "inevitable defeat" over with as soon as possible. The best way for women to fight this tendency is to avoid outtalking their partners. Women should give men the space and leeway to express their thoughts and even to restate them (without incurring a "penalty") if their words do not reflect their true intent. When men are more proficient at emotional expression than their partners, they should take similar precautions.

In short, we should always ask ourselves how the other person's point of view might differ from our own. We should give weight to what we know about their priorities and preferences, to the history of the relationship between us, and to the context of the current situation. Taking a few minutes to answer such questions can save hours of relationship talks to smooth over a situation that could have been prevented had we made the effort to think through the other person's perspective ahead of time.

Treatment Summary: Take the Other Person's Perspective

Dosage: Administer full treatment and practice frequently. Do not get discouraged by initial failures, as building and improving these skills takes both time and practice.

Effective for: Rebuilding and strengthening weak relationship muscles, improving social interactions, and enhancing relationships.

Secondary benefits: Reduces emotional suffering.

Treatment D: Deepen Your Emotional Bonds

Empathy involves stepping into another person's shoes in order to gain an understanding of their emotional experience and then conveying our insights to them convincingly. Rather than merely acquiring their point of view as we do when perspective taking, we seek a deeper understanding so we can glimpse how they actually feel. Much as we do with perspective taking, we regularly overestimate our capacity to employ empathy successfully. One of the reasons this happens is that empathy is not necessarily an easy skill. It requires a Jedi mind trick of sorts, albeit one we do to our own minds. Specifically, we have to direct our awareness to a place it does not automatically go—to what it actually feels like to be another person—linger there for a moment until we register the other person's emotional landscape, and then return to our own reality.

Surveys of college students have found that their empathy skills have decreased significantly over the past thirty years, which probably reflects a larger societal trend. Most of us could use a tune-up when it comes to both our empathy and perspective-taking skills. For example, Alban had trouble understanding why his wife, Blanca, was so angry with him for leaving the flowers and card he got her for Valentine's Day on the kitchen counter. After all, he'd not only remembered Valentine's Day (as opposed to previous years in which he had forgotten it entirely), but despite the huge amount of work waiting for him when he got home he'd taken the time to stop and get his wife tokens of his affection. When I asked Alban to consider things from Blanca's point of view, he quickly conceded he'd screwed up, but he just didn't understand why his good intentions counted for so little.

How to Access Our Empathy

The only way to gain insight as to how other people feel is to imagine ourselves in their situation, not just for a second or two, but until we can use our own emotional compass to point to how they might be feeling. To do so accurately, we need a good sense of their emotional landscape—the context leading up to the situation in question. For example, I asked Alban to consider Blanca's expectations, how she might have experienced the two hours between the time he arrived home and when she discovered the card and flowers on the kitchen counter.

"She saw me working in the study," Alban said, thinking aloud, "but she didn't see the flowers because they were in the kitchen." Alban's eyebrows shot up and he turned to Blanca. "You thought

I'd forgotten Valentine's Day again! That's why you didn't respond when I said good night."

Blanca nodded. I asked Alban to continue the exercise. "Now, taking that into consideration, how did Blanca react when she saw you in the study?"

"She didn't," Alban said. "She must have been upset, but she didn't say anything because I was working."

"So she was being considerate," I said. Alban nodded. "So how was she feeling right before she discovered the flowers in the kitchen?"

"She was upset and disappointed; but she decided to be considerate and not discuss it with me until I finished working."

"For two whole hours," I pointed out. "She sat on her feelings for two hours. You go to bed and only then does she pass by the kitchen."

"And sees the flowers and cards on the counter," Alban continued. "And . . . damn!" He turned to Blanca. "You must have thought I don't even care enough to hand them to you in person." Blanca nodded. "You made efforts to contain your disappointment all evening and I couldn't even take a moment to hand you the flowers in person." Blanca nodded, exhaling deeply. Alban put his arms around her. Slowly, she softened into his embrace. "I'm such an ass," Alban whispered. "How do you stand me?"

"You do make it difficult," Blanca responded with a brief smile. Alban quickly promised to take Blanca out for a belated Valentine's dinner to make it up to her.

I continued to work with Blanca and Alban for several months. Alban had done a good job exercising his empathy muscles in the session, but it takes more than a single empathy workout to build up relationship muscles to their full strength. Alban continued to practice using empathy, and the more he persisted, the happier he and Blanca became. Over time, and with lots of work, their strained and distant marriage changed to one in which they both felt trusted, supported, and cared for by the other.

Improving our empathy skills will do wonders for our most important relationships. The caring and consideration that empathy conveys can spark a cycle of goodwill, affection, and generosity of spirit that radically deepens bonds of marriage, family, or friendship. Obviously this works best when both people are strengthening their empathy muscles with one another at the same time, but even unilateral efforts can bear significant fruit.

Because of the practice this skill requires, we should endeavor to practice our empathy muscles in a variety of situations and with numerous people. In doing so, we should seek opportunities to anticipate how people might feel about future situations as well as past ones. Keep the following in mind:

Visualize yourself in their situation. The best way to assess another person's emotional experience is to visualize yourself in his or her situation in as immersive a manner as possible. Take notice of the surrounding environment, of who else is there, the time of day, the person's mood, and any physical pains or ills the person may be suffering from. Imagine how you come across to him or her, not how you actually feel but what you actually convey to the other person. Keep in mind that in many situations we experience feelings that are contradictory. For example, when Blanca found the flowers on the kitchen counter she probably felt pleased that Alban had made the effort even though she also felt hurt, disappointed, and angry that he'd executed it so poorly.

Context is key. Understanding someone's feelings involves having at least a rough sense of his or her frame of mind at the time. The following questions are ones you might want to consider: What are the person's previous experiences with similar situations? What fears, doubts, hopes, or expectations might he or she have about the situation? What else is happening in his or her life at the time? What has his or her day been like up to this point? How might other relationships be impacting his or her responses?

Convey your insights thoughtfully. Having insight into another person's feelings only matters if we can convey our understanding convincingly and compassionately. Knowing how someone feels but communicating it poorly is akin to buying him or her flowers and then leaving them on the kitchen counter. Be as descriptive as possible. The more the other person realizes you've put thought and effort into appreciating his or her point of view, the more impact your empathy-informed communications will have.

TREATMENT SUMMARY: DEEPEN YOUR EMOTIONAL BONDS

Dosage: Administer full treatment and practice frequently. Do not get discouraged by initial failures, as building and improving these skills takes both time and practice.

Effective for: Rebuilding and strengthening weak relationship muscles, improving social interactions, and enhancing relationships.

Secondary benefits: Reduces emotional suffering.

Treatment E: Create Opportunities for Social Connection

Loneliness makes us extremely hesitant to create new opportunities for social engagement or to take advantage of existing ones. We feel uncomfortable attending social events (especially those with too many unfamiliar faces), we hate traveling by ourselves, and we are reluctant to sign up for new activities or social groups because we dread showing up alone. We might see options for social activities around us, but we fear coming across as "losers" or "loners" and inviting the very stigma of loneliness we are desperate to escape.

The best way to overcome feelings of vulnerability, reduce our hesitancy, and avoid being labeled as lonely is to approach situations with a larger goal in mind. For example, participating in a speed-dating event would feel far less uncomfortable if we were doing so as research for an article on our blog or college newspaper. We would be far less apprehensive about signing up for a tour with other singles if we were amateur photographers or artists and planned to paint, sketch, or photograph the sites we visited for our portfolios. And we would find it easier to join a swimming, biking, or running group if we were training for a triathlon.

By having an additional agenda, we come across not as someone who is lonely, but as someone who is passionate about our hobby, devoted to our goals, or serious about our creative endeavors. Having a larger goal also helps reduce insecurity and self-consciousness because our attention is focused on the task at hand; documenting our speed dates, creating art for our portfolios, or making it through the triathlon.

Go Online

The Internet allows us to connect to people with whom we might share common interests and experiences without leaving our homes. It also allows us to adopt identities through which we can interact with others and express ourselves in ways that might not be possible in our regular lives. For example, Second Life (secondlife.com) is a three-dimensional virtual world where users interact with one another using a digital representation of their own choosing. Users can switch genders, make themselves older or younger, choose how attractive they would like to be, and give themselves various other characteristics and abilities. The interactions in Second Life cover the gamut from chatting to virtual mating, from conducting business to constructing homes, and participants report having meaningful friendships and relationships with one another.

Relationships and friendships that start online can be substantial and they often translate into in-person interactions. For example, a recent study found that online dating is now the second most common way couples meet (being introduced by mutual friends is the most common), surpassing previous romantic venues, such as bars, clubs, and the vegetable aisle in the local supermarket on Sunday afternoons.

Volunteer to Help Others

Another option for creating new social bonds is to volunteer. Helping others reduces feelings of loneliness, increases feelings of self-worth, and makes us feel more socially desirable to others. Helping others contributes to more happiness and greater life satisfaction, and it can also reduce our fear and hesitancy about engaging with new people (or indeed with people in general). By setting out to give rather than get, we can focus on the person in need instead of on ourselves, which in turn makes us feel less self-conscious, less insecure, and less vulnerable.

Treatment Summary: Create Opportunities for Social Connection

Dosage: Administer full treatment as needed and repeat as necessary.

Effective for: Reducing emotional suffering and increasing opportunities for social interaction.

Secondary benefits: Strengthens weak relationship muscles.

Treatment F: Adopt a Best Friend

In some cases, circumstances may prevent us from creating new social bonds or enhancing existing ones. People with limited mobility, who are isolated geographically, or who cannot reach out to others for various reasons frequently adopt pets to soothe feelings of loneliness. Dogs are great at soothing feelings of loneliness in people who are isolated, elderly, or dealing with a significant illness or psychological injury such as post-traumatic stress disorder. Dogs are also great people magnets, and many friendships and relationships have started with the sentence, "Oh, your dog is so cute! What's its name?"

Attesting to the singular therapeutic powers of our canine friends, one study had lonely people spend time alone with a dog or with another person and a dog together. Those who spent time alone with a dog reported feeling significantly less lonely than those who shared the company of the dog with another person. Whether the "other persons" in the study were informed they came in second to animals that drink out of the toilet and lick themselves is unknown.

Despite the many advantages of dog therapy, adopting any pet, especially a dog, is a huge responsibility and one that some of us cannot undertake for practical reasons. Cats have been studied less frequently than dogs, but they too can provide significant companionship and they are easier to care for than dogs, especially by people who are homebound.

Treatment Summary: Adopt a Best Friend

Dosage: Administer as needed and to the extent circumstances allow.

Effective for: Reducing emotional suffering.

When to Consult a Mental Health Professional

Treating loneliness with the emotional first aid techniques discussed in this chapter should help soothe the emotional suffering loneliness creates, correct the perceptions and behaviors that sabotage our efforts to deepen and expand our emotional and social connections, and provide new opportunities for social interaction.

However, if your emotional pain is so great you have thoughts of harming yourself or others, or if you find yourself thinking about what it would be like if you were no longer around, you should seek the immediate help of a mental health professional or go to your nearest emergency room. If you have not had self-injurious thoughts but nonetheless feel too hopeless or discouraged to apply these first aid treatments, or if you've tried to do so but were unsuccessful, a mental health professional could help you assess factors that might be holding you back and provide the emotional support necessary for you to move forward.

||||||||||||||||||||

CHAPTER 3

LOSS AND TRAUMA

Walking on Broken Bones

Loss and trauma are an inevitable part of life, and their effects are often devastating. Losing a loved one, being victims of violence or crime, becoming disabled, developing a chronic or life-threatening illness, being exposed to terrorism or war, or living through other life-threatening and traumatic experiences can derail our lives and leave deep psychological wounds. Healing such wounds usually involves an extended process of readjustment and recovery that can be different for each of us. Much like broken bones that need to be set correctly, how we go about putting the pieces of our lives back together after loss or trauma makes a huge difference in how fully we recover from such events.

Some of the losses and traumas we experience are so deeply scarring they require the skills of expert mental health professionals and probably extended psychotherapy. As such, this chapter is not intended for those who've suffered extremely adverse impacts, and such readers are strongly advised to seek help from a trained mental health professional if they have not already done so.

However, many of the losses and traumatic experiences we

sustain in life are not severe enough to cause long-term psychological or emotional damage. For example, when we lose our job, when our best friend drops us after a bad argument, or when an elderly grandparent dies, we go through a period of sadness and adjustment but we usually return to our previous level of psychological and emotional health. However, the same loss can have different subjective meanings to different people. For example, if losing our job caused our family to become homeless, if our best friend was also our only friend, or if our grandparent raised us and had been in good health, the loss we experience and the impact it has on our lives can be far more substantial.

Whatever differences we might exhibit in how we cope with loss and trauma, we all face similar challenges when it comes to rebuilding our lives and achieving a full emotional and psychological recovery. We have to reset our broken psychological bones—reassemble the pieces of our lives back into a well-integrated and fully functional whole. Treating the psychological wounds loss and trauma inflict can not only accelerate our recovery but in some cases make it possible to emerge from such experiences with meaningful changes in our priorities, a deeper appreciation of our existing relationships, an enhanced sense of purpose, and greater life satisfaction—a phenomenon known as *post-traumatic growth.*

While many of the variables that determine whether we emerge from loss and trauma with diminished or enhanced emotional well-being are not in our control (such as the severity of the events, our basic psychological makeup, and our previous exposure to hardships), some are. In order to best utilize the emotional first aid treatments in this chapter we will need a clear understanding of the psychological wounds loss and trauma inflict and the challenges they present to our mental health and emotional well-being.

The Psychological Wounds
Loss and Trauma Inflict

In addition to the severe emotional distress they cause and the real-world changes we have to contend with in their aftermath, loss and trauma inflict three psychological wounds, each of which represents a different set of bones that need to be reset. First, loss and trauma can create such havoc in our lives that they threaten our self-perceptions, our roles, and our very sense of identity. Second, tragic events often challenge our fundamental assumptions about the world and our place in it, such that we struggle to make sense of the events or to integrate them into the larger framework of our belief systems. Third, many of us find it difficult to remain connected to the people and activities we used to find meaningful and we might even feel as if reengaging in our lives would represent a betrayal to those we've lost or a discounting of the suffering we've experienced.

Emotional pain engulfs all who experience loss and trauma but the extent to which we encounter these three psychological wounds can vary dramatically. Some of us might experience them only in mild form while others might find their lives profoundly impacted by them for years and even decades. Let's examine each of them in greater detail.

1. Life Interrupted: Overwhelming
Emotional Distress

The emotional distress we experience in the first torturous days following loss or trauma can be utterly paralyzing. We might lose the ability to think straight or to perform even the most basic functions of self-care, such as eating or bathing. Engulfed in emotional pain, we often experience every detail of our lives anew as we are forced to live through a wrenching series of "firsts." Our first meal without the person we lost, our first night alone after being victims of violent crime, our first look in the mirror after the events that altered the course of our lives. This endless array of "firsts" can keep coming at us for weeks and months: our first trip to the supermarket after separating from our spouse without buying his or her favorite foods, our first Christmas after losing our job without money to buy gifts for our children, or our first Thanksgiving without our recently deceased parent.

Every "first" evokes memories, painful longings, and deep yearnings for that which we've lost, and we might find it hard to care about anyone or anything else. Plunged into the depths of despair, our feelings might be darker even than those experienced by people suffering from the most severe clinical depression. However, grief is a normal psychological response to extreme circumstances, not a mental disorder. Regardless of how searing our initial emotional pain, it almost always subsides with time. As we begin to absorb the reality of our loss or trauma, the visceral pain begins to dull, even if by the most minute of measures.

Indeed, time is a hugely important factor in our recovery. We often move past the most acute stages of grief and adjustment after six months—although such timetables are obviously dependent on the nature of the loss or trauma and its tangible as well as its subjective impacts on our lives. But when we do not, whether because the loss or trauma we suffered was too significant or because circumstances prevented us from moving through the healing and recovery process as we should, we risk allowing ourselves to become defined by our experiences. The most unique aspects that made us who we are can become lost, subsumed by our grief, hidden from view such that even we no longer glimpse them. Our interests, our creativity, our joy and enthusiasm can all become obscured by sadness, pain, and endless rumination about the past, and our lives become truly interrupted in every sense of the word.

2. Identity Interrupted: How Loss and Trauma Challenge Our Roles and Self-Definition

Grant was a sales rep with a promising career and a love for shooting hoops with his friends when he wasn't on the road. One winter evening, Grant and two colleagues were driving to the airport after a long business trip when snow and icy conditions contributed to their driver losing control of the car. Grant was dozing off in the middle backseat when it happened.

"I went straight through the windshield, landed in the road, and lost consciousness. I came to a few minutes later. I opened my eyes and saw one of my colleagues lying right in front of me, dead. I tried to get up but I couldn't. I looked down and saw I was covered in blood. And my legs . . . my legs were missing." Grant swallowed hard. This was our first session and, judging by the emotions on his face, these were not events Grant spoke of often.

"Next thing I remember is the hospital and the surgeries, many, many surgeries." Grant spent over a year in various hospitals, where doctors treated his massive injuries and started him on a long road of intense physical rehabilitation. He also attended psychological counseling sessions. Grant's broken body slowly began to heal but his mind did not.

"I can't tell you how many times I wished I had died that night. It would have been easier. People wanted to visit, but I couldn't stand the thought of seeing anyone. I couldn't stand the thought of seeing myself either. Six years later and I still can't look in a mirror. When I do catch a glimpse of myself, all I see is a stranger. The person I used to be died that night. This new person, this broken-bodied cripple, is not me!"

My heart ached for Grant, not just for the horrible injuries he sustained but because six years later he was still in such terrible emotional distress. The psychological wounds inflicted by the loss and trauma he experienced were as raw as ever. His broken psychological bones had never been reset correctly and as a result, he never adapted to the new realities of his life.

Loss and trauma often force a new reality on our lives that, depending on the severity of the events we've experienced, can completely redefine our identities as well as the narrative of our life stories. Before the accident Grant had defined himself by his career, by his outgoing personality, and by his athleticism. But those three pillars of his identity were now completely absent and played no role in his life at all. Grant desperately needed to redefine his identity, to reconnect with the aspects of his personality and character that remained buried beneath his grief, to decide what his life could be about.

The challenge of redefining ourselves and our identities accompanies many experiences of trauma and loss. We might have defined ourselves by our careers and lost our jobs, we might have defined ourselves by our couplehood and lost our partner, we might have defined ourselves by our athletic ability and lost our health, or we might have defined ourselves by our parenthood and seen our last child leave home. In each of these situations we need to take the time to rediscover who we are, to search within for things we find meaningful, and to find new ways of expressing aspects of ourselves that lay dormant, buried under an avalanche of sorrow. When we fail to do so we are left with a terrible void that only amplifies the extent of our loss, fragments our basic sense of self, and sets us adrift in the stormy seas of self-doubt and self-loathing.

3. Beliefs Interrupted: Why Loss and Trauma Challenge Our Perceptions of the World

One of our most compelling human drives is the need to make sense of our experiences in life. We each have our own way of understanding how the world works (even if we've never articulated it to ourselves explicitly), and we filter most of our experiences through that lens. Our beliefs and assumptions about the world guide our actions and our decisions and they often provide us with a sense of meaning and purpose. One person might view everything that happens in life as "God's will," another might believe "We reap what we sow," some might believe "Everything happens for a reason," and others believe "Things happen for no reason at all." Some of us feel the world is generally fair while others are convinced the opposite is true, and some of us believe life is largely predictable while others revel in their belief that events are entirely arbitrary.

Whatever thoughts and perceptions we have about such things, loss and trauma can challenge our basic assumptions about the world and how it operates and cause us significant additional emotional distress as a result. Our struggle to make sense of what happened often compounds our initial shock and sends us on a desperate quest to integrate our new realities into a framework of fundamental beliefs that no longer provide us with the security they once did. Indeed, such "crises of faith" are common. We become flooded with questions and doubts and we often embark on a search for answers.

This intense need to make sense of things can leave us ruminating incessantly about how the events occurred, why they happened the way they did, and what we could have done to prevent them. We might analyze each of a thousand small decisions and moments that, if altered, might have spared us the painful realities we now face. As a psychologist working in New York City during and after the events of September 11, 2001, I heard many such questions expressed by my patients. "If only she had left a few minutes later she would have missed her train and not been at her desk when the plane hit the building," "If he hadn't moved to Boston he would not have been on that plane," and "If I hadn't stopped to look up, the falling debris would have missed me," are all examples of the thoughts and ruminations shared by many people on and after that horrific day.

We often spend months dwelling on such questions as we search for ways to make sense of the events. While many of us begin making sense of tragedy within six months of it occurring, many others fail to do so even years later. Yet, the sooner we reconstruct our worldviews in ways that integrate our experiences of the loss or trauma, the quicker the intensity and frequency of our ruminations will diminish, the better our psychological adjustment will be, and the less likely we will be to exhibit poor emotional well-being and symptoms of post-traumatic stress disorder.

4. Relationships Interrupted: Why We Struggle to Connect to Those Who Remain

Maxine came to psychotherapy to deal with her looming fiftieth birthday. Ten years earlier she had promised her husband, Kurt, she would celebrate the milestone with him by flying to Africa and going on a safari. Maxine had never left the country before, despite Kurt's many pleas for her to do so over the years. "It was ten years in the future, but it still wasn't a vow I made lightly," she explained. "I fully intended to keep it."

A few months after she turned forty, Kurt began to get severe headaches. "They gave him one test after another, but they couldn't figure it out," Maxine explained. "Then they did a brain scan. The doctor told us he had a tumor. They would try to remove as much of it as they could, but basically, they gave him three years at most. We cried each other to sleep for nights. Kurt was terrified of the surgery. He knew there was a lot that could go wrong. Right before they wheeled him into the operating room I promised him that as soon as he recovered from the operation we would go on the safari and that we would travel as much as we could in whatever time we had left together. He smiled for the first time in weeks."

Maxine paused to wipe tears from her eyes. "He died in surgery two hours later," she said, her hands trembling, tears now streaking down her face. "I miss him . . . so much! I still talk to him every day: when I get home from work, when I get up in the morning. I know this sounds crazy, but I even make his favorite dinner once a week. It comforts me, makes me feel less alone." Maxine gathered herself and continued. "I'm here because my fiftieth birthday is coming up in six months . . . and I don't know what to do. A part of me feels as though I have to keep my promise and go on the safari. But to do that without Kurt, to go without him, I'm not sure I could stand it."

Maxine and Kurt had no children, but they had enjoyed a thriving social life organized primarily around their love for camping and the outdoors. However, in the years since Kurt died, Maxine had lost touch with most of their old friends and she had given up camping and even hiking altogether. Her social network consisted of a sister who lived on the west coast and a few casual friends from work with whom she had dinner every few months. When I asked her if she ever considered dating again she dismissed the notion immediately and explained that doing so would feel as though she were betraying Kurt.

Many of us respond to profound loss by withdrawing into ourselves, obsessing about the person who died, talking to the person in our heads, and imagining his or her thoughts and reactions to our experiences. However, such phases are usually temporary. In time, we begin to let go of the person we've lost and move on, either by reengaging with the people and activities that populated our lives previously or by finding new people or experiences in which to invest our emotions and energies. But some of us become stuck. We maintain vivid representations of the person we lost, we hang on to the person's memory, and we keep investing our emotional resources in the dead instead of the living.

As another example, Sean, a young man I worked with in the summer and fall of 2001, lost his first cousin and best friend, a firefighter who died when the North Tower collapsed. In the months that followed, Sean became obsessed with the Twin Towers themselves. He spent all his free time watching hours of documentaries and films about their construction, reading everything he could find about their history, and researching various aspects of the buildings' maintenance and operations. Meanwhile, he withdrew from his large family. He refused to attend family gatherings and generally avoided the very people who shared his loss and grief the most.

While such coping mechanisms are reasonable in the aftermath of tragic events, when they continue too long we risk getting stuck in the past as Sean and Maxine did. In many cases, such habits represent a breakdown in our grieving process. Instead of resetting our broken bones, healing, and redefining ourselves and our lives anew, we end up adrift in our memories, relating more to what no longer exists than to what does. When left untreated, such patterns can persist for years and even decades, putting our lives on hold and keeping our futures tethered to the loss and trauma that have come to define us.

How to Treat the Psychological Wounds Loss and Trauma Inflict

Loss and trauma can shatter the pieces of our lives, ravage our relationships, and subvert our very identities. To put the pieces back together—to reset our broken bones—we first need to recover from the overwhelming emotional distress we feel in the immediate aftermath of loss or trauma. While the treatments in this chapter can help, if the tragedy you've suffered is profound, if years have passed and you have yet to recover from the events, or if you experience symptoms of post-traumatic stress disorder, such as intrusive flashbacks, nightmares, emotional numbness, or jumpiness and agitation, you should seek the counsel of a trained mental health professional. Let's open our psychological medicine cabinet and review our treatment options.

General Treatment Guidelines

Loss and trauma create four psychological wounds. They cause overwhelming emotional pain, they undermine our basic sense of identity and the roles we play in life, they destabilize our belief systems and our understanding of the world, and they challenge our ability to remain present and engaged in our most important relationships.

The treatments in this section are presented in an order that roughly mirrors the sequence of psychological adjustment and recovery we go through as we heal from loss and trauma. Treatment A (soothing emotional pain) suggests guidelines for how to manage emotional pain and discusses common fallacies that can delay our recovery. Treatment B (recovering lost aspects of "self") is focused on reconnecting to aspects of life that might have gotten lost and reestablishing a sense of identity, and should be administered only once we've returned to normal functioning within the home, at work, or in school. Treatment C (finding meaning in tragedy) is focused on making sense of the events and moving closer to finding meaning and even benefit in them. Treatment C should be reviewed first and then completed only after enough time has passed for our initial emotional pain to subside and we feel emotionally strong enough to do so.

If you feel as though any of the exercises and treatments in this chapter would be too painful to complete, please review the section at the end of the chapter that discusses when to seek help from a mental health professional.

Treatment A: Soothe Your Emotional Pain Your Way

Working in New York City during and after the events of September 11, 2001, I found that the majority of my patients, as well as those of most mental health professionals, were personally affected by the tragedy in some way. One of my patients was killed when the plane struck the South Tower, some were injured in the attacks, others' homes were destroyed when the buildings collapsed, and several lost close friends or family members. While many of my patients spent weeks processing their loss and trauma, some of those who were most affected by the attacks chose not to discuss their experiences in therapy at all. For example, one young man who was injured by falling debris clearly stated he preferred not to think about what happened to him that day ever again.

Although many of us believe it is essential to talk about traumatic events after they occur in order to minimize the risk of psychological complications, such is not the case. Indeed, a wave of recent research has demonstrated that many of our most cherished notions about coping with loss and trauma—well-known theories such as the five stages of grief (denial, anger, bargaining, depression, and acceptance) and common wisdoms such as the importance of expressing our feelings and the danger of keeping them bottled up—are largely incorrect.

For example, a technique called critical incident stress debriefing (CISD) is used by both the military and the Federal Emergency Management Agency (FEMA). The technique requires people who experience traumatic events to discuss them in great detail as soon after the events as possible, under the assumption that expressing what happened and how they feel about it should minimize the incidence of post-traumatic stress disorder. However, we now know much more about how memories (including traumatic ones) are actually formed in our brain. Specifically, the mere act of recalling an event changes our actual memory of it in minor ways. When we recall traumatic experiences while we're still flooded with intense emotion, we are inadvertently cementing the link between the memory and our intense emotional reactions to it. By doing so we are making it even more likely the memory will continue to evoke intense emotions going forward. As a result, we risk getting vivid flashbacks and making the traumatic memories themselves even more psychologically central and emotionally impactful than they otherwise would be.

However, that is not to say we should try to repress such memories or that we should refuse to discuss them. Indeed, most experts now believe there is no "right" way to cope with the aftermath of loss and trauma. The best each of us can do is to deal with such experiences exactly as our proclivities, personality, and worldview dictate. If we feel the need to talk, we should, and if we don't feel the need to share our thoughts and feelings with others we should not push ourselves to do so. For example, because my patient who was hit by falling debris on September 11 felt such a strong reluctance to think about the events, choosing not to discuss them was the correct course of action for him. Indeed, there is evidence to suggest that those who find it less pressing to discuss traumatic experiences might benefit from their natural tendency to avoid talking about their thoughts and feelings.

One online study began following over two thousand people in, as it happened, August 2001. Once the tragedies of September 11 occurred, the researchers realized they had a huge subject pool at their disposal. They decided to give the study participants the option of posting their feelings and thoughts about the events on the study website should they wish to do so. Three-quarters of the subjects chose to share their thoughts and feelings and one-quarter did not. The researchers continued to follow the subjects for two years and were able to examine their emotional well-being over time. For people geographically closest to the attacks, those who chose not to express their emotions had fewer symptoms of post-traumatic stress disorder two years later than people who had shared their thoughts and feelings online. Furthermore, the more people wrote (i.e., the longer their posts), the poorer they fared two years later.

These results by no means suggest we should avoid discussing our feelings if we feel the need to do so. The best course of action we can take in the aftermath of tragic events is to do exactly as our feelings dictate. Those who feel the need to share their thoughts and feelings with others should do so, and those who feel the need to remove themselves from such discussions should avoid them as best they can.

Following our natural inclinations might be advisable, but it can also be challenging at times. Those of us who prefer to discuss our feelings and experiences might find it difficult to do so if we lack sources of social support, while those who prefer not to discuss their feelings might find it equally difficult if they find themselves surrounded by vivid reminders. It was practically impossible for those affected by the events of September 11 to avoid thinking about their experiences, as reminders of the tragedy were everywhere. For months one could not step into the streets of Manhattan without seeing evidence of the attacks: the ruined buildings, the dust, the stench of burning materials, and the pictures of missing loved ones that were plastered on every wall, bus stop, and street sign along with heart-wrenching pleas for information about their whereabouts.

My patient avoided these reminders as best he could at the time, by burying his head in a magazine when he was on the subway, stepping away from water-cooler conversations when he was at work, and letting his close friends and family members know they should refrain from discussing the topic in his presence. Indeed, it is always best to let those around us know whether we wish to discuss tragic events or avoid such conversations so they know how best to conduct themselves around us.

For those who feel inclined to share thoughts and feelings with others, doing so can help us come to terms with the realities of our loss or trauma. Indeed, many religious rituals around grieving have exactly such a purpose in mind. For example, both Jewish shivahs and Irish wakes involve the gathering of friends and family to provide an outlet for the bereaved to express their feelings, thoughts, and memories while surrounded by sources of social and emotional support (not to mention copious quantities of food and alcohol).

When sources of social support are lacking or if we prefer to do so, we can also write about our experiences or compose letters to the people we've lost. Expressing thoughts and feelings we had not been able to share with the person before they died can give us comfort and even provide a measure of closure.

Regardless of how we choose to soothe our emotional pain in the immediate aftermath of loss or trauma, the most effective treatment—and one that is available to all of us—is time.

Treatment Summary: Soothe Your Emotional Pain Your Way

Dosage: Administer as soon after the events as possible. Make sure to communicate your preferences with regard to discussing your feelings and experiences to those around you.

Effective for: Managing and reducing emotional pain.

Treatment B: Recover Lost Aspects of Your "Self"

When Maxine lost her beloved husband, Kurt, to brain cancer, she lost substantial parts of herself as well. Her life after Kurt died was completely different from what it had been when he was alive. She and Kurt had been extremely active and enjoyed a thriving social circle, frequent camping and hiking trips, and countless evenings spent with good friends. But Maxine stopped participating in all such events after Kurt died and, as a result, she lost touch with the friends and the activities that had been a substantial part of her life.

Many of us are inclined to avoid people, places, or activities associated with the person we lost or with the traumatic events we faced in the first weeks and months after such events occur. But maintaining such avoidance for extended periods of time is problematic when doing so involves cutting out significant aspects of our lives. Maxine lost touch with many of the very experiences and relationships that had defined her, and consequently lost touch with important parts of herself. Relinquishing so many meaningful roles and functions altered her very sense of identity and these losses were never replaced. She found no new interests and passions to fulfill her and she made few new friends. The void her husband's death left in her life was still as large as it had been almost ten years earlier.

Maxine desperately needed to fill these gaps either by going back to previous activities or relationships or by finding new ones. Many of us face similar challenges. We go through our lives feeling empty and incomplete even years after the tragic experiences that changed us.

EXERCISE TO RECOVER LOST ASPECTS OF YOUR "SELF"

The following writing exercise will help you identify aspects of yourself you might have lost by finding new ways to express these missing parts of your identity and identifying new ways to recover meaningful roles you might have forsaken. I've included Maxine's responses to each of the questions for illustration purposes.

Caution: If the events are still fresh and the emotional distress you feel is still extreme, do not push yourself to complete this exercise unless you feel psychologically ready to do so.

1. List your qualities, characteristics, and abilities that you valued in yourself or that others valued about you before the events occurred (aim for at least ten items).

Maxine's list included the following: loyal, passionate, adventurous, curious, intelligent, leader, outdoors lover, expert camper, bonfire storyteller, compassionate, considerate, supportive, enthusiastic, loving, caring, and communicative.

2. Which of the above items feel most disconnected from your life today or tend to be expressed less today than they had been previously?

    Maxine indicated the following: adventurous, leader, outdoors lover, expert camper, storyteller, considerate, enthusiastic, loving, and caring. (Note that Maxine's list clustered around two aspects that had been central to her life before her husband died: her love of camping and the outdoors, and her close bond with the circle of friends who shared her passions.)

3. For each quality you listed, write a brief paragraph describing why you feel disconnected from the attribute in question or why the quality is no longer expressed as extensively as it had been previously.

    For example, Maxine wrote the following about why she rarely felt "adventurous": "I never thought of myself as a lone adventurer. For me, adventure was always about sharing new experiences with Kurt. What made it exciting was having the adventure together. Having them without him doesn't seem worthwhile and it even seems sad."

4. For each quality you listed, write a brief paragraph describing possible people, activities, or outlets you could pursue that would allow you to express the quality in a more substantial way than you are able to do currently.

When I asked Maxine to do this she struggled. She simply couldn't figure out how she might express her adventurous spirit without Kurt there to share the experience. "You think I should reconnect to my spirit of adventure by going on the safari, don't you?" she said, quickly adding, "But I can't, I really can't!"

"Actually, that's not what I was thinking at all," I responded. "I believe in taking small steps and a safari is hardly a small step. Actually, what caught my attention about your lists was that you stated adventures were experiences to be shared with Kurt. But it wasn't just Kurt. You were both part of a larger group of people who shared the same interests and passions, people with whom you might still share adventures, even if small ones. So here's what I was thinking," I said. "Which of your old camping friends would be someone you could see yourself going on a short hike with?" Maxine exhaled noticeably. She had been so convinced I was going to press her to go on a safari, she was happily willing to discuss taking a short hike with one of her old friends.

As another example, Grant had been very athletic and loved basketball before losing both his legs in a car accident. I pointed out that basketball was an extremely popular wheelchair sport and suggested he get information about local amateur leagues he could join.

5. Rank the items from the previous question according to which of them seem both doable and emotionally manageable.

6. Set yourself the goal of working through the list as best you can and at whatever pace seems most comfortable

(taking into account that taking action on each of the items is likely to cause at least some emotional discomfort at first). By working through the items on your list you will begin to reconnect to meaningful and valuable aspects of yourself and your personality, and by doing so, move forward.

Treatment Summary: Recover Lost Aspects of Your Self

Dosage: Administer once you have returned to normal functioning (e.g., within the home, at work, or in school).

Effective for: Restoring important aspects of one's identity and rebuilding disrupted relationships.

Secondary benefits: Reduces emotional pain.

Treatment C: Find Meaning in Tragedy

Since Viktor Frankl wrote *Man's Search for Meaning*, it has been accepted that finding meaning in loss and trauma is essential for coping effectively with such experiences, and thousands of studies have confirmed these assumptions. Finding meaning was a crucial factor in recovery from every kind of loss and trauma studied, from those with spinal cord injuries to bereaved parents of young children, from victims of violence and abuse to frontline veterans of wars. To recover from our tragic experience we need to set our bones correctly and put the pieces of our lives back together in ways that lend meaning and significance to the events by weaving our experiences into the larger fabric of our life stories.

But the question that arises for many of us is *how* to do so. We might be aware that people with similar experiences reached conclusions such as "I came to accept that it was God's will," "I realized I could help others who went through what I went through," or "I figured out what mattered to me and made big changes," but that doesn't tell us how these people reached their insights or how we might go about attaining our own epiphanies.

Scientists who examined how people go about finding meaning in loss and trauma realized the process includes two distinct phases, *sense making* and *benefit finding*. Sense making refers to our ability to fit the events into our existing framework of assumptions and beliefs about the world so they become more comprehensible to us. We are usually able to begin making sense of tragic events within six months of experiencing them (although completing the process of sense making can sometimes take months and even years). Once we do, we are likely to have far better emotional and psychological recoveries.

Benefit finding refers to our ability to wrestle whatever silver linings we can from our experiences. We might gain a greater appreciation of life and of our own strength and resilience, we might realign our priorities and identify new purpose, and we might recognize new paths that have opened before us as a result of our new realities. Benefit finding occurs only in later stages of our recovery, as it is not something most of us can or should do when still in the grips of severe emotional pain. That said, once sufficient time has passed, people who are able to identify benefits in their loss or trauma tend to display greater emotional and psychological well-being than those who are unable to do so.

How to Find Meaning in Tragedy

Once of the most common ways in which people derive meaning from tragic events is by taking action in ways that are directly related to the loss or trauma they sustained. Family members of someone who died of a rare disease might start a foundation to increase awareness of the illness that took their loved one. A survivor of sexual or physical assault might decide to speak out and educate others about how to avoid such experiences or how to cope with them if they occur. Veterans who've lost a limb in war often volunteer to help recently wounded soldiers adjust to their injuries and support them through their long process of rehabilitation. Many people who lost loved ones in the attacks of September 11, 2001, became involved in planning memorial sites in New York; Washington, DC; and Pennsylvania. Of course, not every loss affords us these options, nor are they appropriate for everyone.

The following exercises will help us identify new avenues of thinking that could make our individual explorations more productive. Two exercises facilitate sense making. The first should be completed only once we've begun to recover from the initial assault of emotional pain. The second should be applied slightly later, when we are emotionally able to contemplate potentially painful "what-if" scenarios. The third exercise facilitates benefit finding and should only be considered once we feel substantially recovered and stronger emotionally. If any of the following exercises are too painful to complete, please refer to the section at the end of the chapter that discusses when to seek the advice of a mental health professional.

Make Sense of Tragic Events by Asking *Why*, Not *How*

We often struggle to accept the basic reality of tragic events when they first occur and we replay *how* things happened over and over again in our minds. For example, Maxine frequently replayed memories of her last conversation with Kurt. Natural as it is to do so, when such ruminations persist, they become unproductive and serve only to reactivate our emotional pain. Going over how things happened and replaying similar scenes tends to add no new insights and does not help us make sense of the events. But tweaking one important aspect of these ruminative thoughts could make them more conducive to attaining new insights and to fostering sense making.

Specifically, numerous studies demonstrate that asking ourselves *why* events happened as opposed to *how* they happened is sufficient to trigger a qualitatively different and more productive thought process. Difficult as it is to answer such questions, by asking why instead of how we widen the scope of our thinking and of our associations and are forced to consider the larger existential, spiritual, or philosophical implications of the events. Such bigger-picture thought processes are more likely to help us find meaning in the events in time, and to reach a greater measure of internal peace as a result.

Almost ten years after losing her husband, Maxine never asked herself the big questions about why Kurt died and whether she could derive any meaning or purpose from losing him. In fact, such questions were so foreign to Maxine's way of thinking that she seemed momentarily confused and disoriented when I first asked them. However, once she was able to begin giving thought to the question of why Kurt died she found that she spent much less time replaying the events of his last weeks and months. For Maxine, asking why opened the door to fresh and meaningful thought processes that helped her move forward in her mourning after being stalled for many years.

Make Sense of Tragic Events by Asking *What Might Have Been*

Another feature of the obsessive thoughts we experience in early stages of loss or trauma is they are often characterized by fantasies about alternate outcomes. We ponder such questions as "What if the person who died in an accident had taken a different route?" "What if the cancer had been found earlier?" or "What if our attacker had chosen a different victim?" Some of us might feel that pursuing thoughts of "what might have been" can only focus us on the randomness of the events and thus make it more difficult for us to accept what *is*. But studies have found the opposite. Rather than eliciting a sense of randomness, thoughts that consider alternatives to the factual realities we've experienced (known as *counterfactuals*) can help us feel like the events were predestined and meant to be, thereby lending them greater meaning.

Much like asking why instead of how, counterfactual thoughts force us to think more abstractly, to make connections between different parts of our lives, to utilize our analytic abilities, and to see the bigger picture. All of these are essential aspects of the meaning-making process. Such exercises can help us break out of rigid perspectives that limit our ability to consider the larger context of our lives so we can arrive at fresh comprehensions and new perspectives.

Our natural tendency is to employ counterfactual thoughts to explore how we might have avoided the loss or trauma, but we can also direct our thoughts to how things could have been worse.

Some experts believe the best way to extract meaning from tragic events (again, once we've recovered sufficiently) is to combine both types of counterfactual thinking and consider both what our lives would have been like had the events not happened and the ways in which things could have been worse.

Thought Exercise: "What Might Have Been"

Caution: Readers should be advised that counterfactual thought experiments can be emotionally painful. *Review the exercise and complete it only if you feel emotionally ready to do so.* Further, those who do not believe in fate or predestination might not benefit from this exercise as much as those who do, and therefore they should not complete it if they feel that doing so will be either unhelpful or too emotionally distressing. For those who feel ready, it is best to complete this exercise in one sitting. Written responses are strongly recommended.

1. How would your life be different today if the events had not happened?

2. In what ways could the outcome of the events have been even worse than they were?

3. What factors prevented these worse outcomes from occurring?

4. How grateful are you that these worse outcomes did not occur?

Once you've completed this exercise, give yourself time to recover and to absorb any thoughts, insights, or fresh perspectives it might have evoked (at least a day or more) before moving on to the benefit-finding exercise. You may also choose to wait weeks or months or to skip the benefit-finding exercise entirely if you feel unready or unable to complete it.

How to Identify Benefits in Loss

Finding benefit in loss and trauma once enough time has passed is an important way to ascribe meaning and significance to the events so we can put them in their place and move on with our lives. Although it can take time to identify any such "silver linings," doing so can open doors to paths and opportunities that can become sources of both meaning and life satisfaction later on. Helping others who've had similar experiences; creating awareness about diseases, societal problems, or other dangers; starting foundations in memory of those we've lost; writing about the events and creating art and performances about them; and becoming para-athletes are all examples of ways in which people have extracted benefit and purpose from tragic events.

While identifying potential pathways for deriving benefit from tragedy can have a positive impact on our recovery it is the real-world application of these benefits that does our emotional and psychological recovery most good. Therefore, we need to find ways to put any benefits we identify into action. For example, we might come away from a tragedy with a greater appreciation of our family, but if we don't take action based on these insights, the benefit we derive from our new perspective will be limited. However, if we make changes that allow us to spend more time with family members or increase the quality of the time we already do spend with them, we are much more likely to have truly gained from our loss and reap the psychological blessings of doing so.

Exercise to Identify Possible Benefits

When completing the following exercise, make sure you have the time and space to relax and let your thoughts explore various possibilities without feeling rushed or pressured.

Imagine yourself ten years in the future. You have been able to achieve something meaningful and significant (not necessarily "Nobel Prize worthy" but meaningful to you). You have a quiet moment to look back and reflect about your journey and how it has led you to this current moment in (future) time. Complete the following sentences.

1. I never imagined back then that such tragic events would lead me to:

2. What I did was significant and very meaningful to me because:

3. The first step of my journey toward the achievement was when I:

4. My achievement was possible because I changed my priorities such that:

5. Changing my priorities led me to make the following changes in my life:

6. Along the way I realized my purpose in life is:

Treatment Summary: Find Meaning in Tragedy

Dosage: Review the treatment and administer it only when you feel you can manage the emotional pain or discomfort it might evoke.

Effective for: Reducing emotional pain, recovering lost aspects of our identity, and reconstructing damaged belief systems.

Secondary benefits: Restores and rebuilds damaged or neglected relationships.

When to Consult a Mental Health Professional

When the loss or trauma we've sustained is significant or when it impacts our lives in extreme or fundamental ways, we should always seek the counsel of a mental health professional. If you think you might be experiencing symptoms of post-traumatic stress disorder, such as intrusive flashbacks, nightmares, emotional numbness, or jumpiness and agitation, seek the counsel of a trained mental health professional who specializes in trauma. Further, if you've applied the treatments in this chapter but doing so has not helped your emotional or mental state or you have not been able to make changes to better your situation or resume your life fully and productively, you should also seek the help of an experienced mental health professional, preferably one who specializes in loss, trauma, or bereavement.

If at any point after tragic events occur you feel as though you are in too much emotional pain and have thoughts of harming yourself or another person in any way, you should seek immediate help from a mental health professional or go to the nearest emergency room.

CHAPTER 4

||||||||||||||||||

GUILT

The Poison in Our System

G uilt is an extremely common feeling of emotional distress caused by the belief that we've done something wrong or caused harm to another person. We all fail to live up to our own standards from time to time and even the best of us can act in ways that offend, insult, or hurt someone, inadvertently or otherwise. How common are guilty feelings? Studies estimate that people experience roughly two hours a day of mild guilt, five hours a week of moderate guilt, and three and a half hours a month of severe guilt. In some cases guilty feelings persist for years and even for decades.

The reason we don't walk around feeling incapacitated by guilty feelings is that we usually experience them for only short durations. Indeed, guilt's primary function is to signal to us we've done or are about to do something that violates our personal standards (such as when we cheat on our diets, buy something that wasn't in our budget, or play video games instead of doing work) or that causes direct or indirect harm to another person. We respond to this signal by reevaluating our plan of action or apologizing to those we've harmed and mending the situation as best we can, and our guilt typically dissipates rather quickly thereafter.

Unpleasant as it is, guilt serves a crucial function in maintaining our individual standards of behavior and in protecting our personal, familial, and community relationships. When our spouse tears up in the middle of a heated argument, guilt makes us soften and reach out. When we're extremely busy and stressed at work and realize we forgot our mother's birthday, guilt swoops in to nag at us until we drop what we're doing and shoot her a highly apologetic e-mail or phone call. And when our friend discovers we revealed something he or she told us in confidence, guilt motivates us to offer a heartfelt apology, a promise of future discretion, and maybe even a nice dinner as compensation.

Guilt does so much to protect our most cherished relationships it practically deserves its own superhero costume and cape. But before we break out the spandex, we should consider that not everything guilt does is psychologically beneficial. In the above examples, the harm we caused the other person was mild and our efforts to apologize or atone for our errors were successful. Therefore our guilty feelings ceased immediately or at least decreased significantly as a result. Similarly, when we fail to live up to our own standards, compensating for our wrongdoing and correcting our behavior is usually sufficient to eliminate our guilt substantially if not entirely.

But there are times when our guilty feelings outstay their welcome and become literal squatters in our minds. While guilt can be heroic in small doses, in larger ones, it becomes a psychological villain, poisoning both our peace of mind and our most cherished relationships. And once the toxins of unhealthy guilt are circulating in our systems, extracting the venom is no easy task.

Unhealthy Guilt and Relationships

Although we feel guilty when we violate our personal standards, such guilt rarely lingers. When we cheat on our diet, when we spend too much money, or when we neglect our duties in some way, we might make efforts to compensate for our actions, but we are rarely traumatized by them. No one wakes up screaming in the middle of the night consumed with guilt about the chocolate cheesecake they wolfed down last Christmas. When emotional distress about violating our personal standards does linger, it usually engenders feelings of regret rather than guilt.

Rather, unhealthy guilt occurs primarily in situations involving our relationships—when there are implications for the welfare of others. Unhealthy relational guilt typically manifests in three primary forms, all of which inflict similar psychological wounds: *unresolved guilt*, which is the most common and often the most damaging, *survivor guilt*, and *separation guilt* (or the closely related *disloyalty guilt*).

Although there are innumerable offenses that can elicit relational guilt, one of the main reasons our guilt might remain unresolved is that we're much less skilled at rendering effective apologies than we tend to realize. Another is that even when our apologies are on point, the harm we caused the other person might simply be too great for that person to forgive us for or the person might want to forgive us but simply feels unable to do so (often a sign our apology was ineffective after all). In some situations circumstances might prevent us from being able to communicate an apology to the person at all. In each of these scenarios, our guilt remains unresolved and unremitting and can quickly become toxic.

Some forms of guilt occur without clear wrongdoing on our part. Survivors of wars, accidents, illnesses, or other tragedies often find it impossible to engage in their lives fully because doing so evokes images or memories of those who perished. They might be consumed by questions about why they survived while others did not. Or they might feel responsible in some way even though there was nothing they could have done to prevent the events from occurring. Many of those with severe cases of survivor guilt also suffer from post-traumatic stress disorder (PTSD). As such, their survivor guilt is merely a symptom of a more complex psychological disorder and the treatments in this chapter would not be appropriate for them. When survivor guilt is related to wars, accidents, and other traumatic events, it is best to consult a mental health professional who is specifically trained in treating PTSD.

Survivor guilt is often made worse by circumstance. We might have argued with a sibling just before he was killed in a driving accident, forgotten to call back a friend just before she committed suicide, or insulted a colleague moments before he was fired. One of the most unfortunate examples of how circumstances can induce survivor guilt involves Waylon Jennings, who was a guitarist for Buddy Holly. Jennings had a seat on Holly's plane the day it crashed, killing all aboard, but he gave up his seat to J. P. Richardson ("the Big Bopper") and took the bus because Richardson was sick. If that wasn't enough to induce survivor guilt, the last exchange Jennings had with Holly was when Holly teased Jennings for having to take the bus by saying, "Well, I hope your ol' bus freezes up!" Jennings retorted, "Well, I hope your ol' plane crashes!" Jennings later became a star in his own right, but he was forever haunted by incredible survivor guilt both by Richardson's death and even more so because of his parting words to Buddy Holly.

Fortunately, many of the situations that cause survivor guilt are far less dramatic or tragic than Jennings's. When we find ourselves more fortunate than others, either because we're doing ex-ceptionally well or because they are faring unusually poorly by comparison, our empathy and conscience can combine to elicit an exaggerated sense of guilt. As a result we might experience psychological disruptions in our lives despite no wrongdoing on our part. For example, we might find it difficult to enjoy a promotion because our friend and colleague had competed for the same position. We might feel unable to celebrate our engagement to the person of our dreams because our older sibling is still single and unhappy. Or we might have trouble celebrating getting into our first choice of colleges because our best friend did not.

What makes survivor guilt especially hard to purge is that there are no actions for which we must atone, no relationship ruptures to mend, and no outstanding apologies to be rendered. As such, our guilt serves no relational purpose and its warning signals constitute nothing more than a deafening false alarm that poisons our quality of life.

Separation guilt involves feeling guilty about moving forward and pursuing our own life when doing so involves leaving others behind. We might find it impossible to enjoy a night out with our spouse because we feel guilty about leaving our children with a babysitter, even one with whom they are familiar and comfortable. We might feel guilty about living far from our aging parents, even when they are well cared for. Or we might feel guilty about taking a job or studying overseas when we know how much our families will miss us.

Disloyalty guilt arises when we feel such binding ties of loyalty to close family members or friends that pursuing our own goals or making choices that deviate from their norms and expectations makes us feel bad. We worry that our families will perceive our choices as hurtful condemnations of their own values and as betrayals of family loyalty. Such guilt is especially common around themes of religious practices and sexual orientation. One mother I worked with turned to her lesbian daughter who had just come out (and had agreed to join her for the session) and cried, "How could you do this to me?!" Her daughter responded by saying, "I'm not doing anything to you! I just want to be happy!" and promptly burst into tears while mouthing to her mother, "I'm so sorry. I'm so sorry."

Family members often feel betrayed in such situations and, unfortunately, they often convey their feelings to us in no uncertain terms. Of course, many adult children feel just as betrayed by their parents' lack of support and empathy, but guilt usually falls far more heavily on their shoulders than it does on those of their parents or other family and community members.

While the consequences to our relationships should obviously be addressed in such situations, what makes our guilt maladaptive is that it arises in response to an otherwise healthy desire to express our autonomy, to live our own lives, to make our own choices and tend to our own emotional and psychological needs.

Regardless of whether our unhealthy guilt results from wrongdoing on our part or not, the more excessive it is or the longer it lingers, the more toxic its effects become and the greater the wounds it can inflict on our mental health.

The Psychological Wounds Guilt Inflicts

Excessive unhealthy guilt causes two types of psychological wounds, each of which can be poisonous to our quality of life. The first involves the impact guilt has on our individual functioning and happiness. In addition to creating paralyzing emotional distress, guilt seriously hampers our ability to focus adequate attention on our own needs and obligations, and it often causes us to resort to blatant self-punishment. The second is that it wreaks havoc on our relationships. The effects of excessive or unresolved guilt impair our communication with the person we've harmed and limit our ability to relate to him or her in an authentic manner; in addition, its toxic effects often ripple outward and create tensions and allegiances that ensnare entire families, social circles, and even communities.

The reason it is urgent to treat unresolved or excessive guilt is that such feelings often intensify and devolve into remorse and shame. Once that happens, we begin to condemn not just our actions but our entire selves, leading to self-loathing, low self-esteem, and depression. In order to treat these two wounds successfully we will need a clear understanding of the impact they have on our lives and the damage they inflict on our relationships. Let's examine them in greater detail.

1. Self-Condemnation: How Guilt Plays Whac-A-Mole with Our Joy and Happiness

Guilty feelings come in a range of severities. On the lighter side, our guilt can manifest as an annoying pest that constantly nags at us and tugs at our shirtsleeves. It can distract us as we labor to attend to our obligations and slow us down as we go about the daily business of our lives. In its more severe form guilt can consume us, paralyze us, and become the central organizing theme of our very existence.

Yoshi, a college student, was only months away from graduating when he came to see me for psychotherapy during his spring break. His parents, both physicians, had immigrated to the United States from Japan in their early thirties, then struggled to find jobs as clinicians and took research positions instead. "My father says the happiest day of his life was when I was accepted into an Ivy League school with one of the best premed programs in the country," Yoshi explained. "They expected me to go straight to Harvard Medical School and eventually open a successful medical practice, so I could fulfill the dream they were denied."

The pressure his parents' expectations were putting on Yoshi was enormous, but as he continued his story I realized he was far beyond stressed—he looked absolutely haunted.

"I hated premed from the first class I took," he continued. "I kept at it for the entire first year and I did well, but I was miserable. Premed wasn't for me. Medical school isn't for me. So I switched majors. Only I didn't know how to tell them without breaking their hearts. They've sacrificed so much for me, for my education, I just couldn't . . . I've been lying to them ever since. But I graduate in a few months and then . . . they'll know!" Yoshi covered his face with his hands. "I feel so guilty I could throw up. I keep imagining their faces when they find out." Yoshi began sobbing. He was unable to speak for several minutes. "They've worked so hard to pay for my schooling. I could have gone to a state school and saved them so much money. They think I'll be hearing from Harvard any day now. They're going to be crushed, just crushed!" Yoshi broke into a fresh round of sobs. "I don't know what to do! I can't concentrate, I can't focus, I can't study . . . it's all I can think about!"

After managing his guilt for three years, Yoshi could no longer keep it at bay. His guilty feelings now consumed him, screamed at him, nagged at him, and made it impossible for him to ignore their presence any longer. They hampered his ability to concentrate, to focus, to think clearly, and to move forward in his studies.

Guilt makes many of us experience mental and intellectual disruptions that are so significant we might struggle to meet our basic obligations and to function at work or in school. Until we take steps to address the cause of our guilt or minimize its impact, we will continue to remain at its mercy.

Unfortunately, unhealthy guilt doesn't only make us feel bad, it prevents us from feeling good as well. In one study involving regular college students (i.e., not ones preselected for guilt issues), scientists flashed words associated with guilt, such as "blameworthy," "culpable," and "guilt-ridden," on a screen at high speed such that the participants did not perceive the words consciously but were impacted by them nonetheless—a process called "priming." A second group of people was primed with words associated with sadness, and a third (control) group was primed with neutral words. Participants were then asked to indicate how they might spend a fifty-dollar coupon. While subjects in the neutral and sadness groups allocated most of their funds to things such as music and movies, subjects who were primed with guilt-related words chose far less indulgent items such as school supplies.

This experiment and others like it serve as testaments to guilt's significant party-pooping powers, as even subliminal exposure to guilt-related words was sufficient to function as a killjoy for people who weren't even feeling guilty at the time. Certainly when we are in the throes of unrelenting or excessive guilt it is extremely difficult for us to enjoy our lives in any substantial way. Things that used to bring us pleasure, joy, or excitement lose their appeal, not because we no longer enjoy them, but because we no longer permit ourselves to do so.

This is especially problematic for people who suffer from various forms of survivor guilt. For example, parents whose children are victims of accidents or chronic illness, children (and even grandchildren) of Holocaust survivors, survivors of other atrocities, and spouses who lose their partners often feel guilty at the very thought of having fun or indulging themselves in any way. Such extended and severe guilt serves no productive purpose other than to unnecessarily diminish our own quality of life.

A Fight Club of One

Another toxic effect of excessive guilt is that we might try to relieve our emotional distress by punishing ourselves for our wrongdoings (consciously or unconsciously) with self-sabotaging or self-destructive behavior. Some of us even resort to punishing ourselves physically. Self-flagellation has a long and particularly stomach-turning history as a form of atonement and was especially popular during outbreaks of bubonic plague in thirteenth- and fourteenth-century Europe. People believed that publically whipping themselves with irons or flaying their own flesh would cleanse them from sins and ward off the Black Death. As civilization advanced, so have our methods of self-punishment, as evidenced by the dearth of people who whip themselves into a bloody mess in public and the abundance of folks who bang their heads against a wall in private.

Head bangers aside, far more of us resort to self-punishment than we might realize. In one study, people who were made to feel guilty by depriving a fellow subject of lottery tickets were willing to give themselves highly uncomfortable electrical shocks, especially when they found themselves in the presence of their "victim." In other studies, subjects who were made to feel guilty were willing to keep their hands submerged in freezing water for painful periods of time (and much longer ones than nonguilty subjects). What makes such findings remarkable is that the participants weren't warding off the plague—they just felt bad about a fellow student missing out on a few lottery tickets!

Seeking self-punishment when we feel responsible for harming someone whom we are unable to compensate for our actions is known as the *Dobby effect* (so named after the self-punishing house-elf in the Harry Potter series). The reason we nonmagical creatures resort to such measures, and the reason we might even do so publicly, is that such actions represent a clear signal of remorse. By making others aware of our emotional distress, we redistribute the emotional (or physical) pain our "victims" felt, even the score with them, and hopefully restore our standing in our social circle, family, or community.

2. Blocked Relationships: How Guilt Poisons Arteries of Healthy Communication

Significant guilt poisons the arteries of authentic communication and connection between us and those we've harmed (or, in the case of guilt trips, those who perceive themselves to have been harmed by us whether they were or not). Even if we don't realize it, unresolved guilt impacts our behavior around the other person, and it usually affects how that person behaves around us as well. In many cases, it also embroils others in our social or family circles, such that the natural flow of authentic communication between all the affected people quickly becomes poisoned and our relationships become extremely strained. The ongoing toxicity of our unresolved guilt in such situations can damage our relationships even more substantially than our original offense did.

We often experience guilt in waves and when it comes to our relationships, the waves are at their highest when we interact with the offended person. In such moments, our guilt can spike so dramatically that it feels like being hit in the face in dodgeball. Understandably, our natural inclination is often to duck these painful encounters whenever we can. In order to minimize any chances of injuring the person further, we avoid any mention of the guilt-inducing incident itself, when interacting with that person and with other family members. We steer clear of any related topics that might segue into the incident, a list that tends to grow as time goes on. We might also avoid people or places that remind us of our wrongdoing, and eventually we begin making efforts to avoid the person altogether.

While such strategies represent ineffective solutions at best, they are all but impossible when the person we've harmed is our spouse. Blake, a stay-at-home dad, and Judy, a pharmaceuticals sales representative, initially came to couples therapy to deal with parenting issues. They had three children, two of whom were diagnosed with attention deficit and hyperactivity disorder and all three of whom failed to respond to any efforts the parents made to set limits. However, their parenting differences were swiftly pushed aside when Blake discovered a text message indicating Judy might have had an affair with a coworker the previous year. He confronted her about it in our next session. Judy was stunned by Blake's ambush but she confessed to the affair right away. "It was a one-time thing and I've regretted it ever since," she said. "We had a drink after work and it just happened. But it didn't mean anything! It was just a stupid mistake, a terribly stupid mistake."

Blake, who had hoped Judy would be able to offer a compelling explanation for the text message, was absolutely shattered. "You slept with another man," he mumbled, shaking his head in disbelief. "You slept with another man. . . ."

Judy's face was a mask of guilt and anguish. "I'm sorry, Blake! I truly am! But I promise you it meant nothing. It was a mistake, that's all. You have to believe me!"

Judy was incredibly relieved when Blake informed her that

he'd decided to stay in the marriage. However, that did not mean he forgave her. In fact, Blake continued to feel so wounded he struggled to think of anything else. Every time Judy looked at him, she saw the terrible hurt in his eyes and she felt incredibly guilty because of it. As the weeks went by, they began to fall back into their normal patterns and routines, but Blake's pain lingered on and so did Judy's guilt. Judy's job in sales required her to be energetic and positive and she was able to adopt that mind-set when she was at work. But at home she felt oppressed by her guilt. She began working longer hours (making sure to call Blake every thirty minutes to reassure him she was legitimately in her office). She found excuses to avoid family engagements, both with his and with her own family, and she became less involved in the kids' extracurricular activities.

I decided to meet with Judy privately to discuss her increasing disengagement. "It's not just your guilt that you're avoiding," I pointed out, "it's your entire marriage." Judy nodded silently. But her guilt had become so overwhelming she simply wasn't sure whether she could tolerate it much longer. She was desperate to receive forgiveness from Blake and he in turn was desperate to forgive her and move on—but he simply couldn't. The cycle of hurt, guilt, and avoidance that played out between them devastated their ability to communicate authentically with one another and presented an even greater threat to their marriage than her affair had. When we play dodgeball with our guilt, we rarely win.

Tripping on Guilt Trips

Guilt trips almost always take place in close relationships and their most common theme is one of interpersonal neglect. "I could be lying here dead and you'd never know it because you never call," "If you get that tattoo it'll break your mother's heart!" and "Your father's been a wreck since your argument with him last week!" are common yet benign examples of everyday guilt trips that are the bread and butter of many family communications. The main reason we seek to induce guilt in others is to influence their decisions and behavior. But guilt trips have a boomerang effect we rarely consider in that, along with guilt, they also induce resentment.

In one survey, 33 percent of people indicated they felt resentful toward those who make them feel guilty while only 2 percent of guilt inducers mentioned resentment as a potential consequence of their guilt-inducing efforts. Indeed, few guilt trippers are aware of the self-defeating consequences of their actions. When we are the recipients of guilt trips we might respond to a person's charges of neglect by engaging with them, but the resentment we typically feel by doing so is likely to motivate us to avoid them even more going forward. Mild as the poisonous effects of most guilt trips are, over the long term, their toxicity can build and cause our interactions and communication to become superficial and perfunctory, and the quality of our relationships to diminish.

How Guilt Poisons Entire Families

When our transgression is significant or when the person we harmed remains unforgiving, it doesn't take much for the poisonous effects of our guilt and the condemnation of the person we hurt to spread to other members of our family or social circle. All it takes is for one person to take sides and invoke unspoken expectations of loyalty in doing so, and a divide is quickly established. Other family members then quickly line up on either side of the rift, poisoning arteries of healthy communication even further and affecting everyone to one degree or another. Many a multigenerational family feud was birthed in just this way.

The most fertile grounds upon which these toxic family dynamics play out are family events and religious holidays. Large gatherings create perfect stages upon which to revive a family's "greatest hits" of past wrongdoings. Of course, aside from inducing powerful guilt in those who committed the transgressions it creates tensions and divisiveness that can mar even the best-planned and most festive events.

Antonia, a twenty-year-old college student, was the third oldest of twelve siblings, ten of whom were girls. By Antonia's own admission, she, of all the siblings, had the most tumultuous relationship with their mother. "I'm from an Italian family," she explained in our first session. "Very Italian, you know? I always give my mother respect but I argue with her too. Anyway, things are really bad between us now and I have to do something." I nodded sympathetically, encouraging Antonia to continue. "I know this sounds terrible and everything," she said, "but the reason everyone is so upset is . . . I mean, what happened was I . . . ran her over with the car."

My eyebrows shot up so hard I thought my forehead would "ding."

"I mean her foot!" Antonia hastily clarified. "I ran over her foot with the car! And it was a mistake. A mistake!"

Antonia had been visiting her parents when she and her mother had one of their "scream-fests." Antonia decided to leave. She was about to pull out of the driveway when her mother ran out because, in Antonia's words, she "still had more scream left in her." Apparently Antonia's mother proceeded to deplete her reserves of "scream" by yelling at Antonia for disrespecting her and walking away in the middle of an argument. It seems her mother delivered her tirade so loudly and with such profanity, neighbors came outside to watch. "I've never seen her so furious," Antonia recalled. "There was spit all over the car window. I mean saliva!"

Antonia, no slouch in the yelling department herself, yelled at her mother to move away from the car. "My mom stood back but she looked scary mad. It really shook me up. She made me so crazy, I forgot to straighten the wheel and didn't realize it was turned." Antonia swallowed hard. "I pressed on the gas and before I could hit the brake, I drove right over her foot." Her lower lip began to tremble. "I thought I would die. Die! I jumped out and saw my mother clutching her left foot and screaming. I almost had a heart attack when I realized I must have driven over it. She had bunion surgery on that same foot just last year! I was, like, 'Ma, I'm sorry! I didn't realize the wheel was turned! I'm sorry!' But she didn't even look at me. She just moaned in pain."

Antonia wanted to drive her mother straight to the emergency room, but her mother refused and insisted Antonia's older sister drive her instead. "I waited for them at home all night," Antonia continued. "I felt so guilty I could vomit. Vomit! Then my sister Maria comes up to me and tells me my mother says I ran over her on purpose! Can you believe that? How could she think that?!"

By the time Antonia's mother got home, her sisters had already divided into camps: those who believed she had run over her mother's foot on purpose and those who were horrified by the mere suggestion. Unfortunately, her mother's foot took months to heal, during which members of the extended family were slowly recruited to one side or the other. All the while, Antonia continued to visit her parents and communicate with her mother, albeit somewhat minimally, such that on the surface things appeared normal. But below the surface, the unspoken accusations and resentments and Antonia's guilty feelings were snowballing. By the time the family gathered for Thanksgiving the tension was so thick, it ruined the holiday for everyone. Antonia decided to seek my advice before their Christmas was ruined as well.

Similar tensions and tests of loyalty are common in work-places, among friends, and in other social circles such as recreational sport teams. When our guilt is substantial and unresolved, the poison that impairs healthy communication and creates stress between ourselves and another person can easily expand and become toxic for the entire group.

How to Treat the Psychological Wounds Guilt Inflicts

Guilt usually serves an important function by alerting us to when we might have harmed another person or when any actions we're considering might do so. Once we modify our plan of action or atone for our transgressions, either by apologizing or in some other way, our guilt subsides. Therefore, we do not need to apply emotional first aid treatments in every situation. However, if our offense is serious or if we've already made significant efforts to apologize to the person we harmed or to atone for our actions in other ways and our guilt remains excessive, or if we suffer from substantial survivor guilt, or separation and disloyalty guilt, emotional first aid is indeed necessary. Let's open our medical cabinet and review our treatment options.

General Treatment Guidelines

The most effective way to treat unresolved guilt is to eliminate it at the source by repairing our relationship with the person we've harmed. Mending the rupture and garnering the person's authentic forgiveness will cause our guilt to diminish significantly, and most likely dissolve completely, soon thereafter. Treatment A (rendering effective apologies) focuses on how to repair damaged relationships by crafting psychologically effective apologies that can detoxify any ill will the other person still harbors and promote relationship repair.

Treatment B (self-forgiveness) focuses on situations in which the circumstances prevent a direct apology to be issued or ones in which it is impossible to repair the relationship for other reasons, and provides other ways to alleviate guilt, and reduce self-condemnation and self-punishment. Treatment B is not as effective as Treatment A in removing the venom that is at the root of excessive guilt but it does provide a form of "psychological anti-toxin" that can deliver much-needed emotional relief. Treatment C (reengaging in life) is focused on survivor and separation and disloyalty guilt (in which there are no relationship ruptures to mend). At the end of the chapter I discuss guidelines for when one should consult a mental health professional.

Treatment A: Learn the Recipe for an Effective Apology

In theory, the solution to toxic relational guilt is simple—you render an authentic apology to the person you've harmed and, assuming your sincerity shines through and your transgression was not

too monumental, all will be forgiven, especially with time. However, research demonstrates that in practice, this simple transaction of apology and forgiveness goes awry far more often than we
might expect, regardless of the area of our lives in which it occurs.
Further complicating matters, both psychologically and commu-
nication-wise, when our apologies are perceived as insincere they
can actually backfire and make a situation worse, spreading even
more poison into an already toxic interpersonal dynamic.

The reason this happens so often is that crafting apologies that
are effective enough to garner authentic forgiveness is far more
complicated than we realize. In fact, until recently, it was far more
complicated than most psychologists realized as well.

How is it possible that something as basic as an apology be-
fuddles so many of us? After all, most of us are taught to say "I'm
sorry" as soon as we can talk. Surely as adults we should be at least
somewhat proficient at offering effective apologies. Alas, we're not.
Although we're taught *when* to say "I'm sorry," we're never really
taught *how* to say it, or at least how to voice it effectively. This exact
issue eluded psychologists for many years. Hundreds of studies
have investigated apologies and forgiveness but the vast majority
of them have examined only if and when an apology was rendered,
not how it was articulated nor what distinguished a successful
apology from an unsuccessful one. Fortunately, relationship experts and researchers have finally begun to investigate the specific
ingredients that make apologies effective and more likely to elicit
authentic forgiveness from the offended party.

The Recipe for Communicating Effective Apologies

Most of us conceive of apologies as including three basic ingredients: (1) a statement of regret for what happened; (2) a clear "I'm sorry" statement; and (3) a request for forgiveness—all of which must be delivered with sincerity (e.g., "Wow, I completely forgot about our date night! I feel really bad about it and hope you can forgive me!" as opposed to "Oops! Was that tonight?"). Although each of these ingredients might seem obvious, it is remarkable how often we end up omitting one of them. When I point out such omissions to my patients, they often respond as if I'm being petty by calling them on a mere "technicality." "Aw, come on!" they often say, "I'm apologizing, aren't I? The 'I'm sorry' part is implied!"

My response is usually to point out that flour is an implied ingredient when we're baking a cake, but if we forget to put it in, what we end up with won't look like cake and it won't taste like cake either. The analogy is important because if we want our apologies to be effective, we have to follow a clear recipe, and the three items above are not the only ingredients we need to include. Scientists have discovered three additional components that also play a vital role in an apology's effectiveness: validating the other person's feelings, offering atonement, and acknowledging we violated expectations. Let's look at these additional ingredients and then examine which of the total of six apology components were present or lacking in the apologies offered by Antonia, Judy, and Yoshi, and how their apologies fared as a result.

Validate Their Feelings

We generally find it hard to forgive people who hurt, angered, or disappointed us unless we believe they really "get" how they made us feel. But if their apology demonstrates a clear understanding of the emotional pain they caused us and if they take full responsibility for doing so, we feel substantial emotional relief and have a much easier time letting go of our resentment because we feel like our feelings have been validated.

Emotional validation is a powerful tool when used correctly, and a great toxin remover when used in apologies. Consequently, we need to put ourselves in the other person's shoes and understand the specific consequences of our actions, how the person was affected by them, and the feelings they caused. Validating the person's emotions by conveying we "get" how he or she feels does not imply we meant for the person to feel that way. Doing so merely acknowledges the person felt wronged, regardless of our intentions.

The reason this ingredient is so often omitted from apologies is because when we've caused someone harm, acknowledging how upset he or she seems strikes us as a risky proposition. The idea of telling someone who's angry, frustrated, or horribly disappointed in us that he or she indeed should feel angry, frustrated, or horribly disappointed seems akin to pouring fuel on the fire. Consequently, our instinct is to avoid addressing the individual's emotional state entirely. Yet, counterintuitive as it might seem, when we validate someone's feelings *accurately*, something quite magical happens. Rather than inciting further fury and pouring fuel on the fire, our message of emotional validation actually douses the flame.

Emotional validation is something we all seek and crave far more than we realize. One of the reasons so many of us feel compelled to discuss our feelings with others when we feel upset, angry, frustrated, disappointed, or hurt is that we hope to *get things off our chest* and ease our internal distress by doing so. However, in order to feel true relief, we need them to "get it," to understand what happened to us and why we feel the way we do. We need them to validate our feelings by conveying that understanding along with a generous dollop of empathy. When we spill our guts to our friends we hope they'll say "Wow," "Gosh," and "That's terrible!" We would find it incredibly unsatisfying if their only response to our heart-wrenching tale was to shrug and say, "Bummer."

How to Offer Authentic Emotional Validation

There are five steps to offering authentic emotional validation. The most important factor is accuracy. The more accurate we are when conveying our understanding of the wronged person's feelings, the more relationship poison we remove by doing so.

1. Let the other person complete his or her narrative about what happened so you have all the facts.

2. Convey your understanding of what happened to this person from his or her perspective (whether you agree with that perspective or not and even if that perspective is obviously skewed).

3. Convey your understanding of how the person felt as a result of what happened (from his or her perspective).

4. Acknowledge that his or her feelings are reasonable (which, given that person's perspective, they are).

5. Convey empathy and remorse for the person's emotional state.

For more detailed instructions on how to access our empathy and accurately assess how another person feels, see the sections on *perspective taking* and *empathy* in chapter 2.

Offer Compensation or Atonement

Although it might not always be relevant, necessary, or possible to do so, making offers to compensate or atone for our actions in some way can be extremely meaningful to the offended party, even if he or she turns down the offers we make. By conveying our recognition that there is an imbalance in the relationship and suggesting actions that can restore a sense of equity and fairness, we communicate a much deeper level of regret and remorse, as well as a strong motivation to repair the imbalance and make things right (e.g., "I'm so sorry I got drunk and ruined your birthday party. I know how much work you put into planning it. Perhaps I could throw a get-together in your honor to make it up to you.")

Acknowledge You Violated Social Norms or Expectations

One huge factor that prevents us from garnering authentic forgiveness from people we've harmed is they don't know whether we've learned our lesson. Are we changed people or are we just as likely to commit the same wrongdoing again? Therefore, we have to clearly acknowledge that our actions violated certain expectations, rules, or social norms and offer reasonable assurances that those will not be violated again in the future. Further, when possible, we should be specific and explicit about the steps we plan to take in order to make sure we avoid repeating our "offense" (e.g., "I've entered your birthday in my electronic calendar so I'll get a reminder every year.")

Effective Apologies in Action

Once I described these six components to Judy, Antonia, and Yo-shi they were each able to identify numerous ways in which their initial apologies fell short. For example, Antonia's apology covered the three basics in that she expressed ample regret for running over her mother's foot, she made numerous "I'm sorry" statements, and she repeatedly begged her mother for forgiveness. Further, Antonia made efforts to atone for her actions (by offering to drive her mother to the hospital and offering to help out around the house), and she even expressed empathy for her mother's physical pain. But she did not do the one thing her mother needed most—Antonia failed to acknowledge that she violated the family norm of never turning her back on her parents and walking away (or in this case, turning the wheel and driving away) and conveying disrespect to them by doing so. Until Antonia offered her mother assurances that she would avoid violating this family rule in the future, her mother would not be able to forgive her.

When Yoshi finally confessed to his parents that he would not be going to Harvard Medical School and that he had not taken premed courses since his freshman year, they were every bit as devastated as he feared they would be. "My mom gasped and burst into tears and my dad just stood there stoically, trying not to break down, saying nothing. I told them how sorry I was, that I knew how much anguish, disappointment, and heartbreak I was causing them. And still he said nothing. I told them I knew how wrong it was to deceive them and to disrespect them by lying and I begged for their forgiveness, but he didn't utter a word. He couldn't even look at me. Every moment of his silence was like a dagger of guilt thrusting deeper into my heart. Eventually there was nothing more

I could say. He just turned, put his arm around my mom, and walked out. They haven't spoken to me since."

Yoshi's apology was extremely sincere and heartfelt and it had a lot going for it in other ways as well. He was extremely sensitive to his parents' feelings and he voiced repeated expressions of empathy. He also acknowledged the many social and family norms he violated. However, the one ingredient he omitted was that he made no offers to compensate his parents for the huge sums of money they would have saved had Yoshi been honest about his aspirations and attended a much less expensive school. Doing so would have impressed upon them how sincere he was about atoning for his transgression and doing the honorable thing. In addition, it would also have allowed them to save face with friends and other family members. They could explain that their son had a change of heart about medical school and that he planned to take full responsibility for his decision and repay the tuition they had invested in his education.

Obviously, even had he done so, the rupture in the relationship with his parents was profound and it would take time for them to reestablish their bond and mend things fully. But garnering even provisional forgiveness and feeling as though he was at least on the path of relational repair would have been sufficient for Yoshi's guilt to begin to diminish.

Judy, who cheated on her husband, Blake, expressed a clear "I'm sorry" statement as well as a statement of remorse ("It was a one-time thing and I've regretted it ever since"). But she kept asking Blake to "believe" her, rather than to "forgive" her. As simplistic as it might sound, if we never ask the other person for forgiveness, we are not likely to receive it. Judy's apology was deficient in other regards as well. Although she acknowledged her actions were wrong ("It was a stupid mistake!"), she did not explicitly address the fact that she broke their marital vows of fidelity.

When I pointed this out to her, she insisted it wasn't necessary to acknowledge something that Blake already knew full well, as it would just upset him further. But the real reason she failed to acknowledge she'd violated their marital contract was that doing so would expose her to an emotional "dodgeball in the face"—a surge in guilt and psychological distress. While her reluctance was understandable, by not making such an admission, Judy failed to come across as taking full responsibility for her actions. Most important, Judy made various offers of atonement (for example, by agreeing to call Blake every thirty minutes when she worked late), but she failed to express sufficient empathy for what Blake was feeling and she demonstrated no insight into his emotional state. As a result, she was unable to validate Blake's emotions in any way. For example, she said nothing to acknowledge how difficult it would be for him to trust her going forward or how challenging it would be for him to recapture his previous feelings for the marriage, even if it were possible for him to do so.

Treatment Summary: Effective Apologies

Dosage: Apply the principles in this treatment fully and thoughtfully to the person(s) you have wronged. Make sure to craft your apology carefully and give thought to the best time and place to deliver it.

Effective for: Reducing guilt and self-condemnation and repairing damaged relationships.

Treatment B: Forgive Yourself

Apologizing to the person we harmed and receiving authentic forgiveness in return can dramatically alleviate our guilt and make it unnecessary for us to continue our avoidant behavior. However, forgiveness is sometimes impossible to secure, either because circumstances do not allow it (such as when the person we harmed is unavailable to us) or because our best efforts to elicit forgiveness have already failed. In such situations our guilt continues to poison our quality of life and our self-condemnation persists.

Although it is always preferable to receive forgiveness from the person we've harmed, when we are unable to do so, the only way to ease our torment is to forgive ourselves. Self-forgiveness is a process, not a decision (granted, it is a process that starts with a decision). We first have to recognize that we've beaten ourselves up enough and that our excessive guilt is serving no productive purpose in our lives and then we have to make the emotional effort necessary to work through it.

Self-forgiveness can be emotionally challenging but the results are definitely worthwhile. Studies have demonstrated that self-forgiveness reduces feelings of guilt and can eliminate our need to avoid the person we harmed. It also increases our ability to enjoy life and decreases our tendency to self-punish or act in ways that are self-destructive. Case in point, people who forgave themselves for procrastinating when they should have been studying were found to procrastinate significantly less than procrastinators who did not explicitly forgive themselves.

The Steps for Attaining Self-Forgiveness

Self-forgiveness by no means implies our behavior was acceptable or that it should be condoned or forgotten. Rather, self-forgiveness should be the outcome of a conscious process, an effort to come to peace with our wrongdoing. The danger of self-forgiveness is that we might forgive ourselves too easily or too readily or that we might fail to implement the changes, mindfulness, and caution necessary to prevent us from repeating our transgressions. Therefore, self-forgiveness requires us first to take full responsibility for our actions and give ourselves an honest and accurate accounting of the events causing our guilt. We must be able to explicitly acknowledge both our wrongdoings and their impact on the person we harmed, both practically and emotionally.

Coming to terms with our actions and their consequences can be emotionally uncomfortable if not painful but unless we go through such self-examination any self-forgiveness we grant ourselves will not be authentic. In cases in which our wrongdoing caused significant harm (e.g., we drove under the influence and caused an accident that resulted in people dying or suffering grave bodily harm) and we are unsure of whether we can or indeed if we should find self-forgiveness, we should seek the counsel of a mental health professional.

Once we take full responsibility for our actions and their consequences, we will be ready to take the second step and work on forgiving ourselves. In order to come to peace with our actions we will need to make some form of amends or reparations for the harm we've caused and find ways to minimize the likelihood of committing a similar transgression in the future.

Exercise for Self-Forgiveness, Part 1: Accountability

To create a clear divide between accountability and atonement the following writing exercise is presented in two parts. The first will help you accurately assess your part in the events so you can find ways to forgive yourself for your wrongdoings in part 2 of the exercise. You may complete both parts of the exercise as a single unit.

1. Describe your actions or inactions that led to the other person feeling harmed.

2. Go through your description and take out any qualifiers or excuses. For example, "She claimed she was insulted" should read, "She felt insulted." Items such as "He did the same thing to me once" or "She made it into a bigger deal than it was" should be omitted entirely.

3. Summarize the harm the other person sustained both tangibly and emotionally. For example, if you criticized a fellow employee unfairly and that person was fired as a result, you should mention aspects such as his or her economic hardship, the time and effort the person will need to invest in order to find another job, the blow to the individual's self-esteem, and his or her feelings of embarrassment, resentment, and demoralization.

4. Go through your above description of harm and make sure it is as realistic and as accurate as possible. It is important not to give yourself too much of a pass, but you should not beat yourself into a pulp either. Counterintuitive as it may seem, while some of us minimize the consequences of our transgressions, plenty of us exaggerate

them. For example, when Antonia first told me about the incident with her mother she didn't say, "I ran over her foot," she said, "I know this sounds terrible . . . I ran her over with the car," which made me immediately envision Antonia mowing down her mother while white-knuckling the wheel and doing sixty. Yes, she caused her mother serious pain, emotional distress, and a frustrating healing process—but that's still vastly different from what most of us envision when we hear someone was run over.

One way to make sure your descriptions are realistic is to imagine that an objective stranger will film the description you write as if it were a script. Would the film depict an identical rendition of the actual events? If not, make whatever corrections are necessary.

5. Now that you have an accurate and realistic description of the events and your responsibility in them, it is fair to consider extenuating circumstances. Did you intend for events to unfold as they did? If so, why? If not, what were your original intentions? For example, Antonia never intended to run over her mother's foot, and Yoshi's original intent was not to wait three years before telling his parents he was not going to medical school. He just avoided the confrontation until his impending graduation prevented him from keeping up the pretense. If your intention was to harm, it is important to explain what drove you to do so and you will need to work on any character flaws in part 2 of the exercise. If your intentions were benign, what went wrong?

6. What extenuating circumstances, if any, contributed to your actions or to their consequences? For example, Judy

had met her colleague for drinks during a particularly stressful period at work, and at a time she and Blake were struggling with their three children. She proceeded to have too much to drink and thus was more receptive than she might have otherwise been to her colleague's advances. The idea is not to excuse your actions, but to understand the context in which they occurred so you can ultimately find ways to forgive yourself for them.

Exercise for Self-Forgiveness, Part 2: Atonement

Now that you have a fair formulation of your actions, their consequences, and their causes, you can focus on self-forgiveness. When you cannot make amends to the person you've harmed, the best way to purge excessive guilt is to "even the score," first by making sure you don't repeat your transgression and then by atoning for your actions in some way. Studies have found that both atonement and reparations are effective mechanisms for purging excessive guilt, as long as you feel as though the actions you take represent a fair way to "balance the scales."

7. What changes do you need to make in your thinking, your habits, your behavior, or your lifestyle that would minimize the likelihood of you repeating the transgression in the future? For example, a parent who feels guilty for disappointing his or her child by missing a basketball game or school concert for the fifth time might decide to reevaluate his or her work priorities and make changes that allow for fuller participation in the children's lives (i.e., switching jobs, taking a different role, or just rearranging their work schedule).

8. Once we've minimized the likelihood of committing the same transgression in the future, we need to purge our remaining guilt by atoning for our actions or making meaningful reparations. One way to do this is to strike a deal with ourselves and identify significant tasks, contributions, or commitments that would make our self-forgiveness feel well earned. For example, one fifteen-year-old girl I worked with who felt guilty about repeatedly stealing money from her parents' wallets decided to make reparations when she discovered they had been struggling financially. She was convinced that simply admitting to the theft would shatter her parents' image of her as a "good girl" and cause them significant emotional distress during an already difficult time. Since they never realized she had stolen any money to begin with, her solution was to increase her babysitting shifts and sneak the cash back into her mother's wallet as she earned it. Keep in mind that most teens who steal money from their parents' wallets feel no guilt whatsoever, let alone put themselves on a work detail reparations program.

As another example, a young man I worked with was driving through a "bad neighborhood" late at night when he scratched and dented two parked cars while making a tight turn. He panicked and fled the scene without leaving a note. He felt extremely guilty about his wrongdoing later on, especially when he realized it was likely the owners of the two vehicles might not be able to afford to repair the damage he had caused. He decided to atone for his actions by donating money (an amount significantly larger than what he estimated would have been the cost of the repairs) to a community center in the area, as well as to a local youth program.

What atonement or reparations could you make so that, once completed, your efforts would feel substantial enough to earn self-forgiveness?

9. Create a short ritual to mark the completion of your atonement. For example, once the teenage girl who'd stolen money from her parents snuck the last ten-dollar bill into her mother's wallet, she planned to surprise her parents by making dinner so she could enjoy her first guilt-free evening with them. You might remove a photograph of the person you harmed from an album and return it only once your task is complete and then literally close the book on your guilt. Or if you decide to donate time or money to a charity, find a way to note the completion of the task in some way, so as to signal to yourself that your penance is now complete.

TREATMENT SUMMARY: FORGIVE YOURSELF

Dosage: Administer this treatment fully if you are unable to administer Treatment A for whatever reason or if you've administered Treatment A but were not successful in eliciting authentic forgiveness.

Effective for: Reducing guilt and self-condemnation.

Treatment C: Reengage in Life

Treating survivor or separation or disloyalty guilt is challenging because there is nothing for which we need to take responsibility or atone. Ironic as it may sound, it is easier to induce self-forgiveness when we've done something wrong than it is when our hands are clean and there is nothing for which we actually need to forgive ourselves. Nonetheless, while we cannot undo the suffering and loss of others, we can take steps to end our own.

The best way to move past our guilt when we didn't do anything wrong is to remind ourselves of the many reasons it is crucial we do so. The following three exercises are composed of sentiments my patients expressed over the years that allowed them to shed survivor, separation, and disloyalty guilt. Taken together, they represent powerful rationales for reengaging in life and they offer various avenues through which we can each seek to do so.

EXERCISE FOR SUFFERERS OF SURVIVOR GUILT

The following writing exercise includes sentiments expressed by people who suffered from survivor guilt but found ways to manage and overcome it. Write a brief paragraph about how relevant sentiments might apply to your own circumstance.

1. Morris was seventy-two when he lost his wife of fifty-one years to a heart attack. "I realized it was unfair of me to mourn for so long. She would have wanted me to enjoy the life I had left."

2. Sylvia, a breast cancer survivor, lost her best friend to the disease. "If I don't live my life to the fullest it would be as if the cancer claimed another victim. I decided it would be wrong to let cancer claim another victim."

3. Joey was a father of three who lost his wife in a car accident when she was running an errand he was supposed to

do himself. "I felt dead inside for many months. But I realized I had to get out of it. Otherwise my kids would feel as though they had lost both parents."

4. Jeremiah was the only member of his high school football team to get a full scholarship to a top university. He felt guilty about it for months and then spoke with his pastor. "He made me realize it would be ungrateful of me to deny the gifts and chances I was given. The best way for me to show gratitude is to take full advantage of them."

5. Shandra was the sole member of her department to survive a brutal round of layoffs. "I decided I'm going to excel, advance, and get to a position of authority so I can make sure good employees don't get fired."

Exercise for Sufferers of Separation Guilt

The following writing exercise includes sentiments expressed by people who overcame or learned to manage the separation guilt that arose when focusing on their own lives meant being less focused on the needs of a loved one. Write a brief paragraph describing how relevant sentiments might apply to your own circumstance.

1. Billy is the father of a severely disabled child. "Caregiving is emotionally stressful and extremely depleting. I figured out that when I make time to do things that bring me satisfaction and, yeah, even joy, I have much more to give."

2. Wanda looks after an elderly parent. "I always keep the airplane demonstrations in mind. In case of emergency, first put on your own oxygen mask and then tend to the

other person. You can't take care of others if you don't take care of yourself."

3. Marsha's severely depressed husband would break down in tears whenever she went out with friends. "I stayed home for months until I realized that by going out and enjoying life I'm not projecting callousness, I'm modeling optimism."

4. Cam and Bev felt guilty about leaving their twin toddlers with a babysitter. "They cried like they were being slaughtered the first time we left. But we realized that the more we coddled them the less resilient and the less independent they would be. Even if it hurts sometimes, we have to be able to have date nights both for our sakes and for theirs."

EXERCISE FOR SUFFERERS OF DISLOYALTY GUILT

The following writing exercise includes sentiments expressed by people who overcame or learned to manage their disloyalty guilt. Write a brief paragraph describing how relevant sentiments might apply to your own circumstance.

1. Levi, an accountant, was an orthodox Jew who fell in love with and married a non-Jewish woman. His entire family felt betrayed but none more so than his father. "His feelings are understandable. But if I let him dictate how I should live my life he'd be basically leading two lives and I'd be leading none—and that isn't fair either."

2. Juan's Catholic father refused to accept his homosexuality. "I supported my dad when he got fired from his job even

though I was a kid and it made it hard on me too. Remembering that made me realize I deserve the same support from him. So instead of apologizing, I started demanding he show me respect for having the honesty to live the life I believe in."

3. Lucas came from a long line of home-schooled children. When he enrolled his daughter in first grade at a private school, his mother, a home-schooling advocate, took it as a personal rejection. "It didn't matter how much I tried to explain, she simply couldn't get over it. But I realized I was not willing to sacrifice doing what I know is right for my child because it might hurt someone's feelings."

TREATMENT SUMMARY: REENGAGE IN LIFE

Dosage: Administer this treatment fully and repeat as necessary whenever you feel surges of guilt about moving on or living your own life.

Effective for: Reducing guilt and self-condemnation.

When to Consult a Mental Health Professional

If you have applied the treatments in this chapter and you still feel overwhelming guilt, if you are unable to apply them for whatever reason, or if your guilt still impairs your quality of life and your relationships, consult a mental health professional to assess whether there might be other psychological factors at play, such as depression, anxiety, or post-traumatic stress disorder.

If you find the exercises in Treatment B too difficult to complete, or if you're concerned about your ability to come up with accurate assessments of your responsibility, you might benefit from discussing the events and your feelings about them with a trained mental health professional. If your guilt is so severe you have thoughts of hurting yourself or another person, consult a mental health professional immediately or go to the nearest emergency room.

CHAPTER 5

||||||||||||||||||||

RUMINATION

Picking at Emotional Scabs

When we encounter painful experiences we typically reflect on them, hoping to reach the kinds of insights and epiphanies that reduce our distress and allow us to move on. Yet for many of us who engage in this process of self-reflection, things go awry. Instead of attaining an emotional release we get caught in a vicious cycle of rumination in which we replay the same distressing scenes, memories, and feelings over and over again, feeling worse every time we do. We become like hamsters trapped in a wheel of emotional pain, running endlessly but going nowhere. What makes rumination a form of psychological injury is that it provides no new understandings that could heal our wounds and instead serves only to pick at our scabs and infect them anew.

Unfortunately, our tendency to ruminate is set off almost solely by painful feelings and experiences and rarely by positive or joyful ones. Few of us stay up nights on end replaying how we had everyone in stitches at a dinner party. Nor do we feel the need to go over every nuance of how our boss complimented our latest efforts at work. But if everyone at the dinner party was laughing at us rather than with us, or if our boss criticized our performance and yelled at us in front of our colleagues, we can stew over it for weeks.

The danger of rumination is not only that it deepens whatever emotional distress we already feel about the events, but that it is linked to a wide range of threats to our psychological and physical health. Specifically, rumination increases our likelihood of becoming depressed and prolongs the duration of depressive episodes when we have them; it is associated with greater risk of alcohol abuse and eating disorders, it fosters negative thinking and impaired problem solving, and it increases our psychological and physiological stress responses and puts us at greater risk for cardiovascular disease.

Despite being aware of these dangers for decades, many psychotherapists struggle when it comes to treating rumination in their patients because their approaches are based on the assumption that the best way to purge ourselves of our preoccupations is to talk them through. But when we have ruminative tendencies, revisiting the same feelings and problems over and over again, even with a therapist, only increases our drive to ruminate and makes matters worse.

To be clear, not every attempt to analyze emotionally painful experiences is doomed to cause us more harm than good. Certainly there are many forms of self-reflection that are perfectly useful and adaptive. The question is, what distinguishes these adaptive forms of self-reflection from the maladaptive ones? Further, can those of us with ruminative tendencies find ways to think about our feelings and problems more productively so that we don't end up picking at our emotional scabs and preventing them from healing?

These questions have been occupying and preoccupying the

thoughts of a new generation of researchers. Fortunately, their ruminations about rumination have yielded fascinating studies and promising new approaches. As a result, we've finally begun to pull back the veil on the mechanisms that underlie both maladaptive rumination and helpful self-reflection and we've begun to learn how we can modify our ruminative tendencies to make them less damaging and more psychologically beneficial. In order to utilize these new discoveries we first need a better understanding of the psychological wounds rumination inflicts.

The Psychological Wounds Rumination Inflicts

Ruminating on our problems and feelings scratches at our emotional scabs and causes four primary psychological wounds: it intensifies our sadness and allows it to persist for far longer than it might have otherwise; likewise, it intensifies and prolongs our anger; it hogs substantial amounts of emotional and intellectual resources, inhibiting motivation, initiative, and our ability to focus and think productively; and our need to discuss the same events or feelings repeatedly for weeks, months, and sometimes years on end taxes the patience and compassion of our social support systems and puts our relationships at risk. Let's examine each of these wounds in greater detail.

1. Supersizing Our Misery: Why Rumination and Sadness Are Best Friends Forever

One of the reasons rumination is so difficult to treat is its self-reinforcing nature. Ruminating about problems tends to make us even more upset about them, and the more upset we are the stronger the urge to ruminate becomes. This dynamic represents the primary reason rumination puts us at risk for developing clinical depression: hyperfocusing on painful emotions and experiences can damage our mood, distort our perceptions so we view our lives more negatively, and make us feel helpless and hopeless as a result. Further, once we have a tendency to ruminate, it becomes easy to trigger a ruminative cycle whenever we self-reflect, even if there is nothing necessarily distressing going on in our lives at that moment.

A simple experiment demonstrates this dynamic beautifully. Scientists asked regular people on a regular day to reflect on their feelings for eight minutes. Many of us can do this without it having any impact on our mood whatsoever, and indeed, we might struggle to fathom why it should. But people who were a little sad to begin with, and those with a tendency to ruminate, reported feeling significantly sadder after this eight-minute exercise than they had been previously. Again, people's emotions were not manipulated in any way in these experiments, they were simply asked to think about their feelings.

My work with Linda, a corporate attorney, provides a good illustration of how persistent ruminations can be. Linda graduated at the top of her class at an excellent law school and was quickly snatched up by one of the best law firms in New York City. A few years later, one of the firm's senior partners requested she transfer to his department and join his team. It was the most exciting moment of Linda's professional career to date. It was also the start of her downfall. Her new boss turned out to be a nightmare. He was critical, dismissive, patronizing, passive-aggressive, and condescending while at the same time incredibly demanding of her time and efforts. He was also a screamer, something to which Linda had not been exposed previously.

A year passed and Linda was utterly despondent. She considered transferring back to her old department, but her new boss made sure to dangle the carrot of partnership in front of her, hinting that if she improved her efforts and worked harder, he would nominate her for the promotion within a few years. He did give Linda above-average yearly reviews, but at the same time he also continually put her down, diminished her contributions, and embarrassed her by publicly belittling her efforts and yelling at her in meetings. Linda found herself regularly crying in the bathroom. With the encouragement of her husband, she decided to confront her boss about when she would be nominated for partnership. He promised that if she continued to perform as she had, he would nominate her by the end of the following year. Linda asked him to put his promise in writing and, much to her delight, he did.

Linda doubled her efforts. When her boss finally invited her to his office to discuss her future she could barely contain her anticipation. But instead of announcing her promotion, he handed her a terrible yearly review, chastised her for "slacking off" (despite her having worked harder than ever before), and told her she had no chance of making partner at the firm. Linda was devastated. She transferred to another firm soon thereafter, taking a large pay cut in the process.

Linda came to see me a full year after starting her new job because although she liked her new boss, she simply could not stop ruminating about her experiences with her old one. "I'm just miserable all the time," she explained. "I keep thinking about how he rolled his eyes whenever I spoke in meetings, the expression of disgust he had when he criticized my work, how angry he looked when he yelled at me in front of my colleagues." The emotional pain these and other experiences evoked was etched plainly on

Linda's face. Linda had sought out psychotherapy previously, but doing so had done little to reduce her ruminations and sadness.

Many traditional therapies involve patients examining their experiences in great detail and from every angle, something that can actually increase ruminative tendencies. Other approaches, such as cognitive therapy, involve less heavy pondering and instead teach people to identify negative thoughts so they can dispute them. However, this approach can also be problematic where rumination is concerned because in order to practice refuting such thoughts one has to keep bringing them to mind.

Illustrating this problem, in a recent study, researchers gave college students at risk for depression either a cognitive therapy workbook or an academic skills workbook. The participants' levels of depression were measured immediately after they completed the workbook and again four months later. Subjects with high ruminative tendencies felt significantly more depressed after completing the cognitive therapy workbook than those who completed the academic skills workbook. Asking people with ruminative tendencies to identify their negative thoughts and feelings, even if for the purpose of learning to refute them, caused them to ruminate about their feelings even more and to become sadder as a result. That their sad feelings persisted even four months later is a testament to the tenacity of ruminative urges once they become entrenched.

2. Anger Inflation: How Rumination and Venting Fan the Flames of Fury

Another emotion that tends to elicit powerful ruminative urges is anger. Many of us replay experiences that elicit our ire over and over in our heads. As with the self-reinforcing cycle that gets triggered with sadness, the more we ruminate about our anger and the more we discuss anger-provoking thoughts and experiences with others, the angrier we feel as a result and the stronger our urge to ruminate about these feelings and problems becomes.

Carlton, a young man I worked with a few years ago, fell prey to this very dynamic. Carlton's father had come from modest means, but after making a fortune in the stock market he insisted his son want for nothing. For example, after graduating from college, Carlton expressed an interest in moving to New York. His father promptly put him up in a newly purchased penthouse apartment and gave him a generous monthly allowance because, as he told Carlton many times over the years, "Nothing but the best for my son!"

Carlton tried his hand at several careers, landing one plum job after another with the aid of his father's connections. However, since he had neither the experience nor the qualifications to succeed in these positions, Carlton usually spent less than a year in each of them before being gently advised by his superiors to "try something else" or to "move on." The suggestion that he wasn't performing adequately caught him by surprise more than once.

"I kept assuming these companies would never offer me a job I was unqualified for. But they were just doing my dad a favor," Carlton explained when we first met. "Since they figured I wouldn't be there for long, they never told me what I wasn't doing well or what I could do to improve. They'd just ask me to leave. You have no idea how humiliating it was each time it happened!" Carlton's nostrils flared at the memory. "I didn't ask my dad for the apartment, I didn't ask for the allowance, and I never asked for help getting a job, not once. I'd just mention I was interested in something and the next thing I knew I'd get a call about a possible opening. No one told me these positions were over my head. Good ol'

Dad just kept setting me up for failure. *Nothing but the best for my son!*" Carlton added in a bitter imitation of what I assumed was his father's voice.

When Carlton was twenty-five he met Solana, a marketing professional. They married a year later. In the fall of 2008, a few months after their wedding, the world entered a global recession and Carlton's father was hit hard. He was forced to sell the apartment in which Carlton and Solana were living and to cut off every penny of his allowance. Carlton was between jobs at the time and he and Solana found themselves having to manage with Solana's salary and the small sum of money Carlton had left in the bank.

"I started looking for work like crazy," Carlton explained. "I applied to hundreds of jobs over the next six months and got rejected by all of them. No surprise there, my resume looked like one failed career choice after another. My dad was so into being the hero, he didn't care if it made me totally financially dependent. He didn't care if it screwed up my professional life. He didn't care that it could leave me with no chance of getting anywhere!" Carlton's face was red with anger. "I'm twenty-seven years old and I have no skills, no qualifications, and no prospects! He ruined my life! I'm angry all the time and poor Solana gets the brunt of it. She tells me to stop obsessing about my father, but each time I get rejected from a job I hear his voice in my head: *Nothing but the best for my son!* It's making me crazy! If I don't stop yelling at Solana she'll leave me. She's even said as much. And then I'll really have nothing!"

Getting stuck in an angry ruminative loop can leave us awash in fury and resentment and make us feel irritable and on edge much of the time. Angry feelings activate our stress responses and our cardiovascular systems such that over the long term, having consistent and intense anger ruminations can place us at greater risk for developing cardiovascular disease.

An even more insidious consequence of anger ruminations is that the general irritability they cause can make us overreact to the mildest provocations. As a result we often end up taking out our frustrations on our friends and family members. We snap at them, jump down their throats, and respond in exaggerated ways to minor and everyday irritations.

As an illustration of how easily we displace our anger onto innocent people, one study put people through a frustrating experience and then induced some of them to ruminate about it. Participants who ruminated after the frustrating experience were far more likely to display aggressive behavior toward an inept but innocent confederate compared to those who had been through the same frustrating experience but had not been induced to ruminate about it afterward. Even though the confederate had nothing to do with the situation that caused their frustration, the angry ruminators went as far as to sabotage the confederate's chances of getting a job they knew was hugely important to his livelihood and career.

Although it is no treat for our partners and family members when we get caught in a depressive ruminative loop, their quality of life (as well as ours) tends to take a much greater hit when the ruminative cycle holding us hostage is one of anger and irritability.

3. Cognitive Leakage: How Rumination Saps Our Intellectual Resources

Rumination involves such intense brooding it consumes huge amounts of our mental energies. By doing so it impairs our attention and concentration, our problem-solving abilities, and our motivation and initiative. Further, the faulty decision making we employ in its wake often proves incredibly costly to our physical and mental health. For example, women with strong ruminative tendencies were found to wait two months longer than women without ruminative tendencies to see a physician after discovering a lump in their breast—a potentially life-threatening difference. Other studies found that cancer and coronary patients with ruminative tendencies had poorer compliance with their medical regimens than people with similar disease profiles who were not ruminators.

Rumination causes us to stew in our negative feelings until we become so consumed with them that we begin to see our entire lives, histories, and futures more bleakly. Our negative outlook then causes us to view our problems as less manageable, to come up with fewer solutions to them, and to avoid implementing the solutions we do find. We might be able to recognize that certain mood-enhancing activities would be helpful to us but we are far less willing to pursue such activities nonetheless.

This leads some of us to soothe our pain with alcohol or other substances. Many of the ruminators I've worked with over the years claimed that drinking eases their irritability and makes life more manageable for those around them. While having a drink might take the edge off our irritability and make us more agreeable to others, the question is whether someone can stick with one drink or whether they tend to go for two, three, or more. When we use alcohol to manage our mood, our consumption is unlikely to remain at moderate levels for long. The more inebriated we get the less impulse control we have and the more likely we are to express our anger and aggression in destructive ways.

Our first steps onto the path toward alcohol abuse or dependence are often prompted by a misguided effort to manage the emotional distress and anger our ruminations cause. Some of us might turn to binge eating or purging instead. But whether we turn to food or to alcohol or other substances to manage such feelings, the ruminations causing them remain unaddressed and we only increase the risk of sustaining long-lasting psychological damage.

4. Strained Relationships: How Our Loved Ones Pay a Price for Our Ruminations

Our ruminations are often so consuming, we fail to consider how our need to constantly discuss them can impact our friends and families and put a strain on our most important relationships. In addition, we usually fail to spread our efforts evenly and prefer to share our feelings with those who have been most supportive and compassionate in the past, making them shoulder a disproportionate load of supportive duties. Even if these individuals care for us tremendously, repeating the same discussions over and over will eventually tax their patience and compassion and risk making them feel resentful and angry toward us as well. When I point out these risks to my patients they grudgingly acknowledge why someone might lose patience but not why that person might become resentful or angry.

To understand why this might happen we need to consider that lending emotional support and assistance to people who are close to our hearts is one of the most rewarding aspects of close friendships and relationships. Helping others we care about makes us feel better about ourselves, it fosters stronger relationship bonds, it increases trust and loyalty for both parties, and it allows us to feel valuable and meaningful in the world.

Consider, then, that by bringing up the same thoughts and feelings we've discussed many times before we cannot help but communicate to those around us that their previous efforts to help us were ultimately lacking because here we are asking them to do so all over again. At best they were able to provide us with a measure of relief but it clearly didn't last long if we're expecting them to repeat their efforts. Our supportive friends and family members might not pick up on this embedded "insult" consciously but they are likely to find themselves feeling vaguely angry and resentful nonetheless.

Further, we each have an internal statute of limitations when it comes to how long we feel it's fair for someone to be distressed about certain events. Once that period has expired and we're asked to listen and be supportive again nonetheless, we might offer our support and compassion out of duty, obligation, or guilt but we'll probably feel somewhat resentful and angry about having to do so.

I once worked with a young man whose fiancée had left him only weeks before their wedding, and he spoke about little else with his buddies for over a year. From what I gleaned, his friends were showing every sign of losing patience with his constant obsessions and soliloquies about his ex. They started changing the nature of their get-togethers with him so that instead of activities that fostered conversation, like golf, dinners, or meeting at bars, they suggested movies and activities such as basketball or football. Unfortunately, the young man did not heed any of his friends' hints nor my own warnings about their rising resentment. When he broached the subject for the umpteenth time during a game of basketball, one of his friends became so exasperated he stopped the game and yelled, "Come on, dude! Just man up already!" and punctuated his statement by throwing the basketball straight into my patient's face, breaking his nose in the process.

Clearly the friend's resentment had been building up over many months and had reached a boiling point. But he hadn't said a word about feeling burdened by my patient's incessant ruminations. Indeed, none of his friends had. The assaultive friend did receive his comeuppance, however, as he spent the next five hours in the emergency room, listening to my patient replay nasal renditions of the breakup while avoiding sprays of bloody gauze from his nose.

Of course, few of our friends throw things at us in exasperation when we chew their ears off, but that doesn't mean they don't feel like doing so. Intense ruminations can often make us so focused on our own emotional needs that we become blind to those of the people around us and our relationships often suffer as a result.

How to Treat the Psychological Wounds Rumination Inflicts

It is natural to reflect on upsetting events after they occur and to mull them over in our minds. The intensity and frequency of normative preoccupations should decrease with time and as such they do not usually require treatment. But when time has passed and the frequency and emotional intensity of our preoccupations continue unabated, we should make efforts to break the cycle of rumination and apply emotional first aid. Let's open our psychological medicine cabinet and examine the treatment options available to us.

General Treatment Guidelines

In order to break the self-reinforcing nature of ruminative thoughts and allow our wounds to heal we must interrupt the cycle of rumination once it gets triggered, and we should weaken the urge to ruminate at the source by diminishing the intensity of the feelings that fuel it. We must also make efforts to monitor our relationships and to ease the emotional burden we might be placing on our loved ones.

The following treatments are listed in the order in which they should be administered. Treatment A (changing perspective) is focused on reducing the intensity of the urge that compels us to ruminate, and Treatment B (distraction from emotional pain) is focused on reducing the frequency of ruminative thoughts (which is easier to do once the urge to ruminate is less intense). Treatment C (reframing anger) targets the anger and aggressive impulses ruminations can evoke, and Treatment D (managing friendships) is useful for monitoring our relationships with those who provide emotional support.

Treatment A: Change Your Perspective

When scientists began investigating the mechanics of how we self-reflect on painful feelings and experiences in an effort to understand what distinguishes adaptive from maladaptive forms of self-reflection, one factor emerged as hugely significant—the visual perspective we use when going over painful experiences in our minds.

Our natural tendency when analyzing painful experiences is to do so from a self-*immersed* perspective in which we see the scene through our own eyes (also known as a first-person perspective). Analyzing our feelings in such a way tends to allow our memories to unfold in a narrative form (i.e., the play-by-play of how things happened) and to elicit emotions at a level of intensity similar to when the events occurred.

But when the researchers asked people to analyze a painful experience from a self-*distanced* perspective (a third-person perspective) and actually see themselves within the scene from the point of view of an outside observer, they found something quite remarkable. Instead of merely recounting the events and how they felt about them at the time, people tended to reconstruct their understanding of their experience and to reinterpret it in ways that promoted new insights and feelings of closure. This result was amplified even further when they suggested people employ a self-distanced perspective while reflecting not on *how* things happened but on *why* they happened.

In numerous studies, subjects who were asked to analyze painful experiences this way experienced significantly less emotional pain than those using self-immersive perspectives. In addition, their blood pressure was less reactive (it rose less and it returned to normal baseline more quickly), indicating that using self-distanced perspectives lowers our stress responses and causes less activation of our cardiovascular systems. The good news didn't end there. Follow-ups one week later indicated that people using self-distanced perspectives reported thinking about their painful experiences significantly less often, and they felt less emotional pain when they did ruminate about them than people who used self-immersed perspectives. These findings held true for both depressive and anger ruminations.

When I first read about these findings I immediately thought of Linda, the lawyer who ruminated about her abusive ex-boss.

Linda's descriptions of how she saw her boss's face (e.g., "I keep thinking about how he rolled his eyes whenever I spoke in meetings") clearly indicated she reflected on her experiences using a self-immersed as opposed to a self-distanced perspective. I was curious as to whether changing her perspective would impact her ruminations. I told Linda how to tweak her ruminative thoughts so she was using a self-distanced perspective and suggested she be as judicious as possible in doing so until we met next two weeks later.

Linda walked into our next session with a huge smile on her face. "It worked!" she announced before she even got to the couch. Linda reported that for the week following our session she had been diligent about employing a self-distanced perspective whenever she thought about her ex-boss; then she added, "But soon after that something shifted. It took me a few days to realize it, but I was thinking about him far less than usual." Even better, when Linda did think about her ex-boss, she reported feeling much less upset than she had before and she was able to put such thoughts aside more easily. She also found it easier to use distraction (Treatment B) when the thoughts did persist. The combination of the two approaches, perspective change and distraction, helped significantly reduce her ruminations in a short amount of time.

EXERCISE FOR CHANGING PERSPECTIVES

Switching visual perspectives to ones that afford us greater psychological distance from the topics of our ruminations requires practice. Complete this exercise when you have the time and space to do so without interruption and practice the technique for each topic or experience that elicits unproductive ruminations.

Sit or lie comfortably, close your eyes, and recall the opening snapshot of the scene or the experience in question. Zoom out so you see yourself within the scene, or if the scene involved two locations (e.g., if you were on the phone) imagine a split screen so you see both yourself and the other person or locale. Once you see yourself within the scene, zoom out even further so you can watch the scene unfold from an even greater distance. Allow the scene to unfold as you observe it from afar, as if you were a stranger who happened to pass by as it occurred.

Make sure to use this same perspective every time you find yourself thinking about the events in question.

Treatment Summary: Change Your Perspective

Dosage: Practice the technique in this treatment when you can do so without interruption and then apply it consistently whenever you ruminate. Once the intensity of the feelings the rumination elicits and the urge to ruminate subsides, focus on using Treatment B to cut off any ruminative thoughts as soon as they appear.

Effective for: Reducing depressive and angry ruminations, and restoring impaired intellectual and mental functioning.

Secondary benefits: Reducing physiological stress responses.

Treatment B: Look at the Birdie! Distract Yourself from Emotional Pain

Even once our urge to ruminate is weaker, cutting off a ruminative train of thought once it begins is still quite challenging. The main reason we tend to indulge the urge to ruminate even once we're fully aware of how damaging it can be is that we often catch ourselves ruminating only once our emotions are already churning. Trying to simply suppress our ruminative thoughts is not only difficult, it is inadvisable too. Decades of research on thought suppression demonstrates that nothing compels us to think of something more than trying desperately not to think of it.

In now-classic experiments, people were instructed to see if they could avoid thinking of a white bear for five minutes and to ring a bell if they caught themselves thinking of one (the choice of white bear had no significance other than it was assumed that white bears were not something the subjects thought about often—maybe because the study was done in Texas). Less than a few seconds passed before the average participant rang the bell, and it was usually rung repeatedly thereafter. The more interesting finding was that once the five minutes were over and the subjects were "permitted" to think of whatever they liked, they experienced a rebound effect and found themselves thinking about more white bears than the average Klondike ice-cream truck driver. Since the original white bear experiments, many studies have demonstrated that efforts to suppress unwanted thoughts are likely to cause similar rebound effects, such that the very thoughts we try to banish return with a vengeance the moment our concentration wavers.

While suppression is a dud as far as our war on rumination goes, distraction has proven to be a far more effective weapon. Dozens of studies have demonstrated that distracting ourselves by engaging in tasks we find absorbing or ones that demand our concentration, such as moderate to intense cardiovascular activity, socializing, doing puzzles, or playing computer games, will disrupt a ruminative thought process. Distraction has also been found to restore the quality of our thinking and of our problem-solving abilities because once we cease ruminating, we recover our ability to apply our intellectual skills effectively rather quickly.

While socializing or going to the movies can take our mind off our ruminations, it is not always practical to engage in such time-consuming activities. However, brief and less labor-intensive distractions can also be effective in cutting off ruminative thoughts. For example, spending a few minutes engaging in a brief mental exercise like completing a quick Sudoku puzzle on our phone or imagining the layout of our local supermarket (e.g., *aisle two—cleaning supplies and toiletries, aisle five—Klondike bars*) was found not only to interrupt people's ruminations but to improve their mood as well.

Identifying which distractions work best, given the specifics of our situation (i.e., whether we are at home or at work, trying to study or sitting on the subway) and the nature of our ruminations, can require trial and error, as our assessments of how absorbing various activities or thought exercises will be are not always accurate. Whenever possible, we should test out our arsenal of potential distractions ahead of time so we can identify which work best for the settings in which we tend to ruminate most. The more distractions we have from which to choose, the more effectively we will be able to derail the ruminative train of thoughts that plague us.

Exercise for Identifying Potential Distractions

Complete this writing exercise for each topic or experience about which you tend to ruminate unproductively.

1. List the places and situations in which you tend to ruminate most often.

2. For each place and situation, list as many distractions as possible of both short durations (e.g., a game of Sudoku or supermarket layouts) and longer ones (e.g., a cardiovascular workout or catching a movie).

Once your list is complete carry it with you so you can refer to it when the need arises even if you're convinced you won't have trouble recalling the distractions you chose. Remember, our thinking is not as clear as it could be when we're in the midst of an intense rumination.

TREATMENT SUMMARY: DISTRACTION

Dosage: Create a list of distractions that work for you and apply the treatment as soon as possible whenever you catch yourself entering a ruminative cycle.

Effective for: Minimizing the impact of depressive and/or angry ruminations, and restoring impaired intellectual and mental functioning.

Treatment C: Reframe the Anger

In the film *Analyze This* a psychiatrist (played by Billy Crystal) encourages a patient who has anger issues to "hit a pillow" in order to let off steam. The patient (Robert De Niro), who also happens to be a mobster, pulls out a gun and fires a round of bullets into the pillow. The alarmed psychiatrist recovers his composure enough to ask, "Feel better?" The mobster thinks for a moment and then replies, "Yeah, I do!"

The notion that venting our anger produces a cathartic experience that will reduce our rage and improve our psychological state is widespread even among mental health professionals. Decades ago, therapists like the one played by Billy Crystal began advocating we vent our anger by assaulting benign objects and nary a couch pillow has felt safe ever since.

Indeed, the "catharsis model" of venting anger has spawned entire product lines with numerous forms of "therapeutic" toys for both children and adults. For example, one line of lifelike plastic figures comes with firm plastic bats children can use to express their anger "productively"—*by smashing the humanlike figures in the face and head*. The last time I observed a session in which the therapist used one of these figures it featured a seven-year-old bruiser who pummeled the figure mercilessly while the therapist stood to the side, saying, "Yes, you're very angry at Daddy, aren't you?" Not exactly a recipe for domestic tranquility, if you ask me.

The effectiveness of venting anger by letting off steam has been studied extensively and the verdict of all such studies has been virtually unanimous—the catharsis model is not only wrong, it is actually harmful! In one recent study angered participants were placed into one of three groups. They were instructed either to hit a punching bag while thinking of the person who angered them, to hit the bag while thinking of a neutral subject, or to do nothing at all. Subjects who hit the punching bag while thinking of the person who angered them felt significantly angrier afterward and displayed significantly more aggressive and vengeful behavior than those in the other two groups (bad news indeed for the "daddy" of the bruiser). In fact, it was the participants in the group that took no action at all who felt least angry and who displayed the least aggressive behavior.

Venting our anger by assaulting benign objects only serves to reinforce our aggressive urges in response to anger. These issues should be of special concern for the innumerable parents whose children's aggressive impulses are unwittingly being strengthened with every swing of the bat and every pound of the pillow.

So how should we manage our anger?

The most effective strategy for regulating emotions such as anger involves reframing the event in our minds so that we change its meaning to one that is less infuriating. By formulating a new interpretation of the events to one that is more positive we change our underlying feeling about the situation to one that is less enraging. For example, Michael Phelps, the most decorated swimmer in history, was often subjected to his competitors' taunts in the press before major competitions. Phelps gave several interviews in which he discussed how he dealt with the anger he felt in those situations. Rather than pounding the lane divider in the pool while his coach whispered, "Yes, you're very angry at that German swimmer, aren't you?" Phelps would reframe the situation as one in which he envisioned his rivals' taunts as motivational fuel that spurred him to train harder and to focus even more intently in his actual races.

Despite the effectiveness of reframing, many of us struggle to use the technique because it is not always easy to reinterpret upsetting events in benign ways. For example, Carlton, the man whose father went bankrupt and left him without financial support, was so angry at his father's previous meddling in his career that it was all he could think about. His constant ruminations exacerbated his anger to such a point that he had trouble tolerating even minor frustrations, leaving his wife, Solana, to bear the brunt of his irritability and aggression. Carlton needed to find a less enraging way of thinking about his situation, but even after I explained why it was crucial he do so, he struggled to reframe his situation in positive or more benign terms. I tried pointing him in the right direction.

"Carlton, you have a college degree from a great university and you spent the last five years working in every field in which you expressed an interest. Even if you did so for only brief periods of time, you did get a taste of these fields. Surely those experiences helped you figure out which of those directions holds the most appeal as a career choice."

"Sure. But what's the point? I'll never get the kind of job I really want without my father pulling strings."

"No, you won't. But that's exactly why you're angry with your father. He got you jobs you weren't qualified for instead of allowing you to get the kind of experience you needed. In the real world people don't start where you did, they start at the bottom and work their way up."

"But then these past five years were entirely wasted! That's what kills me!"

"Well, not exactly. They helped you identify what you want to pursue. If you thought of your previous experiences as internships that helped you figure that out, you might be able to see them as time well spent. Now that you know what you want you can start at the bottom and work your way up."

"Don't you get it?" Carlton snapped. "I don't want to start at the bottom!"

"I know," I responded softly, "and your dad didn't want you to either. Was it so terrible of him to want to spare you what you now wish you could spare yourself?"

The color drained from Carlton's face. He looked as if he had been struck. He had never considered that his father's hopes and intentions mirrored his own so closely. But once he was able to reframe his father's meddling as well-intentioned as opposed to controlling, and his professional experiences as instructive as opposed to wasteful, it had a huge impact on him. His ruminations diminished rapidly, as did his anger and irritability. He began searching for positions more suited to his training and lack of experience, and within a few months he landed his first job entirely on his own merit—it was an entry-level position at the bottom rung of the ladder, and Carlton could not have been happier about it.

Reframing requires us to switch our perspective and to perceive the situation in ways that change its meaning and, consequently, how we feel about it. Although the focus here is on reducing anger, reframing can also help us feel less sad, less disappointed, or less victimized. For example, had Linda been promoted in her old law firm she would still be working for her abusive boss. Distraught as she was about taking a step back professionally, doing so did wonders for her quality of life. Reframing her boss's behavior as "useful" rather than as "destructive" allowed her to feel less victimized by her experience.

Exercise for Practicing Reframing

Although your ruminations are unique to your specific circumstance, certain themes and principles are common to many reframing situations. Use the following four suggestions to help identify ways to reframe your situation so that it elicits less anger (or sadness).

1. *Find the positive intention.* Much as Carlton's father had good intentions, most people who cause us to ruminate in anger have some redeeming qualities and might mean well regardless of how their words or actions impact us. Identifying these kernels of good can help us view the situation differently and modify the intensity of our emotions as a result.

2. *Identify the opportunities.* Today, many companies insist their managers reframe areas of weakness as "opportunities" when giving employees feedback. Doing so makes negative feedback easier for the employee to absorb without becoming demoralized. What makes this technique so successful is the universal truth it embodies. Many distressing situations might also provide opportunities for us to improve ourselves, to reevaluate things, to change direction, or to address problems that needed fixing anyway.

3. *Embrace the learning moment.* There is usually much we can learn from the situations that elicit our ruminations. Identifying mistakes we've made and ones we wish to avoid in the future, viewing negative situations as strategic puzzles that require creative solutions, learning who we can count on and who we cannot, and discovering our strengths, weaknesses, and vulnerabilities can provide valuable lessons that will boost our confidence and spare us future heartache and emotional distress.

4. *View the offending person as needing spiritual help.* Those of us with strong religious beliefs can reframe many situations as ones in which the person who caused us emotional distress is in obvious need of spiritual help. As such they deserve not our anger but our prayers. A series of recent studies examined the power of prayer to alleviate anger (using sound scientific principles and blind peer-review processes) and found that it can be an effective way to regulate our emotions, *as long as the nature of our prayer is positive.* Tempting as it may be to do so, praying that the person who angered us gets hit by a Mack truck will not

make us less angry, as it is the spiritual equivalent of shooting a couch pillow.

A secular version of this approach (albeit an untested one scientifically) would be to view the offending person as someone who might be troubled and in need of psychological help or psychotherapy.

TREATMENT SUMMARY: REFRAME THE ANGER

Dosage: Apply to situations, memories, or events that elicit anger or sadness and are the subject of repeated ruminations. Write down the reframed formulations you construct so you can revisit them whenever the rumination occurs.

Effective for: Reducing anger and anger-focused ruminations (as well as the intensity of other emotionally painful ruminations), restoring impaired intellectual and mental functioning, and reducing physiological stress responses.

Treatment D: Go Easy on Your Friends

When we repeatedly discuss the same problems with friends and family members we risk taxing their patience and compassion and we also risk making them feel resentful. In order to preserve these relationships we have to assess whether we are overburdening those who provide us with emotional support.

Exercise to Evaluate Relationship Strain

Answer the following questions for each person in your social support system and take the recommended actions when it is relevant to do so.

1. How much time has passed since the event in question?

    Obviously some life events are extremely traumatic and they might dominate our thoughts and feelings for months and years. However, most of our ruminations do not fall in this category and we should be aware that people expect us to recover within a certain time frame. For example, a general rule of thumb for breakups is that it takes one to two months for every year of a relationship to recover. If we were in a relationship for three years, we should begin to recover from the initial surge of intense ruminations about how and why the breakup happened within three to six months and we should think twice about continuing to discuss the how and why aspect of things with our friends if the topic still dominates our discussions a year later.

2. How many times have you discussed these issues with this person?

    We all have our go-to people when it comes to getting social support. However, they are also the ones most likely to encounter "fatigue" when we discuss the same ruminative thoughts, events, and feelings too often. It might be wise to spread things around and utilize other sources of social support as well so as to avoid overburdening the people we go to most.

3. Does this person feel comfortable bringing up his or her own issues and problems?

If your conversations with a friend are too one-sided and tend to be all about your problems and rarely about his or hers, you might be at risk of jeopardizing the friendship. To assure a balance, make time to ask your friends about their lives and to have entire conversations in which you focus solely on them. If they ask about you when you are trying to do this, respond briefly and refocus the conversation on them.

4. What percentage of your communications with this person is dominated by the subject of your ruminations?

    It is often only in hindsight that we realize the extent to which our discussions with friends were dominated by the subject of our ruminations. Allowing our emotional distress to dominate our relationships and determine what our friendships are about is bad for our friendships, but defining ourselves as victims is damaging to our own mental health as well. Make sure you keep a balance of light conversation, enjoyable moments, and fun whenever possible.

Treatment Summary: Go Easy on Your Friends

Dosage: Apply periodically to evaluate the health of your supportive relationships. Take action to repair any relationship damage when necessary.

Effective for: Evaluating and repairing strained relationships.

When to Consult a Mental Health Professional

If you've applied the treatments in this chapter and your urge to ruminate is still strong, if you find yourself ruminating just as frequently as you had previously, or if your ruminations are so intense and distracting they interfere with your basic ability to function in your professional or personal life, seek the advice of a mental health professional. If your intrusive thoughts are not focused on emotionally painful experiences but on things like catching germs, forgetting to lock the front door, or whether you turned off the gas before you left the house, a mental health professional will be able to assess whether you're exhibiting symptoms of obsessive-compulsive disorder.

Rumination is also strongly tied to depression. If you think you might be depressed and have symptoms such as a persistent low mood, feelings of helplessness about changing your situation, feelings of hopelessness about things getting any better, or disturbances in your eating and sleeping patterns, consult a mental health professional to assess whether you require professional treatment. If at any point you feel so emotionally distressed, sad, or angry that you have the urge to harm yourself or another person, seek immediate professional help or go to the nearest emergency room.

CHAPTER 6

||||||||||||||||||||

FAILURE

How Emotional Chest Colds Become Psychological Pneumonias

None of us reach adulthood without encountering failure thousands of times and many more such experiences await us in life going forward. Failure is so common a human experience that what distinguishes us from one another is not that we fail but rather how we respond when we do. Such differences are especially apparent when observing those who fail more regularly and more frequently than anyone else—toddlers. Trying, failing, and trying again is one of the main ways toddlers learn. Fortunately, toddlers are generally persistent and determined (otherwise we'd never learn to walk, talk, or do much of anything), but they can also display dramatically different responses to failure.

Imagine four toddlers playing with identical jack-in-the-box toys. To open the box and release the cute teddy bear within, they need to slide a big button on the side of the box to the left. They know the button is where the action is, but sliding is a complex skill. Toddler #1 pulls the button. It doesn't move. She pushes the button hard. The box rolls out of reach. She extends her hand toward it but it's still out of reach. She turns away and starts playing with her diaper. Toddler #2 fusses with the button for a few moments without success. He sits back and stares at the box, his lower lip trembling, but makes no further efforts to open it. Toddler #3 tries to pry open the top of the box by force. Then she pulls the button. Undeterred, she keeps experimenting until ten minutes later—success! She slides the button, the top springs open, and Teddy pops out with a squeak. She squeals with delight, stuffs Teddy back into the box, and tries all over again. Toddler #4 sees toddler #3 open her box. He gets red in the face, smacks his own box with his fist, and bursts into tears.

When we encounter failure as adults, we tend to respond in very similar ways (albeit few of us resort to playing with our diapers). Failure can make us perceive our goals as being out of reach, causing us to give up too quickly (like toddler #1, whose box rolled away). Some of us feel so demoralized by failure that we become frozen, passive, and helpless (like toddler #2, who gave up). Some of us fail but keep trying until we succeed (like toddler #3), and some of us become so stressed and self-conscious that we can't think straight (like toddler #4, who burst into tears).

How we deal with failure is crucial to our success in life as well as to our general happiness and well-being. While some of us respond well to failure, many of us do not. Failure always hurts and disappoints but it can also be an informative, educational, and growth experience, as long as we take the failure in stride, figure out what we need to do differently next time, and persist in pursuing our goals. However, as with many of the psychological wounds we sustain in daily life, ignoring the injuries failure inflicts can make a bad situation worse, and at times, far worse.

Although our various ways of coping with failure are established early in our lives, we are by no means doomed to follow in the footsteps of our toddlerhood. Even those who respond to failures in the most unproductive and damaging ways can learn to employ more favorable and psychologically healthy coping styles. However, to do so, we must first understand the impact failure has on us, the psychological wounds it causes, and the emotional challenges we face if we wish to heal them.

The Psychological Wounds Failure Inflicts

Failures are the emotional equivalent of chest colds in that we all get them and we all feel terrible when we do. We usually recover from chest colds because we modify our activities accordingly once we get them—we rest, drink warm fluids, and dress warmly. If we were to ignore a cold entirely it would probably get worse and, in some cases, develop into pneumonia. We face similar dangers to our mental health when we encounter failure, yet few of us are aware of the need to employ the psychological equivalents of resting, drinking warm fluids, and dressing warmly. As a result, many of our failures cause unnecessary psychological damage, the implications of which can harm our emotional well-being far beyond the impact of the original incident.

Failure inflicts three specific psychological wounds that require emotional first aid. It damages our self-esteem by inducing us to draw conclusions about our skills, abilities, and capacities that are highly inaccurate and distorted. It saps our confidence, motivation, and optimism, making us feel helpless and trapped. And it can trigger unconscious stresses and fears that lead us to inadvertently sabotage our future efforts.

One of the reasons so many of us sustain psychological damage from failure is that it often takes only one or two incidents to set the entire vicious cycle into play. Further, when a failure is especially significant or meaningful to us (which it often is), leaving it untreated puts us at risk for developing psychological complications such as shame, crippling helplessness, and even clinical depression. Thus, what starts as a single episode of failure—a small emotional cold—can develop into psychological pneumonia that impacts our general functioning and mental health for the worse.

1. Honey, I Shrunk My Self-Esteem: Why Our Goals Seem Bigger and We Feel Smaller

Baseball players have long claimed that when they're on a hitting streak the ball literally seems bigger to them (and therefore easier to hit). Not surprisingly, when they're in a slump they report the baseball as appearing smaller and more difficult to hit. Most psychologists never took such claims seriously, perhaps because baseball players are a notoriously superstitious lot. Some players refuse to wash their underwear after a win so they don't "jinx" it and others sleep with their bats in bed to break out of hitting slumps. Which of those practices leads to more baseball wives sleeping on the sofa is anyone's guess.

When psychologists finally decided to investigate the players' claims scientifically they ran into a problem. It turns out major league umpires frown at the notion of pausing baseball games to allow players to complete psychological questionnaires. Consequently, scientists decided to test this phenomenon using regular people . . . and football.

Participants were asked to kick an American football through an adjusted field goal from the ten-yard line. They each had ten kicks. Before making any kicks, all subjects estimated the width and height of the goal similarly. But after their attempts, subjects who failed at the task (by scoring two or fewer successful kicks) estimated the goal as being 10 percent narrower and higher, and those who succeeded estimated it as being 10 percent wider and lower. It seems baseball players were right all along. Failure can make our goal seem literally more difficult and more imposing than it had appeared previously.

Failure not only makes our goal loom larger, it makes us feel "smaller" as well. Failing can induce us to feel less intelligent, less attractive, less capable, less skillful, and less competent—all of which have a hugely negative impact on our confidence and on the outcome of our future efforts. For example, if a college student fails a midterm exam, she might view herself as less capable and view the class as more difficult, making her more worried and less confident about doing well on the final. While some students might knuckle down and work harder as a result, others might become so intimidated they begin to question whether they can pass the class at all.

But what if that failed midterm also happened to be the first exam they ever took in college? What if they perceive not just the class but college as a whole as being a greater challenge than they're able to meet? Since they're unaware that failing the midterm has distorted their perceptions (such that the class and college appear harder than they actually are), they might reach premature and inappropriate decisions as a result. Indeed, many students drop out early in their freshman year for this exact reason (and toddler #1 is at risk for doing so as well).

Failure has an even greater impact on our self-esteem. Many of us respond to failures by drawing damaging conclusions about our character and abilities that seem incredibly compelling to us at the time even when they have no merit whatsoever. Many of us react to failure by thinking or voicing incredibly damaging thoughts such as: "I'm such a loser," "I can't do anything right," "I'm just not smart enough," "I'm such an idiot," "I'm a total embarrassment," "I deserve to lose," "People like me never get anywhere," "Why would anyone want to hire/date me?" or similar character assassinations.

Few people would argue that such demoralizing and unproductive thoughts have any redeeming value. Yet too often we allow ourselves to indulge in them, utter them aloud, and give them validity. If our six-year-old failed a spelling test in school and announced, "I'm a stupid loser who can't do anything right," most of us would swoop in, refute every word, and forbid him to say such terrible things about himself ever again. We would have no doubt that such negative thoughts would only make him feel worse in the moment and make it harder for him to succeed in the future. Yet we frequently fail to apply the very same logic and wisdom to our own situations.

The negative generalizations we often make after failing are not only inaccurate but they do more damage to our general self-worth and our future performance than the initial failure that spawned them. Criticizing our attributes so globally makes us hypersensitive to future failures, it can lead to deep feelings of shame, and it can threaten our entire well-being. Further, doing so prevents us from accurately assessing the causes of our failure so we can avoid similar miscalculations in the future. For example, if we blame our inability to attain personal improvement goals on our character shortcomings we are unlikely to identify and correct crucial errors in planning and strategic goal setting that are far more likely to be responsible for our failure.

Why New Year Resolutions Often Nudge Our Self-Esteem in the Wrong Direction

Every New Year we list our resolutions with hopes of improving our lives and feeling better about ourselves, only to abandon our efforts entirely by February (and often by January 2). As a result, instead of our self-esteem being strengthened by our accomplishments, we're left feeling weakened by failure and disappointment, which we quickly attribute to a lack of motivation or ability. We tell ourselves, "I guess I don't want to change," or "I'm just too lazy to do anything about my life," and feel even worse about ourselves than we did on December 31.

What makes such conclusions unfortunate as well as inaccurate is that the primary reason we complete so few of our resolutions is because we neglect to think through how we plan to achieve them. Without a carefully crafted plan in place our resolutions are unlikely to make it out of the starting gate no matter how motivated or capable we are. Indeed, one of the most common goal-planning errors we commit is neglecting to set a start date.

Another common New Year resolution error is goal bingeing. As a general rule, if your resolution list is longer than the one your child made for Santa, you might want to pare it down. Pauline, a recently divorced woman with two school-age children, marched into my office on the first Monday after the New Year and proudly thrust a sheet of paper into my hands. "My resolutions," she explained. "You've been encouraging me to take the wheel and steer my life in the right direction, so here, I'm taking it!" I glanced at Pauline's list and flinched. It had the following items: go to the gym four times a week and lose twenty-five pounds, try harder at work, organize the closets at home, paint the bedroom, make five new friends, post a profile on a dating website and go on at least two dates a month, join a book club, volunteer one afternoon a month, take a wine-tasting class, teach myself how to play the piano, and spend more time with the kids.

"What do you think?" she asked eagerly.

"I think that's what taking the wheel looks like—if you were a NASCAR driver," I said with a smile. "It might be a little much for a soccer mom with a minivan."

I explained that when we set too many goals for ourselves we are unlikely to complete any of them. Pauline's list included an entire smorgasbord of goal-setting errors. Some of the goals on her list conflicted with one another (e.g., getting to the gym four times a week and spending more time with the kids), others were too ambiguous (e.g., "try harder at work"), and others were too difficult (e.g., making five new friends, volunteering one afternoon a month, and going on two dates a month would be a challenging agenda for most single women, let alone a working mother of two).

Having multiple goals would be less of a problem if we took the time to prioritize them according to which were most urgent or most attainable given the circumstances of our lives at the time. We also neglect to break down long-term goals into smaller and more realistic subgoals. Without doing so, many of our goals can appear daunting and overwhelming. Last, we rarely take the time to develop action plans for dealing with the obstacles, hurdles, and setbacks that might arise along the way and we're then ill-equipped to deal with them when they do.

In short, we frequently fail to complete our New Year resolutions (as well as other goals) because we set the wrong goal(s) to begin with, and our self-esteem often suffers as a result.

2. Passivity and Helplessness: Why Not Only Mimes Get Trapped Inside Invisible Boxes

Failures sap our confidence, our motivation, and our hope. They can make us want to give up and forgo any future efforts and possibility of success. As a general rule, the more sweeping and negative our assumptions about our attributes and capacities are, the less motivated we'll be, as few of us make efforts to pursue goals we truly believe are out of reach. After all, if we're convinced we failed because we're not smart enough, capable enough, or fortunate enough, why would we persist?

What we neglect to take into consideration when the sting of failure is still fresh and our self-esteem is still bruised is that the very assumptions and perceptions that form the basis of our impulse to "surrender" are fundamentally incorrect.

Lenny, a thirty-year-old office manager at a sales company, came to psychotherapy after feeling increasingly depressed about his career. Although his day job provided basic financial support for his wife and new baby, Lenny's true passion was magic. He was a slender young man with angular features and a thick mustache (I've worked with numerous magicians over the years and why so many of them have mustaches remains a mystery to me). He wore oversized slacks and jackets, which I admit led me on more than one occasion to hope he would interrupt our session to pull out a stunning white dove, a cute rabbit, or even a string of colored handkerchiefs. Alas, the most exciting thing Lenny ever whipped out of his jacket was a throat lozenge.

Lenny had been performing as a magician since high school, but he never became successful enough to quit his job with the sales company. Although he was thrilled when his son was born, he also realized the added responsibility represented the death knell to his aspirations as a magician. Knowing little about the career path of magicians at that time, it wasn't immediately obvious to me why that would be so.

"There's no way to make a living as a magician without an agent," Lenny explained, "and I've never been able to get one. A couple of years ago I sent tapes to every agent out there, and nothing came of it. Yeah, I know," Lenny said, as if I was about to object, "you're wondering if my signature trick was good enough." Of course I wasn't wondering anything of the sort, but Lenny explained that agents only take on magicians whose signature trick— the one that serves as the magician's calling card—is a killer. Apparently, Lenny's was not.

"I spent the last two years working on my signature trick," Lenny continued. "But a couple of months ago, I turned thirty. Yeah, I know," he said in response to yet another imaginary objection on my part, "thirty isn't old. But I figured it was time to give up magic and focus on supporting my family. I stopped booking shows and I put away my stuff." Lenny took a deep breath. "But not doing magic anymore . . . it's killing me." Lenny swallowed hard. "Yeah, I know," he continued, "it doesn't matter how I feel because there's nothing I can do about it. I tried my best to make magic work, and I failed. I'll never be a professional magician: I have to accept that and move on. That's why I'm here, Doc. I need help. You have to help me accept that my life as a magician is over. Maybe once I do, it won't hurt so much."

Magic was Lenny's lifelong passion, but his failure to secure an agent or come up with a spectacular signature trick made him feel as though he'd exhausted all his options. In his mind, the only choice he had left was to give up his dream. Failure does that to us. It makes us feel hopeless and trapped, and it induces us to give up. We tend to fall prey to this kind of defeatist thinking far more than we realize. We get passed up for a promotion, so we cease making efforts because we believe our boss won't promote us no matter how well we perform. We skip the voting booth because we don't believe the candidate of our choice can win. We refuse to go back to the psychiatrist when our antidepressant medication fails because we assume if one of them didn't work, none of them will. We join a gym, sprain a muscle, and conclude we're too out of shape for physical activity. We break our diet and conclude we're one of those people who "just can't lose weight." When our intimate advances keep getting rebuffed by our spouse we conclude he or she no longer finds us attractive and we stop initiating sex.

In each of these scenarios failure convinces us that we have no chances of getting what we want and so we stop trying. Failure can be very persuasive.

Failure can also be very misleading.

Accurate as we feel our assessments are, in the vast majority of situations, ceasing our efforts only creates a self-fulfilling prophecy. By not taking action we guarantee we won't succeed, and we then view our eventual failure not as a lack of persistence on our part but as a confirmation that success was impossible all along. The fact that our own surrender has brought about the very outcome we feared eludes us, as does the fact that our pessimism has blinded us to the options and possibilities that do exist.

For example, we might have been second in line for the promotion at work and therefore next up for advancement had we continued to perform well. We could have campaigned for the political candidate we favored and by doing so increased that candidate's chances of getting elected. We could have tried another antidepressant, as it often takes trying several medications to find the one that works best for us (just as it does with over-the-counter pain relievers). Becoming more educated about exercise could have helped us avoid injury by planning workouts suited to our fitness level. If we found it too difficult to stay on a diet we could have taken steps to strengthen our motivation. And if our spouse rebuffed our advances we could have discussed things with him or her and resolved any larger issues that were at play.

Succumbing to feelings of pessimism, helplessness, and passivity is as damaging to our mental health as ignoring a worsening cold is to our physical health. Indeed, Lenny's "chest cold" took a rapid turn for the worse the moment he decided to give up magic. He became engulfed in feelings of hopelessness, helplessness, and despair, and he was at risk for developing full-blown depression, a "psychological pneumonia" that could threaten his mental well-being.

3. Performance Pressure: What to Expect When Expecting to Fail

When we fail at tasks in which our expectations for success are low, the psychological wounds failure inflicts are relatively minor. Failing to win a national lottery rarely sends people into a depression and the vast majority of untrained singers do not experience deep feelings of shame when they fail to get on a singing show (although they definitely feel disappointed). But when we possess the necessary skills and abilities to succeed and have expectations of doing so we are likely to feel much stronger pressure to perform well. Performance pressure can be useful in small doses but it becomes extremely unproductive in larger ones, as it can foster test anxiety, a fear of failure, and the risk of choking.

Many of us get anxious in test-taking situations regardless of our intelligence, preparation, or familiarity with the material. One of the reasons test anxiety is so common is that it is relatively easy to trigger. Even one episode of heightened anxiety is sufficient for us to feel intensely anxious when facing a similar situation in the future. Test anxiety is especially problematic because it causes massive disruptions to our concentration, our focus, and our ability to think clearly, all of which have a huge impact on our performance. As a rule, anxiety tends to be extremely greedy when it comes to our concentration and attention. The visceral discomfort it creates can be so distracting, and the intellectual resources it hogs so critical, that we might struggle to comprehend the nuances of questions, retrieve the relevant information from our memory, formulate answers coherently, or choose the best option from a multiple-choice list. As an illustration of how dramatic its effects are, anxiety can cause us to score fifteen points lower than we would otherwise on a basic IQ test—a hugely significant margin that can drop a score from the Superior to the Average range.

One of the more insidious but lesser-known manifestations of test anxiety occurs when we're reminded of negative stereotypes about our gender, race, ethnicity, or other group. Known as *stereotype threat*, such reminders often trigger subconscious worries and fears of conforming to stereotypes, even when entirely unwarranted and even when we believe the stereotype in question has no validity whatsoever. Such worries, even if they barely register in our awareness, can steal away just enough of our attention to hamper our performance on the task at hand.

As an illustration of stereotype threat, consider what happens when girls take math tests. When girls take math tests without boys present, they do substantially better than when taking the test with boys. Even in the twenty-first century, the presence of boys can subtly remind girls of the stereotypical yet false belief that men are innately better at math than women.

We Have Nothing to Fear
but Fear of Failing Itself

For some of us, failure is associated not just with disappointment and frustration but with far more damaging feelings, such as embarrassment and shame. As a result, the prospect of failing can be so intimidating that we make unconscious efforts to lower expectations for our success. While lowering expectations might seem like a reasonable approach, the way we go about doing so can result in our unwittingly sabotaging ourselves and bringing about the very outcome we fear.

Lydia, a woman in her late thirties I worked with some years ago, had taken a ten-year break from her career in marketing to raise three young children. When her youngest child started kindergarten, Lydia and her husband agreed it was time for her to resume working. Lydia quickly leveraged her connections to get job interviews at six different companies. But despite her inside track and impressive credentials, none of them called her back for a second interview. Lydia was horribly embarrassed by her failure, not to mention truly befuddled. Although she believed she had done the best she could, it quickly became apparent that a fear of failure had led her to unconsciously sabotage one opportunity after the other. Or rather, it quickly became apparent to me. Lydia, on the other hand, was convinced she had done all she could to succeed.

"Look, I understand why the first company turned me down," Lydia explained. "I didn't have time to read up on it before the interview because my daughter had an important basketball game and I promised I'd bake brownies for the team." Lydia's account of the second interview revealed an equally unconvincing imperative. "Ah, you see, my mother called the night before and I got stuck on the phone with her for three hours. She was upset about my cousin's wife feuding with her sister, and I felt bad about cutting her off." Lydia's take on what went wrong in the third interview was just as flimsy: "Well, what happened there was my nails were a mess and I thought I'd have time to do a quick mani-pedi before the interview, but I misjudged the time and got there half an hour late. Maybe forty-five minutes. Anyway, they refused to see me. Can you believe it?" I certainly could believe it, but I graciously refrained from nodding.

Lydia continued by explaining that a severe migraine headache kept her up the night before her fourth interview. "I was exhausted! Could you believe I even forgot to bring them a copy of my resume?" Lydia reported being afflicted with sudden "gastrointestinal distress" the morning of her fifth interview. "At some point my stomach was rumbling so loudly I just made a joke about it and apologized. But they hadn't heard a thing so it was kind of an awkward moment. I'm sure I'll laugh about it in the future." I doubted Lydia would ever find the situation chuckle-worthy, but again, I held my tongue.

Lydia claimed her sixth interview would have gone well, except—"My luck, I woke up on the wrong side of the bed, real irritable and impatient. My husband thought I should go to the interview anyway, but I should have listened to my gut and stayed home. The receptionist was so annoying I ended up getting into an argument with her. The interviewer came out to see what the ruckus was about and, whatever . . . it just went downhill from there. You know what they say, if it isn't meant to be, it isn't meant to be."

Most people hearing Lydia's account would immediately recognize an obvious pattern of excuses, avoidance, and self-sabotaging behavior that was sure to guarantee failure. But Lydia was truly oblivious to it. Her unconscious mind knew that by having obstacles to blame for any possible failures she could avoid the shame and embarrassment she feared. Fear of failure makes many of us engage in all manner of self-handicapping behaviors in which we exaggerate or create impediments to success without being aware we're doing so. Indeed, we are often extremely creative in the self-handicapping devices we construct in order to have something to blame for our failure.

Many of us procrastinate and "run out of time" to study before an important test. We might go out with friends and drink too much the night before an important presentation or get too little sleep. We might forget our study materials on the subway or at a friend's house. We might forget the cherries when packing our ingredients for the county fair cherry-pie-baking contest, or we might arrive at the marathon having packed only our left sneaker. And as Lydia demonstrates, there are endless physical ailments we can manufacture. If we do well despite these setbacks we have the added bonus of giving ourselves extra credit for succeeding when the odds were against us.

Of course, self-handicapping rarely leads to success. In addition, such strategies prevent us from examining our failures accurately and drawing useful conclusions about what we need to change or do differently in the future. For example, Lydia's resume might have needed changes or her job-interviewing skills might have needed sharpening, but it is impossible to assess such factors because they were obscured by the array of obstacles Lydia placed in her own way.

The unconscious nature of self-handicapping can blind us to its existence even when someone else points it out to us. Lydia was initially convinced that every one of her excuses was valid and that her failure was due to events over which she had absolutely no control. When I suggested otherwise, she responded with statements such as "You don't expect me to break a promise to my daughter, do you?" and "The problem was I didn't listen to my gut and stay home. My gut never leads me astray."

Fear of Failure in Families

Confronting Lydia's fear of failure was all the more urgent because studies show that parents who suffer from fear of failure often transmit such fears to their children. Most parents view their children as extensions of themselves as well as products of their parenting skills, so that when children fail, parents' own feelings of shame get triggered. They might then respond to their child's failure by withdrawing from them both subtly (e.g., with their tone of voice or body language) and overtly (e.g., expressing disapproval or anger). Children pick up on their parents' withdrawal, which triggers their own feelings of shame and teaches them that failures should be both feared and avoided.

To be clear, in the vast majority of situations, parents are entirely unaware they might be impacting their children so negatively. Lydia had three young children whom she loved dearly. However, the fact remains that unless she treated the psychological wounds failure inflicted and corrected her self-sabotaging habits, she was likely to perpetuate the cycle of fear of failure and pass it on to her children.

Choking Under the Influence

Bill Buckner had a stellar career as a Major League Baseball player, amassing over 2,700 hits, winning batting crowns, and playing as an All-Star. But he is most known for the error he made when playing for the Boston Red Sox in the 1986 World Series against the New York Mets. Buckner was on first when a ground ball that should have been simple to block went by him, costing the Red Sox the game and eventually the World Series. Buckner is hardly the only athlete to choke in a championship game when executing a simple skill they've performed perfectly thousands of times. Non-professional athletes choke in clutch moments just as frequently and choking is also common outside of sports.

Why do so many of us bowl a great game only to gutter the last ball? Why does a gifted vocalist sing flawlessly in a crucial audition only to deliver a cringe-worthy, off-key final note? Why does an advertising executive pitch the perfect presentation to every client, only to stammer incoherently and draw a blank when his company's president steps into the room?

Psychologists began researching why we tend to choke under pressure over two decades ago, but only recently have studies uncovered the psychological mechanisms responsible for these mental gaffes. Choking tends to happen because the stress we feel in high-pressure situations makes us overthink tasks and draw attention away from the part of our brain that executes the task automatically or fluidly. To illustrate this point try the following exercise. Fill a coffee mug with water, hold it by the handle, and walk it across the room. Easy, right? Now do it again, but this time, keep your eyes on the water as you walk and focus on making the adjustments necessary for the water not to spill. Most of us are far more likely to spill the water when we're trying not to than we are when we walk with the mug without thinking about it.

Choking is based on a similar dynamic. The greater the pressure of the situation, the more likely we are to overanalyze our actions and interfere with the smooth execution of a task we've performed or rehearsed hundreds of times. While we all make errors, choking usually occurs when the stakes are extremely high. The ramifications of choking and the self-recriminations that follow can be profound. Bill Buckner is still heckled for his gaffe even twenty-five years later, and many of us have trouble living down our own choking moments for years or even decades.

How to Treat the Psychological Wounds Failure Inflicts

Failures are often painful but not all of them warrant emotional first aid. Many of our failures are minor, and we shrug them off with relative ease, even if they do sting for a short while. Even substantial and meaningful failures might not require treatment if we are able to take them in stride, accurately assess what we should do differently next time, put in the necessary effort, and persist until we reach our goal.

But when we fail repeatedly or when we respond to failures in ways that set back our confidence, our self-esteem, and our chances of future success, we run the risk of allowing our emotional chest cold to turn into psychological pneumonia. Because much of the anxiety associated with failures can build upon itself, it is best to be prudent and apply psychological first aid treatments as soon as possible after meaningful or bothersome failures occur. Let's open our psychological medicine cabinet and review our treatment options.

General Treatment Guidelines

Failures inflict three kinds of psychological wounds. They damage our confidence and self-esteem and make our goals seem further out of reach. They distort our perceptions, make us feel hopeless about succeeding, and compel us to give up or stop trying. And they can create the kind of performance pressure that increases our anxiety and causes us to unconsciously sabotage our future efforts.

Treatments A (getting support) and B (regaining control) help minimize damage to confidence and self-esteem, they prevent the pessimistic and defeatist mind-sets that lead to loss of motivation and giving up, and they also boost our motivation, hope, and chances of success going forward. Treatment C (taking responsibility) is focused on owning the failure as well as the fears and feelings it elicits so as to minimize the likelihood of our self-sabotaging future efforts. Treatment D (managing performance pressure) helps reduce performance pressure, fear of failure, test anxiety (and stereotype threat), and choking.

Treatment A: Get Support and Get Real

Whenever a patient tells me about a disappointing and meaningful failure, my first response is to express sympathy and express warm emotional support—which often makes my patients reach for the tissue box. My second response is to point to some of the lessons they could learn from the failure that would help them going forward—which often makes them hurl the tissue box in my direction. Having silver linings pointed out to us when we're still getting rained on is always somewhat annoying.

Nonetheless, I respond this way for two reasons: First, because I'm really good at ducking. And second, because research has repeatedly demonstrated the most effective way to treat the psychological wounds failure inflicts is to find the positive lessons in what happened. Further, providing social and emotional support alone often makes people who experienced a failure feel *worse*.

But why is that so? Don't we always benefit from empathy when we're hurting?

Receiving concern and emotional support when we're still reeling from a failure can actually validate our (mis)perceptions about the deficits and shortcomings in our character and abilities. But if expressions of social support are quickly followed by realistic evaluations of the failure's implications, we could benefit from receiving emotional validation while still maintaining a realistic and grounded perspective that allows us to "get real."

This one-two combination of getting emotional support and assessing what we can gain or learn from the experience is the most effective strategy we can take in the immediate aftermath of a stinging failure. Most of us are proficient at getting emotional support, but figuring out the relevant takeaways when we still feel bad about ourselves can be challenging.

Exercise to Facilitate Learning from Failure

The following writing exercise will help you identify what you can gain from the failure. There are six general lessons that can be extracted from most failure experiences. Apply each of these lessons to your own situation.

1. *Failure is a great teacher.* Thomas Edison failed thousands of times before he invented the lightbulb and he viewed each failure as a learning experience. In his words, "I

haven't failed once. I've learned ten thousand things that don't work." Failure always tells us something about what we need to change in our preparation or execution of the task. What should you do differently next time?

2. *Failure provides new opportunities.* Henry Ford's first two car companies failed. Had they succeeded he might never have tried company number three, which was when he hit on the idea of assembly line manufacturing and became one of the richest men of his time. What opportunities might your failure possibly present?

3. *Failure can make us stronger.* Diana Nyad was sixty-two years old when in August 2011 she attempted to swim from Cuba to Florida, a distance of 103 miles. Unfortunately, asthma attacks forced her to give up her attempt after covering sixty miles of the distance. Remarkably she tried again less than two months later. This time she swam over eighty miles before painful Portuguese man-of-war stings forced her doctors to pull her from the water. Diana quickly announced she would not try the swim again. But once her exhaustion and initial disappointment wore off she realized that her two attempts had only made her stronger and more likely to succeed if she tried again. She made another attempt in August 2012 and although she swam farther than she had in her previous efforts, dangerous squalls forced her out of the water before completing her quest.

We all get demoralized when we fail. But bouncing back from our failure and learning from the experience will always make us stronger and more likely to succeed in the future. In what ways might your failure make you stronger?

4. *Some failures are also successes.* I've always wondered how the runner-up in the Miss Universe pageant feels once she's had some time to reflect and pick out the confetti from her hair. Does she feel proud to have represented her country so well, or does she feel devastated about coming so close and not winning? It's crushing when our amateur sports team loses the playoff game but does that nullify the accomplishment of getting to the playoffs in the first place? Sure, it's disappointing we didn't get the job offer after so many rounds of interviews but surely we should feel encouraged about being among the top applicants.

    Many of our failures are also successes in some way, except we tend to focus far more on aspects of failure than of success. No matter how disappointed we feel, we should always acknowledge the ways in which we were successful even if we ultimately failed. In what ways could you view your failure as a success?

5. *Failure makes future success more meaningful.* Studies show that the harder we work, the more failures and challenges we overcome, the greater the meaning, joy, and satisfaction we derive when we eventually succeed. Oscar Pistorius is a professional athlete from South Africa who in 2011 ran the four-hundred-meter sprints at the Track and Field World Championships in South Korea. However, unlike the other sprinters in the field, Pistorius is a double amputee; both his legs were amputated when he was a child. Running on metal "blades," he became the first disabled athlete ever to run in an able-bodied world championship meet. He then capped off his achievement by advancing to the individual semifinals and winning a

silver medal in the relay races (as well as setting a national record).

For Pistorius, just being on the track was a triumph. He had spent years fighting in court for the right to run in the world championships and the Olympics, eventually proving that his blades did not give him an "advantage" over the other athletes. Even after winning the legal battle, he struggled to make the minimum qualifying time for the event, failing to do so until the very last race before the deadline—one week before the championships began. When Pistorius took the track for his first race, every camera in the stadium was pointed at him. The sheer awe and joy on his face as his name was announced outshone that of every other athlete there and gave goose bumps to anyone watching. Pistorius then repeated his stunning performance and reached the semifinals of the four-hundred-meter sprints in the London 2012 Olympics. (Sadly, Pistorius gave fans goose bumps of an entirely different kind when he was arrested in February 2013 on charges of killing his girlfriend.)

The more we fail, the greater the impact our eventual success will have on our mood, self-esteem, and confidence. How much more will success mean to you now that you've encountered failure?

6. *Success is not always necessary*. Recent studies have begun to illuminate a surprising aspect about failure: many of the benefits we hope to reap by pursuing our goals are not necessarily dependent on our ability to complete them. In most situations, making steady progress toward our goals contributes more toward our sustained happiness and self-fulfillment than actually reaching them. The satisfac-

tion, excitement, sense of pride, and personal accomplishment we feel by inching ever closer to our target combine to create a heady mix of satisfaction and joy that does wonders for our mood, motivation, and psychological well-being. Can you identify ways in which you derived meaning and satisfaction as you pursued your goal?

Treatment Summary: Get Support, Then Get Real

Dosage: Apply the treatment as soon as possible every time you experience a meaningful failure.

Effective for: Minimizing damage to confidence, self-esteem, and motivation.

Secondary benefits: Reduces performance pressure.

Treatment B: Focus on Factors in Your Control

Failing can make us feel trapped and helpless, as though events are out of our control and we are doomed to fail. Once we believe nothing we do can bring about a different outcome, we tend to give up or make only feeble efforts. However, succumbing to such paralysis can turn an emotional cold into psychological pneumonia, as hopelessness and helplessness often lead to conditions such as clinical depression.

The tragedy of failure is that many of the assumptions and perceptions that lead us to draw incapacitating conclusions about our lack of control are actually false. Further, scientists have repeatedly demonstrated that changing our perspective and focusing on aspects of the situation that are in our control can have a hugely beneficial impact on our hope, motivation, and self-esteem. In some cases, merely acquiring information that refutes our incorrect assumptions of helplessness and lack of control is sufficient to cure our paralysis and prevent our "emotional cold" from getting worse.

One study illustrated this point with a group of seniors over the age of sixty-five. Seniors are often quite sedentary, which can seriously compromise their health (though being sedentary isn't a recipe for good health at any age). The problem is that seniors today often believe that being sedentary is a natural part of aging (which, of course, it isn't). Scientists taught the seniors to attribute their sedentary lifestyle not to age but to factors that were entirely in their control, such as how much walking they tended to do on a daily basis. One month later, this simple intervention led to the seniors increasing their walking by two and a half miles a week (which is hugely significant) and they reported equal improvements in their stamina and mental health.

The best way to regain a sense of control over the circumstances that led to our failure is to reexamine both our preparation (our goal planning) and our performance (how we executed our efforts) so we can identify elements that we perceived as being out of our control that could be in our control if we approached or perceived them differently.

EXERCISE FOR GAINING CONTROL OF OUR GOAL PLANNING

Since it is best to pursue one goal at a time, complete this exercise for each goal separately. I've included the responses of Pauline, the recently divorced woman with an abundance of New Year resolutions, for illustrative purposes. Pauline agreed to prioritize the item "make new friends," as her social circle had been severely reduced over the course of the divorce and she was eager to find new outlets for social engagements and new friends with whom she could enjoy them.

1. Define your goal in as realistic and specific terms as possible.

    Keep in mind: Formulate clear and measurable objectives. For example, "get into shape for summer" is realistic but not specific. "Win the lottery" is specific but not realistic, and "write a best-selling novel" is neither specific (what is the novel about?) nor realistic (few novels become best sellers). Pauline defined her goal as "find three venues to meet people with similar interests."

    In addition, defining your goal in ways that are personally meaningful and that you find inherently interesting and enjoyable will help maximize your motivation over the long term. For example, you might define your weight loss and exercise goal as "develop a healthier lifestyle that gives me greater vitality and stamina so I can enjoy active pursuits with my children and grandchildren for many years to come." Give careful thought to the regimens you choose as well. For example, your motivation to exercise might be stronger and last longer if you joined a hiking group with friends than if you ran on a treadmill in your basement alone.

2. Break down the goal into intermediate steps.

    Keep in mind: How we break down our long-term goals into smaller intermediate steps can have a huge and crucial impact on our motivation. Intermediate goals that require too little effort can cause us to lose interest and enthusiasm and become less engaged in pursuing our larger goal, and thus hamper our motivation. Intermediate goals that are too challenging tend to frustrate us and therefore also lead to a loss of motivation. Try to define intermediate milestones that provide a challenge but aren't too daunting. It is best to get some successes under our belt, so we should ramp up slowly by starting with easier challenges that become (incrementally) harder.

When defining our subgoals it is important to focus on variables within our control (e.g., our performance) rather than those outside our control (e.g., a specific outcome). For example, weight loss or fitness goals should focus on what we eat or how much exercise we get (as those are within our control) and not on how much weight we lose (as we cannot force our bodies to lose weight at a prede-termined rate). If we plan to start a blog we should deter-mine the allotments of time we plan to set aside to work on it, not the actual progress we hope to make (as it is difficult to foresee programming and design problems and other difficulties). It is better to feel we're making progress on our cheese lovers blog because we put in as many hours as we said we would than to feel as though we're failing because it took us half a day to resize a stunning picture of Swiss Flösserkäse.

Pauline broke her goal into the following subgoals: "Make a list of activities that interest me. Search online for possible venues. Explore one new venue a week."

3. Set time frames for the overall and intermediate goals.
    Keep in mind: It is best to go through the intermediate goals on your list and indicate two time frames for each, a starting date/hour and a completion date/hour. Objective deadlines might make it necessary to create a time frame

for our larger goal first and then assign time frames to each of the intermediate goals accordingly (such as when we're training for a marathon or creating a portfolio for an upcoming job or school interview), but when possible we should set time frames for intermediate goals first, as doing so allows for more realistic and attainable schedules. Much as we did when forming our intermediate goals, making the time frames moderately challenging is the best way to maintain our interest, effort, and motivation. Pauline decided to start the next day and to explore one new venue a week until she found a suitable one, after which she would explore a new venue every two weeks.

4. List any potential detours, setbacks, or temptations that might arise.

    Keep in mind: We would be wise to adopt the Boy Scouts' motto and "be prepared" by troubleshooting not only what *might* go wrong but what *could* go wrong as well. For example, if our goal is to minimize our drinking and adopt moderation we might anticipate the need to strategize what to do during holiday parties at work but we should also consider what to do if we're asked to attend a last-minute business dinner with clients who are wine lovers. Pauline anticipated potential problems with her babysitter, who had a history of canceling at the last minute.

5. List the possible solutions for each of the above detours, setbacks, or temptations, including what you can do to avoid them and how you plan to implement these solutions. Phrase your implementation strategies as positive actions (e.g., "If I'm offered a cigarette I will say, *No, thanks,*

I quit," as opposed to, "If I'm offered a cigarette I won't take it").

Keep in mind: Anticipating problems and planning solutions to them ahead of time is crucial for avoiding discouragement and maintaining motivation and morale when difficulties arise. Any solution is only as good as our plan to implement it. For example, asking women intending to get a breast cancer exam to spend a few moments planning how and when they would do so made them twice as likely to follow through with the exam than women who did not make a plan. Pauline's solution was to find a spare babysitter she could call on if necessary.

Reexamining Our Execution of the Task

Not all our failures are due to faulty planning. We also need to identify ways for gaining control of how we execute the task. For example, Lenny abandoned his dreams of becoming a professional magician because he believed he had tried everything he could to develop a great signature trick yet still failed to do so. He spent hours going over lists of all the tricks he knew. He tried brainstorming new combinations and elaborations that could elevate them to a new level. But despite all these efforts, he failed to come up with a show-stopping trick.

After hearing about his efforts, I expressed sympathy for his feelings of disappointment (which made Lenny reach for the tissue box). I then told him I disagreed with his assessment entirely, and prepared to duck. Lenny was surprised by my comment but also extremely curious. I explained that there were still many brainstorming avenues he could explore and that by trying to generate ideas from his existing list of tricks he had actually limited his options and inadvertently rendered his brainstorming efforts ineffective.

I then gave him examples of other ways in which he could approach brainstorming, for example, from the top down, by first identifying conceptual themes he found compelling (family, nostalgia, love, culture, food, etc.) and only then considering how to evoke these concepts using magic. Or he could start with the emotional impact he was trying to elicit (awe, surprise, wonder, confusion, amazement, shock, etc.) as well as the sequence in which he wanted to evoke them. Or he could focus first on unconventional materials or approaches (such as reversals). For example, I suggested that it would be hilarious if instead of holding out cards, putting the chosen one in a hat, and pulling out a rabbit, he held out several rabbits for the audience member to choose from, put the rabbit in the hat, and pulled out a card (alas, Lenny did not share my vision).

Failure had caused Lenny to limit his options in other ways as well. He was convinced audiences were more interested in reality television stars and jokes about celebrities or politicians than they were in magic. However, he never considered integrating these concepts into his existing act and changing his patter accordingly. Lenny soon came to realize there were many more avenues to explore and that it was too soon to give up on his dream. His mood changed the instant he reached the decision and for the first time I saw a sparkle of hope in his eye.

Exercise for Gaining Control of Our Task Execution

The goal in this writing exercise is to identify factors that contributed to the failure and that are in your control and to determine how to address these factors when making future efforts. I've included Lenny's responses for illustrative purposes.

1. Describe the failure in question. Make sure it is a single incident of failure. For example, if you failed a driver's test five times, list only the most recent attempt.

   Lenny wrote "I failed to become a professional magician."

2. List all the factors that contributed to your failure.

   Lenny listed "weak signature trick, no agent, lack of contacts, audiences don't care about magic."

3. Identify which of the factors on your list are in your control and which are not. For example, factors within your control might be "I failed to complete the marathon because I didn't give myself enough time to train," or "My marriage failed because we never learned to communicate with one another." Factors outside of your control might be "I failed the bar exam because I get nervous during important tests," or "I lost the customer because the product we delivered had too many problems."

   Lenny listed the factors outside his control as "No agent will take me on without a stronger signature trick," "I'm not a good enough magician to invent a great signature trick," "I don't have contacts that could help me get more bookings or secure an agent," and "Most audiences don't care about magic." The only factor he listed as within his control was "Giving up magic was my decision."

4. Go through each factor you listed as being outside your control and try to view it differently. See if you can replace the factor with one that is within your control. For exam-

ple, you might replace "I failed the bar exam because I get nervous during important tests" with "I didn't take steps to manage my test anxiety" (because we can always learn ways to do so), and you might replace "I failed to retain the customer because the product we delivered had too many problems" with "I lacked the necessary complaint-handling training to retain the customer" (because complaint-management training is something we can always get).

Lenny switched "I'm not a good enough magician to invent a great signature trick," with "I only tried one brainstorming approach among many." He swapped "I don't have contacts that could help me get more bookings or secure an agent" with "I haven't networked with other magicians, bookers, and club owners as much as I could." And he replaced "Most audiences don't care about magic" with "I haven't restructured my tricks around topics audiences care about."

5. Once you've completed step 4, create a new list of action items that are within your control. For each factor, identify how you might go about addressing the issues or making the necessary changes to improve your chances of future success.

     Lenny decided to try three additional brainstorming techniques for his signature trick and to allot himself an additional year within which to do so. He also decided to focus on networking with other magicians, bookers, and club owners and to increase his presence online using social media platforms.

     Eight months later Lenny left me a message letting me know he would be performing his new signature trick—

on television! The trick he came up with was both moving and visually beautiful. But to me, the most magical thing about his television debut was the sheer joy I saw on his face as he performed.

TREATMENT SUMMARY: FOCUS ON FACTORS IN YOUR CONTROL

Dosage: Apply the treatment as soon as possible every time you experience a meaningful failure. Make sure to revisit the goal-planning and execution exercises before making future efforts and whenever you set new goals.

Effective for: Preventing or reducing feelings of helplessness and hopelessness, increasing hope and motivation, and improving chances of future success.

Secondary benefits: Minimizes damage to confidence and self-esteem and reduces performance pressure.

Treatment C: Take Responsibility and Own the Fear

Although it is tempting to make excuses about our failure, doing so prevents us from learning the many useful lessons it can teach us. Worse, the more we deny any responsibility we might have, the more likely we are to feel as though the situation is outside our control. By recognizing that failure usually evokes at least some measure of fear and anxiety, we can begin to get in touch with such feelings, own them, and thereby prevent them from influencing our behavior unconsciously and destructively.

Lydia, the mother who sought to reenter the workplace after raising three children, struggled because her self-esteem and confidence as a professional were extremely low after a long hiatus from the workplace. Her unconscious self-handicapping served to protect her self-esteem by providing ready-made excuses for any failure she might encounter. Unfortunately, it practically guaranteed her failure, a fact to which Lydia was completely blind. Once she finished telling me about her sixth job interview fiasco (arguing with her prospective boss's receptionist), I decided to share my concerns with her.

"I sometimes get a little anxious about coming back to work after a week-long vacation," I began. "I can only imagine how terrifying it must be to jump back into the workplace after an absence of over a decade."

"Well, sure, yeah, it's a little scary," Lydia admitted.

"I'm sure it must be. Do you discuss that aspect of things with anyone?" Lydia shook her head. I continued, "Feeling apprehensive, anxious, and even scared is entirely natural, Lydia, especially given the changes in the marketing industry over the past ten years. In fact, it would be weird if you weren't a little scared. But the way our fears work, if we don't own them and if we don't talk about them, our mind will find other ways of expressing them."

"Like what?" Lydia asked.

"Like getting into fights with the secretary of the person who has to determine whether you'd fit in well with his staff," I responded with a smile.

"But you don't know how irritating she was!" Lydia objected.

"Actually, I assume she was incredibly irritating," I said. "But you have three young kids, Lydia. I'm guessing you must be pretty used to handling irritating and frustrating situations." Lydia nodded. "Again, I think you weren't expressing your fears consciously so your mind decided to express them for you."

"Wait, you mean like the migraine and bad stomach? Those were real!"

"So is your anxiety about failing," I responded. "But unless you own it and figure out how to address it, I see more headaches and stomachaches in your future." I was relieved to see that Lydia didn't argue this time, she just became thoughtful. Difficult as it was, Lydia was eventually able to own her feelings and take responsibility for each one of her failed job interviews (and the self-handicapping that caused them). Once she did, she was able to reengage in her job search in a much more productive manner. It took her several more months of looking and numerous failed interviews but Lydia eventually found a job in her field and reentered the workplace successfully.

We should all assume that where failure goes, anxiety and fear might follow. The best way for us to own both our feelings and our failures is to talk about them with supportive people. Airing our fears and exposing them to trusted friends or family members will minimize our unconscious need to express them self-destructively. Another option is to write about our fears in a journal or blog, as long as we make sure to balance them with more optimistic assessments.

One of the most effective ways to remove the emotional sting of failures is to joke about them when it is possible or appropriate to do so. In studies, seeing the humor in a failure was found to be an extremely effective way to get over the pain as well as any embarrassment or shame a failure caused. Being able to "see the funny" in a situation also helps reduce performance pressure when making future attempts. By verbalizing our fears in joke form we make it less necessary for our minds to express them unconsciously and in self-defeating ways. Of course, not all failures are ones we can or should laugh about, but many are.

One group of people who regularly practice laughing about their failures is stand-up comedians. Many comics turn their painful experiences of failure into jokes, and in doing so drastically reduce the pain the failure evokes. For example, comic Jim Short found a way to deal with his feelings about his financial failures and shortcomings by talking about them in his act. "I'm thirty-four and I make seven thousand dollars a year. I'm a loser! I was sad and depressed. And then I thought, wait a minute, I'm not a loser! I've tried! I'm a *failure!*"

In 2011 Bill Buckner, the Red Sox player whose choking cost his team a ticket to the World Series, played himself on Larry David's *Curb Your Enthusiasm*. In the episode, Buckner is heckled for not catching that crucial ball at first base (yes, even decades later). Later, he passes by a burning building, where a mother on the third floor is instructed by firefighters to toss her baby into their net below. Reluctantly, the mother complies. The baby drops into the net but bounces high into the air. The gathered onlookers gasp and then collectively wince when they recognize Buckner and realize the baby is headed straight in his direction. But Buckner reaches for the baby, makes the perfect catch, and redeems himself, while the crowd breaks into applause. Buckner's appearance represented a real-life example of someone who was able to laugh at his most painful failure and no doubt heal the psychological wounds it inflicted by doing so.

Treatment Summary: Take Responsibility and Own the Fear

Dosage: Apply the treatment as soon as possible every time you experience a meaningful failure.

Effective for: Preventing or minimizing damaged confidence and self-esteem and taking the sting out of painful failures by finding the humor in them.

Secondary benefits: Reduces performance pressure and fear of failure.

Treatment D: Distract Yourself from Performance Pressure Distractions

Performance pressure can increase test anxiety, it can make us choke at crucial moments, and it can drain our attention with worries about conforming to stereotypes. It does so because the stress or anxiety we feel in the moment steals attention from the task we're executing, hampers our performance, and makes us more likely to fail. We then feel even more stressed and anxious going forward and the cycle deepens.

To treat the psychological wounds of performance pressure we have to fight fire with fire. When stress and anxiety threaten to steal our attention we need to steal it right back. Studies have demonstrated a number of ways to distract ourselves from the distraction of performance pressure, and some of them are as simple as whistling Dixie. In fact, one of them is whistling Dixie, or rather whistling—whether "Dixie" is your warble of choice is up to you. Let's examine these countermeasures in more detail.

1. Whistle While You Choke

The Seven Dwarfs (from the Disney film *Snow White*) believe in whistling while they work. I assume they too feared choking under pressure, because studies have demonstrated that whistling can prevent us from overthinking the kinds of automatic tasks we've done many times before and then choking as a result (such as swinging a golf club, throwing a football, carrying a cup of water, and, yes, Bill Buckner, catching an easy dribbler at first base). The reason this works is that once we're focused on the task at hand, whistling requires just enough additional attention to leave none left over for overthinking.

One word of caution: while you might find whistling incredibly useful in certain situations, those around you might not. So keep in mind you don't have to perform a bird-calling aria to combat performance pressure; whistling softly is just as effective.

2. Mumbling to Yourself During an Exam Does Not Mean You're Crazy

The most important thing we can do to avoid or minimize test anxiety is to prepare and study for the test as best we can and avoid procrastinating when doing so. The better prepared we are the less anxious we will feel on exam day. However, test anxiety can strike us even when we're well prepared, hampering our ability to focus during exam time.

We therefore need to do two things: quell our anxiety and regain our focus. The first will require us to sacrifice a tiny bit of exam time to calm ourselves down. Even if we don't realize it, anxiety can cause shallow breathing that limits the oxygen we take in and increases our sense of panic. To restore normal breathing and lower your panic you should put down your pen, look away from the exam, and focus on your breathing for one minute as you inhale and exhale to a count of three (count "in-two-three out-two-three" in your head while doing so). As you count, notice how the air feels filling your lungs and how it feels as you exhale. Roughly a minute should be sufficient to stabilize your breathing and take the edge off your anxiety.

Next, we need to redirect our attention back to the task at hand and we need to prevent our mind from worrying about how well or poorly we're doing and the implications thereof. The best way to keep our focus on the specific steps required to answer the questions is by reasoning through them aloud (but quietly—a whispered mumble will do). By vocalizing the questions and reasoning aloud, we use just enough attentional resources to deprive the part of our brain that wants to focus on worrying.

3. Neutralize the Stereotype

When we're reminded of negative stereotypes about our gender, race, ethnicity, or other group, it can trigger a subconscious worry about conforming to these stereotypes that can prevent us from giving our full attention to the task at hand. The best medicine in such situations is to neutralize such worries by affirming our self-worth.

In a series of recent studies, four hundred seventh graders in a socioeconomically diverse school were asked to choose a personal value (e.g., athletic ability, close friendships, or strong family ties) and write a brief essay about it at the start of the school year. Half the students were instructed to choose a value that mattered to them and write about why it mattered and how they expressed it, and half (as a control group) were told to choose a value that did not matter to them and write about why it might matter to someone else. The results were no less than astonishing. Students who wrote about values that mattered to them narrowed the achievement gap between black and white students by 40 percent and the effects lasted through the eighth grade (two years). A similar experiment was done with college women taking physics (women are chronically underrepresented in the hard sciences). Women who did the self-affirmation exercise did significantly better than their female counterparts who did not.

Of course, stereotype threat does not affect everyone, but the lower our confidence the more likely we are to become distracted by such concerns when reminders of them are present. If you feel you might be susceptible to such worries, take time before the exam to write a brief essay about an aspect of your character you value highly and about which you feel confident and proud. Doing so is a good investment, as it requires little time and it can make you more resilient to any irrelevant worries and anxieties a previous failure might trigger.

TREATMENT SUMMARY: DISTRACT YOURSELF FROM PERFORMANCE PRESSURE DISTRACTIONS

Dosage: Apply the treatment before and during situations in which you might experience performance pressure or anxiety or in which stereotype threat might come into play.

Effective for: Reducing performance pressure, test anxiety, stereotype threat, and risk of choking.

Secondary benefits: Minimizes damaged confidence and self-esteem and eases fear of failure.

When to Consult a Mental Health Professional

Treating the psychological wounds failure inflicts should bring you emotional relief, foster your future preparation and performance, and allow you to persist in making efforts toward your goals. However, if you've applied the treatments in this chapter and still struggle with feelings of hopelessness, helplessness, shame, or depression, you should seek the help of a mental health professional. You should also seek professional help if these treatments have not helped you lower performance pressure or if you continue to fail at tasks at which you should be succeeding. Finally, if your mood and outlook have become so bleak and despondent that you have thoughts of harming yourself or others, please seek immediate help from a mental health professional or go to your local emergency room.

CHAPTER 7

||||||||||||||||||||

LOW SELF-ESTEEM

Weak Emotional Immune Systems

Everyone desires high self-esteem and if we were to judge by the vast assortment of magazines, books, programs, products, and self-proclaimed gurus that promise to deliver it, everyone can have it as well. That this billion-dollar industry exists at all is remarkable given that decades of research and thousands of scientific studies have demonstrated repeatedly that the overwhelming majority of self-esteem programs simply don't work. It is a shame they don't, because having low self-esteem is akin to having a weak emotional immune system: it renders us more vulnerable to many of the psychological injuries we sustain in daily life, such as failure and rejection. Further, people with low self-esteem are often less happy, more pessimistic, and less motivated than their higher-self-esteem counterparts. They also have much worse moods; they face a greater risk of depression, anxiety, and eating disorders; and they experience their relationships as less fulfilling than people with higher self-esteem do.

The good news is that despite the many failed promises of the self-esteem industry, researchers have found ways to boost our self-esteem and to strengthen our emotional immune systems by doing so. While such approaches cannot catapult someone's low self-esteem into the extremely high self-esteem range, that is probably for the best. Having very high self-esteem has its own set of pitfalls. For example, people with very high self-esteem tend to blame others for their own mistakes, they reject negative feedback as unreliable, and they often struggle to accept the consequences of their own actions. These tendencies render them likely to repeat the same mistakes and have significant problems in the workplace and their relationships and personal lives as a result.

At the very high end of self-esteem, narcissists possess an overly high and grandiose opinion of themselves but are also quick to feel extremely hurt and angry when criticized or devalued even if the criticism is minor (i.e., there are no small insults to a narcissist). Because they feel so crushed by even insignificant slights, they often have the nasty habit of seeking to retaliate against the people who "punctured" their inflated sense of self. Perhaps scientists should be seeking remedies for narcissism instead of for low self-esteem, but then again, life often finds ways to serve humble pie to those who need it most.

While few of us are true narcissists, there has been a general "grade inflation" in our collective self-esteem over the past few decades, spurred in part by the lavish attentions of the self-esteem industry. Consequently, studies indicate that today most of us are of two minds when it comes to our self-esteem: we feel inadequate as individuals on one hand, yet believe we're better than "average" on the other.

Indeed, the word "average" itself has developed strangely negative connotations. I say "strangely" because by definition, two-thirds of the population is "average" at any given thing (with one-sixth of people being above average and one-sixth below).

Yet, these days, telling a student, an employee, or a lover that his or her skills and abilities are "average" would constitute an insult and a blow to the individual's self-esteem. Most of us believe we're better drivers than average, that we're funnier, more logical, more popular, better looking, nicer, more trustworthy, wiser, and more intelligent than average as well.

Ironically, while we've been developing an aversion to being average, self-esteem scientists have been amassing one piece of evidence after another indicating that where our self-esteem is concerned, being average (not too high, not too low) is the best thing for us. Ideally, our self-esteem should lie in a range where our feelings of self-worth are both strong (not too low) and stable (not too high and fragile). Indeed, people with strong and stable self-esteem have more realistic evaluations of their real-world strengths and weaknesses and relatively more accurate assessments of how they're perceived by others, and they are usually the "healthiest," psychologically speaking.

Of course, this raises another question. How realistic are our self-assessments to begin with? In other words, does our self-esteem reflect the real-world value of our skills and attributes compared to others or does it reflect our subjective and often inaccurate assessments of these qualities based on our own psychological biases?

Let's use physical attractiveness as an example. Studies clearly demonstrate that people with higher self-esteem believe they are more attractive than people with lower self-esteem profess themselves to be. But when scientists compared stripped-down photographs of higher- and lower-self-esteem people (no jewelry or makeup, just faces) it quickly became clear that such is not the case. People with lower self-esteem were found to be just as attractive as people with higher self-esteem were. But because low self-esteem can cause us to underestimate our attractiveness we often downplay our strengths and we get less positive feedback about our appearance as a result. On the other hand, people with higher self-esteem might dress more attractively than their low self-esteem counterparts, which brings them more positive feedback and fuels their self-esteem even more.

Is Our Self-Esteem Low if We Don't Think Much of Anyone Else Either?

An athletic young man I once worked with came to therapy to deal with his "terribly low self-esteem." He went on to describe his own body in extremely critical terms and then quickly proceeded to discuss celebrities known for having beautiful bodies while pointing out their "obvious and disgusting flaws" (which were "obvious and disgusting" only to him). "I don't think you have low self-esteem," I said to him as soon as he finished savaging Brad Pitt for having "skinny arms and chicken legs." "True, you hate your body, but you hate everyone else's body as well," I pointed out while sucking in my stomach. "You might have low self-esteem, but the larger problem is your general negativity and unhappiness. Let's discuss whether you might be depressed." Depression can cause us to feel generally negative about everyone and everything (as well as a host of other symptoms) and it can masquerade as low self-esteem.

Of course, not everyone with a negative outlook on life is necessarily depressed, nor does such negativity necessarily indicate low self-esteem. For example, years ago scientists thought people with low self-esteem were also more prejudiced because they rated people of groups different from their own negatively (e.g., people of different race or gender). However, the scientists forgot to account for the fact that people with low self-esteem also rated their own groups negatively, which means their assessments of other groups weren't prejudiced but rather part of their larger negativity. Once they accounted for people's ratings of their own group the researchers found that people with low self-esteem were in fact less prejudiced than people with high self-esteem were.

One last point of clarification is that our self-esteem includes both a general sense of self-worth and how we feel about ourselves in specific domains of our lives (as a spouse, parent, friend, lawyer, nurse, golfer, video game player, etc.). When we think of ourselves as having low or high self-esteem we are usually referring to our global sense of self-worth. That being said, how we feel about ourselves in the specific domains we consider personally meaningful or important has a big impact on our general self-worth. For example, an aspiring chef might be much more bothered at the thought that she was a terrible cook than a professional athlete would be. Therefore, failures and success in meaningful domains of specific self-esteem can lead to changes in our global sense of self-worth as well.

Now that we've covered some of the basic foibles of our self-esteem, let's turn our attention to the psychological injuries we sustain when our self-esteem is low.

The Psychological Wounds Low Self-Esteem Inflicts

Low self-esteem can inflict three types of psychological wounds: It makes us more vulnerable to many of the emotional and psychological injuries we sustain in daily life, it makes us less able to absorb positive feedback and other "emotional nutrients" when they come our way, and it makes us feel insecure, ineffective, unconfident, and disempowered.

Boosting our self-esteem would strengthen our weakened emotional immune system and buffer us against many of these threats to our psychological well-being. Most of us know this from our own experience. When we feel good about ourselves we are often able to shrug off the kinds of setbacks, disappointments, or criticisms that on a "low self-esteem day" would have a much greater impact. In order to apply emotional first aid treatments successfully and boost our self-esteem we need to have a better understanding of how each of these wounds operates. Let's examine them in greater detail.

1. Egos Under Siege: Greater Psychological Vulnerability

Low self-esteem makes us more vulnerable to the psychological slings and arrows of daily life as even minor failures, rejections, or disappointments can sail over our emotional walls, get through our psychological defenses, and smash into our gut. When our self-esteem is low, normal "insults" like our boss frowning at us disapprovingly in a meeting, losing the office football pool, or a friend canceling plans to hang out with us impact our mood and disposition far more than they should. We blame ourselves for such events, we take them too personally, and we bounce back from them more slowly than we might were our self-esteem higher. Indeed, when our self-esteem is low, the barrage of hurts and slights we sustain on a regular basis can make us feel as though our egos are under siege from every angle.

Although there is an ongoing discussion about the extent to

which high self-esteem functions as a general buffer (studies have only recently begun distinguishing high self-esteem from too-high and fragile self-esteem), a substantial body of research demonstrates that having high*er* self-esteem (i.e., not too low) can make us more psychologically resilient and boost our emotional immune systems on at least several different fronts.

For example, rejection hurts at all levels of self-esteem but brain scans have demonstrated that people with low self-esteem experience rejection as more painful than people with higher self-esteem do. Also, our psychological responses to rejection are far less adaptive when our self-esteem is low, as we typically withdraw and create more distance between ourselves and others to minimize the risk of further rejection and pain. In some cases, our psychological vulnerability and our efforts at self-protection can lead us to push others away so consistently that we become socially or emotionally isolated and place ourselves at risk for acute loneliness. Having low self-esteem also makes us more vulnerable to discrimination and the further loss in self-esteem such experiences cause.

We are also more vulnerable to failure when our self-esteem is low. Failing causes larger emotional blows and sharper declines in motivation in people who have low self-esteem than it does in those with higher self-esteem. In addition, we are likely to be less persistent after failing and to overgeneralize the meaning of the failure such that we perceive it as indicative of a wider and more serious set of shortcomings than it actually is. Failing also sets in motion a vicious cycle of pushing low self-esteem even lower and therefore making it even more vulnerable to future failures.

Having low self-esteem can also make us more vulnerable to anxiety. One study examined reactions to emotionally arousing situations. Participants were told they would be receiving "un-

pleasant electric shocks" (not that an electric shock is ever "pleasant," but these days it always falls short of being outright painful;
and most studies never actually shock participants at all, as researchers are more interested in the anxiety generated by the anticipation of a shock than people's actual responses to being
"zapped"). One group of waiting participants was given an intervention to raise their self-esteem (they were told they'd scored ex-
ceptionally well on a measure of verbal intelligence) and the other
group was not. The group that received the self-esteem boost demonstrated significantly less anxiety when waiting to be "shocked"
compared to the group that did not.

We also respond to stress much less effectively when our self-
esteem is low than we do when our self-esteem is higher, making
us more vulnerable to depression and anxiety as well as to a host of
stress-related physical ailments and conditions. Straightforward
observations of stress hormones such as cortisol have demonstrated that people with low self-esteem generally respond to stress
more poorly and maintain higher levels of cortisol in their blood
than people with high self-esteem do. High cortisol levels are associated with high blood pressure, poor immune system functioning, suppressed thyroid gland function, reduced muscle and bone
density, and poor cognitive performance.

One of the reasons higher self-esteem buffers the effects of
stress on both our psychological and physiological systems is that
when our self-esteem is low we tend to make negative feedback
even more stressful by exaggerating its implications and potential
consequences. Further complicating matters, the more stressed we
are, the less able we are to exert self-control. We are then likely to
encounter slips and failures, judge ourselves too harshly for them,
and damage our self-esteem even further.

Self-Esteem, Stress, and Self-Control

Rudy, a commodities broker who had an extremely stressful job, came to therapy to deal with a long-standing gambling problem. As stress built at work, Rudy would have a powerful urge to spend the night gambling in Atlantic City. He was able to resist this urge as long as the pressure at work remained high, but as soon as the stress level subsided, Rudy's willpower gave out and off to gamble he would go. Rudy's gambling binges often cost him thousands and even tens of thousands of dollars, which he could not afford. What made his self-loathing even greater after such episodes was that he was well aware of the role stress played in this cycle and he knew the triggers that preceded it (a reduction in stress after an intense period). Yet despite recognizing the pattern that led to his destructive behavior, Rudy was still powerless to stop it.

By the time Rudy showed up in my office he had gambled away his home, his entire savings, and most of his retirement, and he'd moved in with a friend. Needless to say, his self-esteem was at an all-time low. Determined as Rudy was to change his ways, his company was a breeding ground for cycles of heavy stress. But what made his situation even more urgent was that some years earlier Rudy's aging parents had signed a power of attorney that granted Rudy access to their finances and Rudy worried that his parents' home might be in jeopardy as well. Given his parents' fragile health and their complete lack of awareness about how bad their son's problem had become, Rudy worried that coming clean and nullifying the power of attorney would cause them such significant emotional distress it might even endanger their health.

Rudy's reactions to stress were extreme in their self-destructiveness but not unusual. Stress can substantially weaken our willpower and self-control and make us revert to automatic and old habits without even realizing it. For example, a stressful day might make a dieter leave the supermarket and drive all the way home before snapping out of his daze and realizing that instead of a salad he'd just purchased a large bucket of fried chicken.

When our self-esteem is low, we are far less likely to attribute slips in willpower to mental and emotional fatigue (which are the more likely culprits) and far more likely to assume they reflect fundamental character deficits. Our self-esteem then drops yet another notch and we are even more likely to blame ourselves unnecessarily when our willpower fails us in the future.

The good news is that manipulations to boost self-esteem have been found to help people better manage failure, rejection, anxiety, and (especially) stress. Encouraging as such findings are, they illuminate only the benefits of boosting our self-esteem, not how we might actually go about doing so. Scientists tend to boost research subjects' self-esteem by methods such as giving them bogus feedback about their score on a test of verbal intelligence. Obviously, we can't go around lying to ourselves about how smart we are, or, at least, most of us cannot. But the results of these experiments represent a "proof of concept" that boosting self-esteem can strengthen our emotional immune systems and make us more emotionally resilient.

2. No Dessert for Me! Why We Resist Positive Feedback and Emotional Nourishment

It's bad enough that having low self-esteem makes us more vulnerable to negative psychological experiences but researchers have also demonstrated that low self-esteem limits our ability to benefit from positive ones. In one study, people were exposed to sad music to put them in a bad mood and were then given the option to watch a comedy video to cheer up. Although people with high self-esteem jumped on the chance to have a laugh, people with low self-esteem agreed that watching the video would improve their mood, but they declined to do so nonetheless.

When our self-esteem is low, the resistance we have to positive experiences and information is quite sweeping. Unfortunately it includes exactly the kind of feedback that could play a vital role in rebuilding our self-worth and confidence and strengthening our emotional immune systems. Yet, thirsty as we are for such information, when our self-esteem is low, we are likely to reject it, avoid it, and at times even recoil from it.

Bo was a single man in his late twenties, a Southern gentleman who seemed to have everything going for him. He was tall and handsome with a stable job and in good health. But when it came to his personal life, Bo was miserable. He had no "social circle" to speak of and the few separate friends he did have seemed to walk all over him. His friends often stood him up, leaving Bo waiting on the street or in the movie theater or restaurant. They threw parties they told him about only after the fact. They criticized him relentlessly and they borrowed hundreds and at times thousands of dollars without paying him back. Bo was desperate to meet a woman he could settle down with, but here too his friends were more of a hindrance than a support. On the few occasions Bo tried talking to women at social events, his friends would join the conversation and "jokingly" put him down. At times, they even resorted to flirting with women in whom Bo had already expressed an interest. Although on the surface Bo had everything going for him, he rarely dated, and when he did, the relationships never lasted for more than a few weeks.

Bo knew his biggest problem was his extremely low self-esteem. In fact, one of the first things he told me when he came to therapy was that he was an admitted "self-help junkie" with a penchant for positive affirmation programs. Affirmations are positive statements about our self-worth, goals, and futures, which one reads, listens to, or states aloud. They are widely believed to contribute to healthy self-esteem, greater personal empowerment, and increased motivation and well-being, and Bo had tried all of them. He read *The Secret* and practiced the "law of attraction," he sipped *Chicken Soup for the Soul*, he spent weeks sleeping with expensive headgear via which personalized messages realigned his "neuroprocessing" and "corrected his brainwaves" (alas, the only thing they ended up "correcting" was his bank account), and he listened to countless subliminal messages, such as "I am worthy and able," which he assured me maintained their "subliminal" powers despite the messages being listed in bold print on the packaging in which they arrived.

But after investing many years and thousands of dollars in positive affirmation programs, Bo, like many other positive affirmation devotees, felt as worthless and disempowered as ever. This raises two questions: First, why did Bo keep investing time and money into positive affirmation programs when none of them worked? And second, why did these programs weaken Bo's emotional immune system rather than strengthen it?

One reason Bo stuck with it is that because our self-esteem is so subjective, our ability to assess whether it has changed for the better is rather limited (unless we use more objective measures such as scientifically established self-esteem questionnaires or other tangible criteria). In fact, numerous studies have demonstrated that we are very likely to unconsciously distort our memories of how we felt before starting a self-esteem program such that we believe the program helped us improve when it actually did not.

For example, one study investigated a popular self-esteem product that used audiotaped positive affirmations. Researchers measured participants' self-esteem before and after they completed the program and found that their self-esteem had not improved at all and had even declined in some cases. But despite this stark reality, the participants happily reported feeling significant improvements in their self-esteem because they unconsciously distorted their memory and believed they had felt worse previously. This is why so many bogus self-esteem programs have such glowing testimonials and commercial success despite being entirely ineffective.

This brings us to the second question: why do positive affirmations leave so many of their users feeling worse about themselves rather than better?

The answer requires a brief detour into the science of persuasion. Persuasion studies have long established that messages that fall within the boundaries of our established beliefs are persuasive to us, while those that differ too substantially from our beliefs are usually rejected altogether. If we believe we're unattractive, we're much more likely to accept a compliment like "You look very nice today" than "Why, your beauty is breathtaking!" Since positive affirmations are supposed to change how we feel about ourselves, whether they fall inside or outside the boundaries of our own self-concept is crucial to their effectiveness. When people with low self-esteem, like Bo, are exposed to positive affirmations that differ too widely from their existing self-beliefs, the affirmation is perceived as untrue and rejected in its entirety and it actually strengthens their belief that the *opposite* is true.

Recent research into the usefulness of positive affirmations has investigated these ideas and verified their potential to cause more harm than good. In one experiment, subjects were asked to complete a variety of questionnaires and then identify a trait they would like to possess but believed they lacked. Researchers then told subjects the good (albeit fictitious) news that they actually did possess the trait they desired. But hearing the "good" news made subjects feel worse and register drops in self-esteem. In other words, the very people who most need positive affirmations (like Bo) are those least likely to benefit from them (and most likely to be harmed by them) because they are likely to find such messages too discrepant from their current self-concepts. Rather than strengthening our emotional immune systems, positive affirmation programs are likely to weaken them even further.

When our self-esteem is chronically low, feeling unworthy becomes part of our identity, something with which we feel comfortable, a way of being to which we become accustomed. People with low self-esteem often feel more comfortable with negative feedback, because it verifies their existing feelings about themselves. One study found that poorly performing college students who were given messages to bolster their self-esteem actually declined academically as a result. Another found that when college students with low self-esteem had roommates who thought better of them than they did of themselves, they tended to look for new roommates. Indeed, one of the areas in which low self-esteem and our resistance to positive messages is especially problematic is in our relationships.

Low Self-Esteem and Relationships

People with low self-esteem have greater doubts about their partners' affections for them than people with higher self-esteem do, and they report less satisfaction in their marital and dating relationships as well. When our self-esteem is low, we are quick to perceive any signs of rejection and disapproval from our partners. We not only interpret many such messages too negatively, we also tend to overgeneralize them and read far greater disapproval into them than is intended.

Although our relationships could and should be sources of support, praise, and, hence, increased self-esteem, people with low self-esteem have tremendous difficulty taking in positive messages from their partners and they often bristle against such emotional nutrients. In one study, praising people with low self-esteem for being considerate boyfriends or girlfriends (which is pretty mild as far as compliments go) was enough to make them feel more insecure about their partners and view their entire relationship more negatively.

Regardless of how parched we might be for positive feedback and affirmation, when our self-esteem is low, compliments, reassurances, and praise from our partners makes us feel pressured to live up to their heightened expectations. We worry we will not be able to sustain such efforts, that we will disappoint them (even when their expectations are well within our capabilities), and that their love is conditional on our being able to keep it up. As a result, rather than enjoy the closeness and intimacy that compliments should evoke, people with low self-esteem often respond to praise by shutting down, withdrawing, and becoming more distant. Unfortunately, pulling away and acting defensively often "succeeds," as it lowers our partners' expectations, tarnishes their perceptions of us, and undermines the integrity and longevity of the entire relationship.

Indeed, many of Bo's dating experiences took a turn for the worse when a woman he considered attractive and successful made the mistake of complimenting him for being sweet, kind, or considerate. "Boy, she doesn't know me at all!" Bo would joke self-disparagingly. "She has no idea of how screwed up I am!" Bo would then make all kinds of unconscious efforts to demonstrate exactly how "screwed up" he was, which, unsurprisingly, ended in the woman breaking off their brief courtship. Bo would then take her rejection as further proof that he could only "hide" his true (and unacceptable) self for so long. The fact that the only unacceptable thing about Bo was his terribly low self-esteem was a reality he was tragically unable to acknowledge.

3. Chronic Backbone Pain: How Low Self-Esteem Makes Us Feel Disempowered

Bo's emotional immune system was extremely weak, affording him poor resiliency against the many rejections and betrayals he sustained from his "buddies." Although he did his best to hide it, each backstabbing incident upset him tremendously and left him feeling more defective, more undeserving, and more inadequate than he had previously. Bo recognized he was being taken for granted, taken advantage of, and generally mistreated by his friends, but he felt completely disempowered to do anything about it. Not only was he unable to limit his exposure in such situations (for example, by refusing to lend people money), but he also felt incapable of avoiding the company of people that were bound to hurt his feelings. "I'd rather have bad friends than no friends" was how Bo justified his reluctance to make any changes in his social life.

Studies have repeatedly demonstrated that people with low self-esteem tend to speak up less in groups and social settings and take less initiative to extricate themselves from unhappy relationships and friendships when they find themselves embroiled in them. Having low self-esteem makes us feel fundamentally insecure, unconfident, and undesirable in social situations and our "beggars can't be choosers" mentality leaves us feeling tremendously disempowered and unassertive as a result. We become convinced that setting limits, making demands, or stating expectations, however reasonable, will cause the other person to reject us immediately and drop us like a hot potato. Of course, others quickly recognize our reluctance to speak up, object, or cry foul, which encourages them to take us for granted and be even less considerate of our needs and feelings going forward.

The reality of Bo's predicament was that some of his friends might indeed reject him if he stood up to them or spoke up about their mistreatment of him. However, others would not. I tried to impress upon him that speaking up would constitute an important litmus test as to the quality and potential of the friendship each person offered him. Those who did indeed care about him, even somewhat, would respond to his objections by demonstrating some kind of accommodation or consideration that Bo could build upon. Those who did not were not worthy of his friendship to begin with.

To be clear, Bo's friends were not necessarily terrible people, although they were unlikely to win any humanitarian awards. Most of us only put in as much effort as a situation requires from us. If we can "get away" with being less considerate or less reciprocal, and various other forms of "getting without giving," many of us will, not because we're evil, but simply because we can. If people demanded or expected more of us we would do more, but when they don't, we don't make the effort. This dynamic is true in practically every relationship we have. When our self-esteem is low and we expect very little of others, we are likely to get very little from them as well.

Changing this dynamic once a relationship is already established is difficult because we're in essence "changing the terms of the deal" after the other person has already been operating under a specific set of assumptions and expectations. That is why it is crucial to pay great attention to the expectations we set up when our friendships and romantic relationships first begin. Bo's challenge was to identify which of his friends were worth keeping and to find ways in which he could change the terms of "the deal" so he could enjoy more reciprocity and mutual support from those who did care about him and eliminate the ongoing damage his self-esteem was sustaining from those who did not.

Gladys, a forty-year-old breast cancer survivor, is another example of someone who had low self-esteem, although, unlike in Bo's case, hers was not a lifelong struggle but rather the result of horrific emotional blows she had sustained over recent years. Without any prior warning, Gladys's husband had left her midway through her chemotherapy treatments some years earlier. Demonstrating truly despicable cruelty, he chose to serve her divorce papers by having someone wait for her outside the hospital the day she was released after having a double mastectomy.

Although Gladys's body recovered from the cancer, the chemotherapy, the double mastectomy, and the several reconstructive surgeries that followed, her self-esteem was not as fortunate. She never got over the blow of her husband abandoning her while she was fighting for her life nor the manner in which he did so. When I met Gladys, there was little evidence of the fighter who'd survived a terrible disease, the high school track athlete who had a closet full of medals and trophies, or the successful Web designer who'd built her own business from scratch after her divorce. Instead, Gladys came across as timid, insecure, and extremely unassertive.

Gladys did have a close circle of friends (many of whom were also breast cancer survivors) but she had not gone on a single date since her divorce, especially since she worked from home and had few opportunities to meet eligible men. However, what finally convinced her to start psychotherapy was that her low self-esteem began to have an impact on her business and her income as well.

"I've never been terribly assertive but I became much worse after my husband left. My business suffers because I often don't get paid what I deserve and I get talked into doing too many unpaid extras. I'm just not very good at standing up to demanding people. I try but they bully and pressure and I always end up giving in." Gladys went on to describe how her biggest client was also the worst offender. Despite already extracting huge concessions and discounts for the services she provided, the client kept demanding more. Gladys feared that refusing the requests would incite the company to take its business elsewhere, a loss that would have significant financial implications for her.

Much as Bo felt he had no room to make demands or set limits in his friendships, Gladys felt too insecure, unconfident, and disempowered to do so in her business. They were both convinced that their impoverished self-worth was an accurate reflection of their character and attributes, such that they basically "got what they deserved." Their lack of assertiveness and backbone was a direct result of a weak emotional immune system that led them to believe that any acts of assertion on their part would only bring intolerable hurt, rejection, and disaster.

How to Treat the Psychological Wounds Low Self-Esteem Inflicts

Our self-esteem fluctuates regularly and even people with generally high self-esteem can have days in which they feel poorly about themselves. Such temporary dips in self-worth rarely require emotional first aid as we usually recover from them fairly swiftly. However, when our self-esteem is regularly low, or when we feel unable to stand up for ourselves and to set limits with friends or family members who treat us poorly or with disrespect, we need to treat our psychological wounds and boost our self-esteem.

The treatments in this chapter should help "stop the bleeding" and set us on the path to bolstering our sense of self-worth. However, improving our self-esteem in deep and fundamental ways requires both time and substantial effort. Higher self-esteem is essentially an outcome of doing well in our lives and relationships. Internalizing the lessons of this chapter and applying them cannot change our self-esteem overnight but it can give us the tools to establish a track record of success that, over time, will strengthen our self-esteem and make it more stable. Therefore, in addition to providing initial emotional relief, the treatments that follow should be adopted as daily strategies and life habits. Let's open our psychological medicine cabinet and examine the treatment options available to us.

General Treatment Guidelines

Having low self-esteem weakens our emotional immune systems and inflicts three kinds of psychological wounds: it makes us more vulnerable to psychological injuries, it makes us dismissive of positive feedback and resistant to emotional nutrients, and it makes us feel unassertive and disempowered. The five treatments suggested in this chapter should be administered to correct self-critical habits and negative self-perceptions, especially following blows to self-esteem or if entering periods of increased stress.

Administer the treatments in the order in which they are

presented. Treatment A (adopting self-compassion) helps prevent the self-critical mind-sets that damage our already weakened emotional immune systems. Treatments B (identifying and affirming strengths) and C (increasing tolerance for compliments) are focused on recognizing, acknowledging, and reconnecting to neglected or marginalized strengths, qualities, and abilities. Treatments D (increasing personal empowerment) and E (strengthening self-control) focus on rebuilding self-esteem and feelings of empowerment. At the end of the chapter, I provide guidelines for assessing when one should consult a mental health professional.

Treatment A: Adopt Self-Compassion and Silence the Critical Voices in Your Head

Imagine witnessing an emotionally abusive parent berating her child for getting a poor report card. The parent verbally attacks the child, mocks him, and mercilessly belittles him without displaying a whit of empathy, support, or compassion. Meanwhile, the child's face registers utter devastation as he absorbs one emotional blow after another. Most of us would find such a scene extremely distressing to witness (especially those of us who grew up with such parents) and we would immediately vow never to treat our own children in such an abusive, cruel, and destructive manner.

And yet when our self-esteem is low, that is exactly how we treat ourselves. We blame ourselves for our mistakes, failures, rejections, and frustrations in the most harsh and self-punitive terms. We call ourselves "losers" and "idiots," we give ourselves stern "lectures," and we replay the scenes in our mind while ruminating on our inadequacies and deficiencies. In other words, we treat ourselves even worse than an emotionally abusive parent would. When I catch my patients running such damaging internal sound tracks in their minds and point it out to them, they are usually quick to respond, "I know I shouldn't beat myself up about it but—" and then they go on to justify why they should beat themselves up about it. When I ask if they would ever treat their own children, their spouse, or their friends in a similar manner they look at me horrified, as if doing so would be unthinkable.

When our self-esteem is low, this double standard is a trap we easily fall into. Our reason abandons us and we struggle to implement the premise that if we consider it abusive to speak to others a certain way we should never direct such thoughts toward ourselves either. The first step we need to take on the path toward self-compassion is to embrace the most simple and basic fact that when our emotional immune systems are weak we should do everything in our power to strengthen them, not devastate them even further. Purging the emotionally abusive voices in our heads and adopting kinder, more supportive ones instead is an absolute imperative.

People with low self-esteem often bristle at the notion of adopting self-compassion when I first suggest it. They worry that switching off self-punitive thoughts and replacing them with soothing and compassionate ones will cause them to "slack off" and function more poorly, making their self-esteem even weaker and more vulnerable as a result. But such worries are entirely unfounded, as studies demonstrate that exactly the opposite is true. Practicing self-compassion actually strengthens our emotional immune systems. In one study, self-compassion was found to buffer incoming college students against homesickness, depression, and general dissatisfaction with their choice of school. In others, individuals who practiced self-compassion had quicker emotional recoveries from separation and divorce, and they recovered more quickly from failure and rejection experiences.

Despite the obvious benefits of adopting self-compassion, it remains challenging to do so when our self-esteem is low because the practice is so foreign to our ordinary way of thinking, it can cause discomfort and even an initial uptick in anxiety. Therefore, we must be determined to put an end to the destructive sound tracks that make up the current playlists in our minds. Once we truly accept that we require soothing and compassion far more than we do emotional abuse, we can turn to the following exercise.

EXERCISE FOR ADOPTING SELF-COMPASSION

Complete the following writing exercise three times, each time describing an event from your past (if possible, include at least one from your recent past). Try to write about one event each day so that you complete the exercise over three consecutive days.

1. We've all experienced failures, embarrassments, humiliations, or rejections that made us feel self-critical and badly about ourselves. Choose one such event and detail what actually happened and how you felt about it.

2. Imagine that the event happened to a dear friend or close family member who then felt terrible about herself (or himself) because of it. Describe that person's experience of the event, how she would react and feel in the very same situation.

3. You hate seeing this person in emotional pain and you decide to write her a letter with the explicit purpose of making her feel better about herself. Make sure to express

kindness, understanding, and concern about the experience she went through and how she felt as a result, and remind her of why she is worthy of compassion and support.

4. Now describe your own experience and your feelings about the event again, but this time, try to be as objective and understanding as you can about what happened and about how you felt. Make sure not to sound judgmental or negative. For example, you might note that your date never called you back, as that is factual, but not that your date thought you were a loser, because that is judgmental and nonfactual. Or that you made mistakes during a presentation, but not that your colleagues disrespect you as a result, because, regardless of how you perceived their reactions, when our self-esteem is low we tend to misinterpret people's facial expressions too negatively.

TREATMENT SUMMARY: SELF-COMPASSION

Dosage: Apply the treatment over three days and repeat regularly until the principles of self-compassion become engrained and automatic.

Effective for: Increasing emotional resilience and decreasing emotional vulnerability and self-criticism.

Secondary benefits: Decreases resistance to positive feedback.

Treatment B: Identify Your Strengths and Affirm Them

Positive affirmation die-hards like Bo, the Southern gentleman with low self-esteem, need not forsake them entirely. Although positive affirmations can be damaging to people with low self-esteem, many positive affirmation routines can be tweaked to make the affirmations easier for us to digest (e.g., by affirming our need to take action when we've been wronged). Bo was hesitant to dispense with positive affirmations altogether but he agreed to adapt them to include action-oriented items such as "When I lend someone money, asking him to pay me back is far less rude than his failing to repay me in a timely manner," and "When a friend upsets me I am entitled to speak up."

That being said, a much more effective way to use affirmations is to use *self*-affirmations that identify and affirm valuable and important aspects of ourselves we already know to be true, such as our trustworthiness, loyalty, or work ethic (in contrast to *positive* affirmations, which affirm qualities we would like to possess but don't believe we do). Reminding ourselves that we have significant worth regardless of any shortcomings we perceive in ourselves provides an immediate boost to our self-esteem and renders us less vulnerable to experiences of rejection or failure.

Another advantage of self-affirmations is they benefit us even when the quality we're affirming has nothing to do with the situation of the moment. For example, if we're hurting because we've been turned down for a promotion we do not have to affirm our value as an employee in order to feel better (which would be a hard sell in that moment anyway). Instead, affirming that we are a good parent or a great wife, a thoughtful friend or a champion quilter, a supportive brother or a great listener is sufficient to make us feel better about ourselves as we walk out of our boss's office without the new title we had hoped to secure.

Ideally, we should employ self-affirmation exercises before we go into situations that might provide a blow to our self-esteem (i.e., before our big date, before the exam, before the job interview). This is also why it is best to use such exercises on a regular basis, as we cannot always predict when blows to our self-esteem might occur. Nonetheless, completing such exercises after the fact still has significant value.

EXERCISE FOR SELF-AFFIRMATION

Complete the following writing exercise as regularly as possible (weekly is good; daily is better). It is especially important to do the exercise when facing situations of heightened stress (e.g., for tax accountants, during tax season; for college students, during finals) or situations that pose potential threats to self-esteem (e.g., when applying to schools or jobs), as that is when our self-esteem might be most vulnerable. You will need two sheets of blank paper.

1. On the first sheet of paper, make a list of your important attributes and qualities, including any achievements you have that are significant or meaningful to you. Aim for at least ten items and preferably many more.

2. If while brainstorming items for your list you think of responses that are negative (e.g., "My boss thinks I'm a terrible employee"), critical (e.g., "I'm a loser"), or sarcastic (e.g., "What am I good at? Let's see, there's napping . . . and I'm a champ at breathing too!"), write them down on the second sheet of paper.

3. Choose one item from the first sheet of paper that is especially meaningful to you and write a brief essay (at least one paragraph) about why this specific attribute, achievement, or experience is meaningful to you and what role you hope it will play in your life.

4. Once you've completed the essay, take the second sheet of paper, crumple it into a ball, and throw it in the garbage where it belongs.

5. On subsequent days, choose other items from your positive attribute list and write about them, preferably each day, until you've completed the list. Feel free to add to your list at any time or to write about specific items several times.

TREATMENT SUMMARY: IDENTIFY YOUR STRENGTHS AND AFFIRM THEM

Dosage: Apply the treatment until you complete your initial list and repeat it whenever you anticipate stress or experience a blow to your self-esteem.

Effective for: Increasing emotional resilience, decreasing emotional vulnerability, and minimizing feelings of disempowerment.

Secondary benefits: Decreases resistance to positive feedback and reduces self-criticism.

Treatment C: Increase Your Tolerance for Compliments

Having low self-esteem makes it difficult for us to absorb compliments and positive feedback from others, especially our loved ones, and to use such communications to rebuild our self-esteem. Instead, we are more comfortable scanning the environment for any hints of negative feedback that might confirm our (mis)perceptions of ourselves as being fundamentally unworthy or inadequate.

Because this resistance to compliments operates on both conscious and unconscious levels, some of us are aware we feel uncomfortable receiving positive feedback from others but many of us are not. Our lack of awareness is especially problematic when it comes to our romantic partners, because when our self-esteem is low, we not only rebuff positive communications from them but we also respond by withdrawing and devaluing the relationship. I should note that the subject pool used in much of this research was composed of college students and young adults. In my experience, long-term couples tend to be more aware when one or both members of the couple are resistant to compliments and they refrain from voicing positive feedback to the resistant person. Of course, that only exacerbates the problem for the person with low self-esteem, as hearing fewer compliments and receiving little positive affirmation from the person who knows us best is itself not conducive to building feelings of self-worth.

On a positive note, several studies that used subjects of all ages have demonstrated that by affirming aspects of our selves that are related to our worth as relationship partners, we can bolster our "relationship self-esteem." Doing so renders any compliments we receive from our partners less discrepant from our current self-views and makes us less likely to reject or rebuff them. Affirming our value as relationship partners not only makes us feel better about ourselves (by boosting our self-esteem), it also makes us feel better about our partners and even about the relationship itself.

EXERCISE TO INCREASE OUR TOLERANCE OF COMPLIMENTS

The following is a writing exercise that can and should be completed on a regular basis (weekly or more when possible).

1. Think back to a time your partner, family member, or friend conveyed that he or she appreciated, liked, or enjoyed something about you, such as a personal quality you have or something you did that the person felt strongly about. Describe the incident and explain what made the person feel positively about you when it occurred.

2. What does displaying this attribute or behavior mean to you?

3. What benefits does having the attribute or behavior bring to your relationships and friendships?

4. What other significant or meaningful functions or roles can the attribute or behavior contribute to your life?

TREATMENT SUMMARY: INCREASE TOLERANCE FOR COMPLIMENTS

Dosage: Apply the treatment regularly until you become more comfortable with receiving compliments. Make sure to repeat whenever you experience a blow to your self-esteem.

Effective for: Decreasing resistance to positive feedback and increasing relational self-esteem.

Secondary benefits: Increases emotional resilience, decreases emotional vulnerability, and minimizes feelings of disempowerment.

Treatment D: Increase Your Personal Empowerment

The vast majority of articles, books, and programs that promise to help us feel more personally empowered fail to recognize a critical flaw in their thinking—personal empowerment is not something one *feels* but rather something one *has*. Sure, we might feel empowered after reading a book about improving marital relationships, but unless we're able to initiate a productive dialogue with our partner and create actual changes, we are no more empowered than we were when we started. To have an impact on our self-esteem, feelings of personal empowerment must be supported by evidence of having actual influence in the various spheres of our lives, whether in our relationships, in our social or professional contexts, as citizens, or even as consumers.

Converting our low self-esteem into assertive feelings of empowerment might sound like a tall order but there is one aspect of personal empowerment we can use to our advantage. Acting assertively and getting results in one area of our lives tends to empower us in other areas of our lives as well. Choosing our battles wisely and starting with smaller and simpler acts of assertiveness can quickly get the ball of empowerment rolling, as even small triumphs provide a significant boost to our self-esteem and make us feel generally more powerful, effective, and assertive.

For example, many of us have had the experience of feeling so "pumped up" by resolving, say, a consumer or customer service complaint (successfully removing charges from our bank statement, perhaps) that we walked straight over to our teenager's bedroom and told her to do something about the mess with such conviction that, for the first time in months, she actually did as we asked without arguing.

Because one successful act of assertion and personal empowerment encourages another, we need to identify areas for potential assertive action that have both a high likelihood of success and manageable consequences in the event of failure. The best way to do so is first to gather as much information as we can about how to attain our goal and to formulate well-thought-out strategies and plans for proceeding. We can then begin a process of practicing assertive actions in lower-stakes situations so we can refine our technique, our approach, and our skills as we go.

EXERCISE FOR IDENTIFYING OPTIONS FOR ASSERTIVE ACTION

1. Think about aspects of your life that tend to make you feel frustrated. Try to include situations in your community life, work life, family and personal life, social life, and life as a consumer. Describe at least three examples for each of these domains. For example, when thinking about your married life you might feel frustrated about a spouse's personal habits, the division of labor between you, your partner's style of communication, or his or her approach to parenting.

2. Rank your items according to which of them have both a high likelihood of success and manageable consequences

in case of failure. For example, Bo decided to speak up about the two thousand dollars he had lent his friend Timothy; Timothy had promised to return it within three months, and a year had passed. Timothy was Bo's "least-close friend" and Bo felt justified enough in the situation to be willing to risk the friendship and discuss the matter with him. And Gladys decided to speak up about a couple of "website tweaks" her client had asked her to "throw in" free of charge; Gladys felt the "tweaks" in question were not crucial enough to prompt her client to fire her if she refused to do them without compensation.

The final list represents your master plan for practicing assertive actions and attaining personal empowerment. Now that you've identified and prioritized your goals, it's time to consider any additional information or specific skill sets that can help you execute them successfully and to plan your strategy accordingly.

Gathering Information and Strategic Planning

To maximize our chances of attaining each goal, we need to consider how the systems or people we plan to challenge operate. In other words, we need to gain a grasp of the priorities and mindsets of any relevant people; the complaint management systems of any relevant businesses, companies, or local municipalities; or the politics, hierarchy, and human resource practices in our workplace.

For example, I asked Bo and Gladys to describe the situation from the other people's perspectives in order to gain some insight about their mind-sets. Bo explained that Timothy had always been slightly resentful and jealous of his income because he earned substantially less than Bo did. Bo assumed he felt entitled to borrow money from him because Bo could afford it, and therefore, Timothy saw no urgency to pay him back. Bo indicated that Timothy spent hundreds of dollars a week going out so that he certainly could afford to pay him back, even if it were at the rate of a few hundred dollars a month. And Gladys told me that her clients were hoping to launch a minor redesign of their website in the near future and that they were unlikely to shop around for an entirely new Web designer unless they absolutely had to.

Examples of other kinds of information gathering we might do include finding out what human resource channels are available if we have a complaint about a work colleague, looking up relevant departments in our municipality so we know who to call about a missing stop sign on our street, finding out who in our cell phone company is authorized to deal with the dollar amount we're disputing (most customer service representatives are only authorized to deal with small amounts), or inquiring whether our teenager has an exam the next day before we demand he spend the rest of the evening completing his chores.

Once we've gathered the necessary information, we need to formulate and think through our plan of action and anticipate any reactions. For example, we might want to figure out how we can ask a friend why she hasn't returned our phone calls without sounding too accusatory or hostile (because even though we might feel hurt by her disappearing, being accusatory simply wouldn't be productive) or how to phrase a complaint to our spouse so he doesn't get too defensive (because even though we might have the right to be annoyed, we also know he doesn't respond well when we approach him in anger). We might think through the best time and place to talk to a colleague about why he never gave us credit for our part in the team presentation and give careful consideration to what we want to achieve by doing so (e.g., rather than just venting frustration we can suggest that we should take the lead on the next presentation as compensation for his omission).

Practice, Patience, and Persistence

Personal empowerment is a process and not something we attain in a single step. We have to be prepared for the reality that not all our efforts will yield immediate results and that we'll need to persist, practice our skill sets, and sharpen our tools before we're able to wield them both effectively and consistently. Bo's first plan to talk to Timothy at a social gathering failed because Timothy promised to chat later in the evening and then claimed he was too tired to do so. Bo learned that he needed to create the space to talk with Timothy without distractions and that he would have to be on the alert for any attempts Timothy made to prevent the conversation from happening.

When Gladys finally called her clients about the extra work they expected her to do, they steamrolled her, barely let her get a word in, and reassured her it wouldn't take her long to make the tweaks they required. Gladys was extremely demoralized at first but once she reflected on the exchange, she realized the best way for her to convey her message was via e-mail, as her clients would not be able to cut her off and she would be able to express her thoughts fully and assertively.

Practice, patience, and persistence are key ingredients in developing personal empowerment. Once we begin speaking up, we will be able to assess our strengths and weaknesses and learn which of our skills and tools still need work. Each setback will also teach us how to devise more effective plans. Bo decided to propose a manageable payment schedule and send it to Timothy in the mail along with self-addressed stamped envelopes. The factual and nonaccusatory tone Bo used in his letter led Timothy to respond with an apology and a check for the first payment. Gladys continued communicating with her clients by e-mail until she extracted additional payment for the work they wanted her to do.

While both Bo and Gladys were elated by their successes and felt quite empowered as a result, their triumphs were only the first step on their respective paths to stronger self-esteem. Over the next year, Bo continued to "clean house" with his old friends, and he made new ones who were more supportive and loyal. Gladys formulated tighter guidelines for compensation that she distributed to all her clients before she agreed to start work. In time, her self-esteem improved to the point where she felt able to start dating. Although she had made no efforts to improve her self-esteem in the dating domain, feeling more empowered as a businesswoman had created a greater sense of self-worth that boosted her feelings of confidence in her personal life as well.

Once we've tackled the first item on our lists and met with success, we should use the boost we get to our self-esteem and turn to the next item as soon as possible so we find success there as well. Although it will take time for our emotional immune systems to strengthen and to function more effectively, our small successes will soon begin to add up. Receiving a raise or promotion at work, resolving conflicts with friends, working out problems with our partners and family members, and getting satisfaction as consumers will each contribute to significantly strengthening our self-esteem and improving our general quality of life.

TREATMENT SUMMARY: PERSONAL EMPOWERMENT

Dosage: Apply the treatment in each of the different spheres of your life when possible (i.e., your home and work life, your friendships, and as a consumer and community member) and repeat until you complete your list. Add new items to your action list when they arise.

Effective for: Increasing feelings of assertiveness and competence, strengthening weak feelings of entitlement, and demonstrating personal empowerment.

Secondary benefits: Increases emotional resilience and general self-esteem and decreases emotional vulnerability.

Treatment E: Improve Your Self-Control

Demonstrating self-control and willpower increases personal empowerment and helps us make progress toward our goals, both of which are extremely beneficial to our self-esteem. Although many of us assume willpower is a stable character trait or ability (i.e., we either have strong willpower or we do not), self-control actually functions more like a muscle. As such, learning how this muscle functions will allow us to use it wisely, strengthen it, and build our self-esteem as a result.

The most important thing to keep in mind about our self-control muscles is that they are subject to fatigue. Some of us might have bigger willpower muscles than others but even the most bulging willpower muscle will tire and become ineffective if we overwork it. Further, using this muscle in one context will tire it and make it weaker when we try to use it in another. For example, if we spend our day squelching the urge to rip off our tyrannical boss's hairpiece and throw it across the conference room like a Frisbee, our willpower will be depleted by the time we get home and we are likely to find it difficult to stick to our diet and eat a healthy dinner.

Complicating matters further, the limited reservoir of emotional energy that fuels our willpower muscles is shared by other complex mental functions such as those responsible for making choices and decisions. Strange as it might sound, using these seemingly unrelated intellectual abilities saps our willpower and weakens our self-control. For example, when we spend the day making decisions about clothing and accessories for an upcoming photo shoot we're styling, we might find it challenging to marshal the willpower to go to the gym when we get home. Indeed, our self-control often fails us at night after the energy reservoir fueling our willpower runs low and causes it to function less effectively.

In order to maximize the effectiveness of our willpower and use it to build our self-esteem we need to do three things: strengthen our basic willpower muscles, manage the energy reservoirs that fuel our self-control so they don't get depleted, and minimize the impact of the many temptations that exist around us.

Pump Up Your Willpower Muscles

The downside of our willpower being a general muscle is that exerting willpower in one area will cause fatigue and make it harder to exert willpower in another. But this "limitation" has an upside. Exercising our willpower by practicing acts of self-control in insignificant areas will increase the strength and endurance of our willpower muscles in more meaningful and important areas as well. Scientists have investigated several such "willpower workouts," including focusing on our posture (great for slouchers); avoiding cursing (more effective for potty mouths than it is for the "gosh darn it!" set); avoiding sweets, cookies, or cakes (great if you have a sweet tooth); squeezing a handgrip twice a day for as long as we can (handgrips are cheap and can be found in sporting goods stores); and the one I think works best—using our nondominant hand.

Practicing any task that requires us to regularly inhibit an automatic impulse (e.g., to slouch, use our dominant hand, curse, eat sweets, or let go of the handgrip when it becomes difficult) can be effective if we "train" for a sufficient period of time (at least four to eight weeks). In a variety of studies, such exercises provided significant benefits for smokers who were trying to quit, people with aggressive impulses who struggled to manage their anger, and compulsive shoppers who were trying to reform.

Exercise for Building Willpower

Use your nondominant hand for as many tasks as possible every day between the hours of 8:00 a.m. and 6:00 p.m. for four to eight weeks (the longer the better). Adjust these hours accordingly if your schedule requires (e.g., if you work the night shift or if you only wake up around noon). Include tasks such as brushing your teeth, opening doors, using a computer mouse or trackball, drinking (other than hot drinks, which can spill and cause burns), carrying things (other than babies and other breakables), stirring, combing your hair, using a fork (when you're not using a knife), moving objects (other than breakable ones), and any other action for which you typically use your dominant hand.

If you are ambidextrous: Use the posture improvement exercise instead. Monitor your posture so that you are sitting as erect as possible at all times. Avoid slouching, lying down, reclining, or leaning on a desk during the hours of 8:00 a.m. to 6:00 p.m. (adjust the hours accordingly if necessary).

Make Sure You Have Fuel in the Tank

One of the most essential fuels our willpower muscles require (as do many of our other muscles, both cognitive and physical) is glucose (sugars). Scientists have known for a while that when our glucose levels are low, effortful mental processes such as asserting willpower and self-control are impaired (automatic and noneffortful processes such as washing the dishes are not). In one study, people were put through effortful mental exercises to deplete their brain of glucose levels and then given a glass of lemonade. Half of them received lemonade sweetened with sugar and half got lemonade with an artificial sweetener (which tastes similar but has no glucose). After fifteen minutes (the time necessary for the drink to get absorbed into their systems) subjects who were given lemonade with real sugar recovered from their mental fatigue and were able to display significantly greater willpower than those who drank lemonade with artificial sweetener.

In short, for our willpower to operate best we require optimal levels of glucose. Previous exertions of self-control or lack of caloric intake will make our blood glucose levels drop below optimal levels and our willpower will be weak as a result. Sleep and rest also have a big impact on our willpower's ability to function at its capacity and being tired or sleep deprived will cause serious impairments in our ability to exhibit self-control.

Avoid Temptations and Manage Them When You Cannot

The average person spends three to four hours a day exerting some form of willpower. Dieters are surrounded by fattening foods, smokers trying to quit walk by people smoking outside most buildings, problem drinkers are never far from a bar or liquor store, students studying for finals face innumerable distractions from friends and electronic devices, and individuals with anger management issues encounter frustrating and provocative situations daily. The best way to manage temptations is not to overestimate our ability to manage them but to avoid them when possible. But there are also techniques we can use when it is impossible to do so.

1. Play One Side of Your Brain Against the Other

Our brain uses different systems to process rewards and risks. When faced with temptations, the reward system (go for it!) can drown out the system that evaluates risk (don't!). While we can't lower the volume on our cravings and urgings in such situations, we can turn up the volume on our risk assessment. For example, if we're trying to quit drinking and we find ourselves at a dinner where alcohol is served we can remind ourselves that the last time we had a drink we made a royal mess of things because we never stop at just one. We can consider how demoralized we'll feel if we allow alcohol back into our lives and how empowered and thankful we'll feel the next day if we resist. We can replay snapshots of our spouse's face the last time we fell off the wagon and see the disappointment in the eyes of our friends, or we can remind ourselves of our commitment, of why we started our journey in the first place, and the reasons we've been able to resist our urges so far. Beefing up our risk assessments by preparing a list of them in advance, which we can then refer to in the moment, can buy us just enough time to get through the situation.

2. Minimize the Damage

Many of us become extremely demoralized when we slip and succumb to temptation. "I've fallen off the wagon" or "I've blown my diet" is a thought that serves no useful purpose other than to give ourselves permission to indulge. After all, if we've blown our diet, we might as well eat whatever we want because we'll have to start all over again anyway.

Viewing slips as simple alerts that our willpower is fatigued and needs to recover (instead of as indications of failure) will allow us to acknowledge the lapse without getting further off track.

3. Avoid the Triggers

Many of our bad habits are prompted by triggers. For example, researchers in one study gave moviegoers stale popcorn and sat them down to watch a movie. They ate just as much of the stale popcorn as they typically ate fresh popcorn—but only because they were watching a movie! When the researchers gave the same participants stale popcorn while watching a music video in a conference room, they barely touched it. Our habits always have triggers, such as lighting up a cigarette when we have a beer, doing recreational drugs when we hang out with certain friends, or biting our fingernails when we sit on the couch to watch television. If we wish to change the habits, we have to avoid the triggers, at least until the new habit becomes well engrained. Sad as it may be, we might have to skip the beers, avoid the drug-using friends (which is not a bad idea in general), or watch TV on a laptop in the kitchen.

4. Practice Mindfulness to Tolerate Urges, Impulses, and Cravings

Mindfulness involves a form of mediation in which we observe our feelings without judging them, in essence becoming anthropologists in our own minds. We act like outside observers, noting the strength of our emotions and the sensations they create in our bodies but without dwelling on them or their implications. Rudy, the stressed-out gambler who was in danger of gambling away his aging parents' home, had an extremely stressful job that sapped his willpower and made it difficult for him to resist the urge to gamble. I suggested Rudy use a mindfulness technique, not just because it is effective for general stress management but because certain mindfulness exercises can be extremely useful for managing cravings, impulses, and urges (including the urge to gamble).

When learning to manage our cravings and urges we must first accept that such impulses, strong as they are, always pass with time. I suggested Rudy use one of our sessions to practice and instructed him to do the following: "Relax and focus on your breathing. Feel free to close your eyes. Study the urge to gamble as its waves wash over you, as if you were an alien who was interested in the human experience." (Rudy was a sci-fi fan.) "Visualize the amplitude of the urge's intensity like a seismograph readout that measures earthquake activity. As the waves come, follow the rise and fall of the dial on the readout; note when one wave intensifies and weakens and where another begins. Observe how different parts of your body feel when the urge intensifies and how the same parts of your body feel when it subsides. Continue to monitor your physiological responses this way, tracking one wave of urges after another as they rush toward you and over you, until the intensity of the waves eventually subsides as every earthquake does."

Focusing on our breathing, visualizing the seismographic readout, and noting the sensations in our bodies can help us ride out the "quake" and resist acting on our cravings, urges, and impulses until they pass. Practicing this technique when we are not in the grips of our impulses will help us apply it more successfully when we are. Fortunately, Rudy was able to get in several weeks of daily mindfulness practice before the work stress subsided again and the urge to gamble swept in. When it did, Rudy was ready for it and he was able to ride it out. He described the situation as "touch-and-go for a while," but the confidence he gained by resisting the urge to gamble when he had succumbed to it many times in the past provided a huge boost to his self-esteem.

Treatment Summary: Improve Your Self-Control

Dosage: Apply this treatment daily toward goals that require willpower and self-control.

Effective for: Increasing willpower and feelings of empowerment, facilitating progress toward self-improvement goals, and boosting self-esteem.

When to Consult a Mental Health Professional

Self-esteem is a deeply rooted psychological construct and applying the treatments in this chapter such that they yield significant results requires time, effort, and dedication. If you feel unable to apply these techniques or if you've invested the time and effort to do so but have not been able to boost your self-esteem as a result, you should consider seeking the advice of a mental health professional.

If there are ongoing circumstances in your life that are contributing to your low self-esteem (e.g., if you have an emotionally abusive boss or partner or if you're struggling to find work despite making consistent efforts to do so), a mental health professional could help you assess whether you should take steps to change your circumstances (as it is hard to rebuild your self-esteem if it is still actively "bleeding"). Finally, if your self-esteem feels so damaged that you have thoughts of harming yourself or others in any way, seek immediate help from a mental health professional or go to the nearest emergency room.

CONCLUSION

||||||||||||||||||||

Create Your Personal
Psychological Medicine Cabinet

We sustain frequent psychological wounds as we go through life. Unfortunately, until now, few of us have had the awareness and the know-how to treat them effectively. Instead we tend either to ignore them entirely or to unwittingly react in ways that deepen them and allow them to cause damage to our mental health over time. The treatments in this book (all of which are based on current research by experts in the field) represent a psychological medicine cabinet starter kit, a set of emotional balms, ointments, bandages, and painkillers that we can apply to emotional and psychological injuries when we first sustain them.

However, being a good self-practitioner means developing our own individualized set of mental-health-hygiene guidelines and you should endeavor to personalize your medicine cabinet whenever possible. Although we all sustain psychological injuries when faced with events such as loss, failure, or rejection, the extent of our wounds and the emotional first aid treatments to which they respond best can vary from person to person. The same is true when it comes to the pills and treatments we use to treat our physical ills. For example, there are numerous over-the-counter pain relievers from which we can choose to treat headaches, backaches, and general pain, but we rarely stock all of them in our homes. Trial and error teaches us that one specific brand of pain reliever works better for us than others do and that is the one we are likely to have on hand.

Similarly, you might find that some of the emotional first aid treatments in this book are more effective for your individual psychological makeup than others. Or you might find that a specific treatment works best for you in some situations but that in a different set of circumstances it is more effective to apply another. Taking note of such things will help you refine your choices when applying emotional first aid techniques and make your future efforts more effective.

Psychology is a young science and one in which new approaches and treatments are continually being discovered and updated. That being said, the suggestions in this book are based on sound and fundamental assumptions about psychology and mental health that are unlikely to be radically revised in their entirety. Even if we find a cure for the common cold, neglecting to treat a cold when we first experience symptoms of one will always put us at risk for developing a more severe respiratory illness such as pneumonia. Similarly, even if we discover more effective strategies for dealing with a psychological injury such as failure, neglecting the psychological wounds failure inflicts will always risk damage to our mental health, self-esteem, and emotional well-being. Therefore, although the contents of our psychological medicine cabinet might need to be updated at some point in the future, having one and using it regularly will always be necessary and beneficial.

It is my sincere hope that prioritizing our mental health and taking the steps necessary to enhance and maintain it will become a daily practice, a habit we all integrate into our lives from an early age. Teaching our children to practice mental health hygiene and instructing them on how to apply the principles of emotional first aid can have an extraordinary impact on their lives and on society at large. All it would take is for the practice of mental health hygiene to become as ubiquitous as the practice of dental hygiene is today, and we could witness, in our lifetimes, a new generation of emotionally resilient and psychologically sophisticated people who confront life's hardships with both strength and resolve, who recover from them rapidly and more completely, and who enjoy far greater happiness and life satisfaction than the average person does today.

If such notions seem foolish or romantic, consider that the goal of leading happy and satisfying lives was one few people even considered several generations ago. Most people were too busy struggling to fulfill basic needs such as food, shelter, and survival to worry about whether they were happy. Perhaps several generations from now, our descendants too will look back at us and marvel at how we took better care of our teeth than we did our minds, of how few of us thought to apply emotional first aid techniques when we sustained common psychological injuries.

Of course, until now, we've lacked the resources and the know-how to adopt such general practices and we've been unable to create a revolution in how we think about and care for our mental health and emotional well-being on a large scale. But we are limited no longer. Anyone who wishes to lead an emotionally healthier and happier life need only open his or her psychological medicine cabinet and reach for the treatments within.

Acknowledgments

For years, I lamented how advances in psychological science would go ignored because cutting-edge research is buried in professional journals and has little impact on the day-to-day life of the average person. I bemoaned how we marginalized emotionally damaging experiences when there was so much we could do to treat them. And I expressed repeated exasperation that we took better care of our teeth than we did our minds and our mental health. Not that I have anything against dental hygiene. I love teeth. I simply felt there was something wrong about the fact that we know so much about brushing and flossing and so little about how to take care of our emotions and our psychological well-being.

Fortunately, two people decided to do something about it. And by "it" I mean my incessant whining about this subject. My agent, Michelle Tessler, and my brother and colleague, Dr. Gil Winch, suggested (more like insisted) I follow the very advice I championed in my first book, *The Squeaky Wheel*, and replace my ineffective complaining with constructive action. "Write a book!" they said. "Distill the information and tell people what they need to know!" they said. So I did. Of course, their duties did not end there, as their encouragement and support was invaluable throughout. Michelle Tessler is truly an amazing agent and I am incredibly fortunate to work with her. My brother Gil, who is also my identical twin, loves, supports, encourages, motivates, and inspires me every day. He has always been the first to read and comment on every word I write, and I could not have written this book without him.

My editors at Hudson Street Press, Caroline Sutton and Brittney Ross, have been enthusiastic, responsive, and supportive from the very inception of this project when Caroline pushed me to find the right frame for the book. Every suggestion they made has been spot-on and their editorial comments have been straightforward, useful, and extremely constructive.

My readers invested a great amount of time and effort to make comments and suggestions that significantly improved the manuscript. I am extremely grateful to Maayan Klein, Yael Merkel, and my dear colleague Dr. Jennifer Hofert for their invaluable professional perspectives. Richard Leff, Frank Anderson, James A. Barraclough, and especially Danny Klein had wonderfully useful and well-organized suggestions. Jessica Rackman went above and beyond the call of duty and took time out of her incredibly busy schedule to give page-by-page comments that were insightful, encouraging, and incredibly helpful as always.

I would like to thank my family and close friends for being enthusiastic, supportive, and extremely patient as I worked on the book, and especially for tolerating me responding to their phone calls and texts with "Writing, can't talk," for so many months.

I owe much to my patients who were willing to try new techniques and emotional first aid treatments when I suggested them, who provided useful and insightful feedback about the work we were doing, and whose openness, trust, hard work, and dedication to their own mental health and emotional well-being I deeply appreciate and respect. I disguised the names and identifying information of people I used as case studies but you know who you are and I'm incredibly grateful to you for serving as examples to me and hopefully to many readers for how employing emotional first aid treatments can truly help us heal, grow, and better our lives in every way.

Notes

Chapter 1: Rejection

5   But when psychologists investigated this very situation: K. D. Williams, "Ostracism," *Annual Review of Psychology* 28 (2007): 425–52.

6   when psychologists asked people to compare the pain of rejection: Ibid.; Z. Chen, K. D. Williams, J. Fitness, and N. C. Newton, "When hurt will not heal: Exploring the capacity to relive social and physical pain," *Psychological Science* 19 (2008): 789–95.

6   The answer lies in our evolutionary past: G. MacDonald and M. R. Leary, "Why does social exclusion hurt? The relationship between social and physical pain," *Psychology Bulletin* 131 (2005): 202–23.

6   brains developed an early-warning system: K. D. Williams and L. Zadro, "Ostracism: The indiscriminate early detection system," in *The Social Outcast: Ostracism, Social Exclusion, Rejection, and Bullying*, edited by K. D. Williams and W. Von Hippel (New York: Psychology Press, 2005), 19–34.

6   the very same brain regions get activated when we experience rejection: N. I. Eisenberger, M. D. Lieberman, and K. D. Williams, "Does rejection hurt? An fMRI study of social exclusion," *Science* 302 (2003): 290–92.

6   when scientists give people acetaminophen (Tylenol): N. C. DeWall, G. McDonald, G. D. Webster, C. L. Masten, R. F. Baumeister, C. Powell, D. Combs, D. R. Schurtz, T. F. Stillman, D. M. Tice, and N.

L. Eisenberger, "Acetaminophen reduces social pain," *Psychological Science* 21 (2010): 931–37.

7   finding out the rejection wasn't even "real": L. Zadro, K. D. Williams, and R. Richardson, "How low can you go? Ostracism by a computer lowers belonging, control, self-esteem, and meaningful existence," *Journal of Experimental Social Psychology* 40 (2004): 560–67.

7   people who'd excluded them were members of the Ku Klux Klan: K. Gonsalkorale and K. D. Williams, "The KKK won't let me play: Ostracism even by a despised outgroup hurts," *European Journal of Social Psychology* 37 (2007): 1176–86.

7   replacing the cyber*ball* with an animated cyber*bomb*: I. Van Beest, K. D. Williams, and E. Van Dijk, "Cyberbomb: Effects of being ostracized from a death game," *Group Processes and Intergroup Relations* (2011): 1–16.

8   Rejections impact our ability to use sound logic: R. F. Baumeister, J. M. Twenge, and C. K. Nuss, "Effects of social exclusion on cognitive processes: Anticipated aloneness reduces intelligent thought," *Journal of Personality and Social Psychology* 83 (2002): 817–27; R. F. Baumeister and C. N. DeWall, "Inner disruption following social exclusion: Reduced intelligent thought and self-regulation failure," in *The Social Outcast: Ostracism, Social Exclusion, Rejection, and Bullying,* edited by K. D. Williams and W. Von Hippel (New York: Psychology Press, 2005), 53–73.

8   Rejections often trigger anger and aggressive impulses: M. R. Leary, J. M. Twenge, and E. Quinlivan, "Interpersonal rejection as a determinant of anger and aggression," *Personality and Social Psychology Review* 10 (2006): 111–32.

10   In 2001 the office of the surgeon general of the United States issued a report: Office of the Surgeon General 2001 *Youth Violence: A report of the Surgeon General, U.S. Department of Health and Human Services.* http://www.mentalhealth.org/youthviolence/default.asp.

10   also play a huge role in violence between romantic partners: G. W. Barnard, H. Vera, M. I. Vera, and G. Newman, "Till death do us part: A study of spouse murder," *Bulletin of the American Academy of Psychiatry and the Law* 10 (1982): 271–80.

10   Studies of school shootings: M. R. Leary, R. M. Kowalski, L. Smith, and S. Phillips, "Teasing, rejection, and violence: Case studies of the school shootings," *Aggressive Behavior* 29 (2003): 202–14.

10–11 In fact, the mere act of recalling a previous rejection: L. Vandevelde and M. Miyahara, "Impact of group rejections from a physical activity on physical self-esteem among university students," *Social Psychology of Education* 8 (2005): 65–81.

13   we are wired with a fundamental need to feel accepted by others: R. F. Baumeister and M. R. Leary, "The need to belong: Desire for interpersonal attachments as a fundamental human motivation," *Psychological Bulletin* 117 (1995): 497–529.

21   One aspect receiving increased attention from scientists: N. L. Penhaligon, W. R. Louis, and S. L. D. Restubog, "Emotional anguish at work: The mediating role of perceived rejection on workgroup mistreatment and affective outcomes," *Journal of Occupational Health Psychology* 14 (2009): 34–45.

23   One of the best ways to mitigate the hurt rejection causes: D. K. Sherman and G. L. Cohen, "The psychology of self-defense: Self-affirmation theory," in *Advances in Experimental Social Psychology*, Vol. 38, edited by M. P. Zanna (San Diego, CA: Academic Press, 2006): 183–242.

28   In one study, even a brief exchange with a friendly experimenter: J. M. Twenge, L. Zhang, K. R. Catanese, B. Dolan-Pascoe, L. F. Lyche, and R. F. Baumeister, "Replenishing connectedness: Reminders of social activity reduce aggression after social exclusion," *British Journal of Social Psychology* 46 (2007): 205–24.

28   In another, instant messaging online with an unfamiliar peer: E. F. Gross, "Logging on, bouncing back: An experimental investigation of online communication following social exclusion," *Developmental Psychology* 45 (2009): 1787–93.

28   Estimating visceral and physical pain: N. L. Nordgren, K. Banas, and G. MacDonald, "Empathy gaps for social pain: Why people underestimate the pain of social suffering," *Journal of Personality and Social Psychology* 100 (2011): 120–28.

29   A recent and compelling study found that teachers: Ibid.

29   Seeking support from members of our group after being the target of discrimination: S. Noh and V. Kasper, "Perceived discrimination and depression: Moderating effects of coping, acculturation, and ethnic support," *American Journal of Public Health* 93 (2003): 232–38.

30   Cancer patients and those with other illnesses: S. E. Taylor, R. L. Falke, S. J. Shoptaw, and R. R. Lichtman, "Social support, support groups, and the cancer patient," *Journal of Consulting and Clinical Psychology* 54 (1986): 608–15.

31 Social snacking: W. L. Gardner, C. L. Pickett, and M. Knowles, "Social snacking and shielding: Using social symbols, selves, and surrogates in the service of belonging needs," in *The Social Outcast: Ostracism, Social Exclusion, Rejection, and Bullying*, edited by K. D. Williams and W. Von Hippel (New York: Psychology Press, 2005), 227–42.

Chapter 2: Loneliness

37 The 2010 U.S. Census: http://www.census.gov/newsroom/releases /archives/families_households/cb10-174.html.

38 What determines our loneliness is not the quantity of our relationships: J. T. Cacioppo and L. C. Hawkley, "People thinking about people: The vicious cycle of being a social outcast in one's own mind," in *The Social Outcast: Ostracism, Social Exclusion, Rejection, and Bullying*, edited by K. D. Williams and W. Von Hippel (New York: Psychology Press, 2005), 91–108.

38 it is also associated with clinical depression, suicidal thoughts: C. M. Masi, H. Chen, L. C. Hawkley, and J. T. Cacioppo, "A meta-analysis of interventions to reduce loneliness," *Personality and Social Psychology Review* 15(3) (2011): 219–66.

38 More important, loneliness has an alarming effect on our general health: Ibid.

38 otherwise healthy college students: S. D. Pressman, S. Cohen, G. E. Miller, A. Barkin, and B. Rabin, "Loneliness, social network size, and immune response to influenza vaccination in college freshmen," *Health Psychology*, 24(3) (2005): 297–306.

39 just as large a risk factor for our long-term physical health as cigarette smoking: J. Holt-Lunstad, T. B. Smith, and J. B. Layton, "Social relationships and mortality risk: A meta-analytic review," *Public Library of Science Medicine* 7 (2010): 1–20.

39 loneliness is contagious: J. T. Cacioppo, J. H. Fowler, and N. A. Christakis, "Alone in the crowd: The structure and spread of loneliness in a large social network," *Journal of Personality and Social Psychology* 97 (2009): 977–91.

41 Over 40 percent of adults will suffer from loneliness in their lifetime: L. C. Hawkley and J. T. Cacioppo, "Loneliness matters: A theoretical and empirical review of consequences and mechanisms," *Annals of Behavioral Medicine* 40 (2010): 218–27.

43–44 simply asking college students to recall a time in their life when they felt lonely: R. F. Baumeister, J. M. Twenge, and C. K. Nuss, "Effects of social exclusion on cognitive processes: Anticipated aloneness reduces intelligent thought," *Journal of Personality and Social Psychology* 83 (2002): 817–27.

44 Another study videotaped students as they interacted with a friend: S. Duck, K. Pond, and G. Leatham, "Loneliness and the evaluation of relational events," *Journal of Social and Personal Relationships* 11 (1994): 253–76.

44 lonely people are easily recognizable to others: K. J. Rotenberg and J. Kmill, "Perception of lonely and non-lonely persons as a function of individual differences in loneliness," *Journal of Social and Personal Relationships* 9 (1992): 325–30.

44 Lonely people are often seen as less attractive: S. Lau and G. E. Gruen, "The social stigma of loneliness: Effect of target person's and perceiver's sex," *Personality and Social Psychology Bulletin* 18 (1992): 182–89.

44 physical attractiveness provides no immunity: J. T. Cacioppo and L. C. Hawkley, "People thinking about people: The vicious cycle of being a social outcast in one's own mind," in *The Social Outcast: Ostracism, Social Exclusion, Rejection, and Bullying*, edited by K. D. Williams and W. Von Hippel (New York: Psychology Press, 2005), 91–108.

46 loneliness also drives us into cycles of self-protection: Ibid.

62 The following three errors are the most important: N. Epley and E. M. Caruso, "Perspective taking: Misstepping into others' shoes," in *Handbook of Imagination and Mental Simulation*, edited by K. D. Markman, W. M. P. Klein, and J. A. Suhr (New York: Psychology Press, 2009) 295–309.

63 we typically give almost exclusive priority to whether *we* find the joke funny: Ibid.

63 sincere versus sarcastic phone messages: N. Eply, C. Morewedge, and B. Keysar, "Perspective taking as egocentric anchoring and adjustment," *Journal of Personality and Social Psychology* 87 (2004): 327–39.

64 Once we consider how this dynamic might play out in gift-giving scenarios: D. Lerouge and L. Warlop, "Why is it so hard to predict our partner's product preferences: The effects of target familiarity on prediction accuracy," *Journal of Consumer Research* 33 (2006): 393–402.

64 Unfortunately, it is the couple's very familiarity: W. B. Swann and M.

J. Gill, "Confidence and accuracy in person perception: Do we know what we think we know about our relationship partners?" *Journal of Personality and Social Psychology* 73 (1997): 747–57.

65 Women should give men the space and leeway to express their thoughts: J. Flora and C. Segrin, "Affect and behavioral involvement in spousal complaints and compliments," *Journal of Family Psychology* 14 (000): 641–57.

67 Surveys of college students: S. H. Konrath, E. H. O'Brien, and C. Hsing, "Changes in dispositional empathy in American college students over time: A meta-analysis," *Personality and Social Psychology Review* 15 (2011): 180–98.

71 The Internet allows us to connect to people: T. Fokkema and K. Knipscheer, "Escape loneliness by going digital: A quantitative and qualitative evaluation of a Dutch experiment in using ECT to overcome loneliness among older adults," *Aging and Mental Health* 11 (2007): 496–504.

72 online dating is now the second most common way couples meet: E. J. Finkel, P. W. Eastwick, B. R. Karney, H. T. Reis, and S. Sprecher, "Online dating: A critical analysis from the perspective of psychological science," *Psychological Science in the Public Interest* 13 (2012): 3–66.

72 Helping others reduces feelings of loneliness: M. Cattan, N. Kime, and M. Bagnall, "The use of telephone befriending in low level support for socially isolated older people–an evaluation," *Health and Social Care in the Community* 19 (2011): 198–206.

73 Those who spent time alone with a dog: M. R. Banks and W. A. Banks, "The effects of group and individual animal-assisted therapy on loneliness in residents of long-term care facilities," *Anthrozoos* 18 (2005): 396–408; interview with the study's author: http://www.slu.edu/readstory/more/6391.

Chapter 3: Loss and Trauma

76 a phenomenon known as *post-traumatic growth*: R. G. Tedeschi and L. G. Calhoun, "Posttraumatic growth: Conceptual foundations and empirical evidence," *Psychological Inquiry* 15 (2004):1–18.

78 We often move past the most acute stages of grief and adjustment after six months: J. M. Holland, J. M. Currier, and R. A. Neimeyer, "Meaning reconstruction in the first two years of bereavement: The role of sense-making and benefit-finding," *Omega* 53 (2006): 175–91.

80   The challenge of redefining ourselves: R. A. Neimeyer, "Restorying loss: Fostering growth in the posttraumatic narrative," in *Handbook of Posttraumatic Growth: Research and Practice*, edited by L. Calhoun and R. Tedeschi (Mahwah, NJ: Lawrence Erlbaum, 2006), 68–80.

81   loss and trauma can challenge our basic assumptions about the world: R. Janoff-Bulman and C. M. Frantz, "The impact of trauma on meaning: From meaningless world to meaningful life," in *The Transformation of Meaning in Psychological Therapies: Integrating Theory and Practice*, edited by M. Power and C. R. Brewin (Sussex, England: Wiley, 1997), 91–106.

82   Yet, the sooner we reconstruct our worldviews: Ibid.

87   Indeed, a wave of recent research has demonstrated that many of our most cherished notions . . . the five stages of grief: J. M. Holland and R. A. Neimeyer, "An examination of stage theory of grief among individuals bereaved by natural and violent causes: A meaning-oriented contribution," *Omega* 61 (2010): 103–20.

87   Specifically, the mere act of recalling an event changes our actual memory: see Jonah Lehrer's article from February 2012 in *Wired*: http://www.wired.com/magazine/2012/02/ff_forgettingpill/all/1.

87   there is no "right" way to cope with the aftermath of loss and trauma: M. D. Seery, R. C. Silver, E. A. Holman, W. A. Ence, and T. Q. Chu, "Expressing thoughts and feelings following a collective trauma: Immediate responses to 9/11 predict negative outcomes in a national sample," *Journal of Consulting and Clinical Psychology* 76 (2008): 657–67.

88   One online study began following over two thousand people in, as it happened, August 2001: Ibid.

94   Finding meaning was a crucial factor in recovery: L. C. Park, "Making sense of the meaning literature: An integrative review of meaning making and its effects on adjustment to stressful life events," *Psychological Bulletin* 136 (2010): 257–301.

95   Scientists who examined how people go about finding meaning: J. M. Holland, J. M. Currier, R. A. Neimeyer, "Meaning reconstruction in the first two years of bereavement: The role of sense-making and benefit-finding," *Omega* 53 (2006): 175–91.

97   Specifically, numerous studies demonstrate that asking ourselves *why* events happened: O. Ayduk and E. Kross, "From a distance: Implications of spontaneous self-distancing for adaptive self-reflection," *Journal of Personality and Social Psychology* 98 (2010): 809–29.

98   Rather than eliciting a sense of randomness: L. J. Kray, L. G. George, K. A. Liljenquist, A. D. Galinsky, P. E. Tetlock, and N. J. Roese, "From what *might* have been to what *must* have been: Counterfactual thinking creates meaning," *Journal of Personality and Social Psychology* 98 (2011): 106–18.

100   it is the real-world application of these benefits: S. E. Hobfoll, B. J. Hall, D. Canetti-Nisim, S. Galea, R. J. Johnson, and P. A. Palmieri, "Refining our understanding of traumatic growth in the face of terrorism: Moving from meaning cognitions to doing what is meaningful," *Applied Psychology: An International Review* 56 (2006): 345–66.

Chapter 4: Guilt

103   Studies estimate that people experience roughly two hours a day of mild guilt: R. F. Baumeister, H. T. Reis, and P. A. E. G. Delespaul, "Subjective and experimental correlates of guilt in daily life," *Personality and Social Psychology Bulletin* 21 (1995): 1256–68.

103   Indeed, guilt's primary function is to signal to us: Ibid.

105   Rather, unhealthy guilt occurs primarily in situations involving our relationships: R. F. Baumeister, A. M. Stillwell, and T. F. Heatherton, "Guilt: An interpersonal approach," *Psychological Bulletin* 115 (1994): 243–67.

105   we're much less skilled at rendering effective apologies: R. Fehr and M. J. Gelfand, "When apologies work: How matching apology components to victims' self-construals facilitates forgiveness," *Organizational Behavior and Human Decision Processes* 113 (2010): 37–50.

110   Guilt makes many of us experience mental and intellectual disruptions: M. J. A. Wohl, T. A. Pychyl, and S. H. Bennett, "I forgive myself, now I can study: How self-forgiveness for procrastinating can reduce future procrastination," *Personality and Individual Differences* 48 (2010): 803–8.

111   In one study involving regular college students: Y. Zemack-Rugar, J. R. Bettman, and G. J. Fitzsimons, "The effects of nonconsciously priming emotion concepts on behavior," *Journal of Personality and Social Psychology* 93 (2007): 927–39.

112   Some of us even resort to punishing ourselves: R. M. A. Nelissen, "Guilt-induced self-punishment as a sign of remorse," *Social Psychological and Personality Science* 3 (2012): 139–44.

112   people who were made to feel guilty by depriving a fellow student of lottery tickets: Ibid.

112 keep their hands submerged in freezing water: B. Bastian, J. Jetten, and F. Fasoli, "Cleansing the soul by hurting the flesh: The guilt-reducing effect of pain," *Psychological Science* 22 (2011): 334–35.

113 known as the *Dobby effect*: R. M. A. Nelissen and M. Zeelenberg, "When guilt evokes self-punishment: Evidence for the existence of a Dobby effect," *Emotion* 9 (2009): 118–22.

115 their most common theme is one of interpersonal neglect: R. F. Baumeister, A. M. Stillwell, and T. F. Heatherton, "Personal narratives about guilt: Role in action control and interpersonal relationships," *Basic and Applied Social Psychology* 17 (1995): 173–98.

116 In one survey, 33 percent of people indicated they felt resentful: Ibid.

120 The most effective way to treat unresolved guilt: C. E. Cryder, S. Springer, and C. K. Morewedge, "Guilty feelings, targeted actions," *Personality and Social Psychology Bulletin* 38 (2012): 607–18.

121 this simple transaction of apology and forgiveness goes awry: R. Fehr and M. J. Gelfand, "When apologies work: How matching apology components to victims' self-construals facilitates forgiveness," *Organizational Behavior and Human Decision Processes* 113 (2010): 37–50.

122 Scientists have discovered three additional components: Ibid.

129 self-forgiveness reduces feelings of guilt: J. H. Hall and F. D. Fincham, "Self-forgiveness: The stepchild of forgiveness research," *Journal of Social and Clinical Psychology* 24 (2005): 621–37.

129 people who forgave themselves for procrastinating: M. J. A. Wohl, T. A. Pychyl, and S. H. Bennett, "I forgive myself, now I can study: How self-forgiveness for procrastinating can reduce future procrastination," *Personality and Individual Differences* 48 (2010): 803–8.

133 Studies have found that both atonement and reparations: H. Xu, L. Beue, and R. Shankland, "Guilt and guiltless: An integrative review," *Social and Personality Psychology Compass* 5 (2011): 440–57; J. J. Exline, B. L. Root, S. Yadavalli, A. M. Martin, and M. L. Fisher, "Reparative behaviors and self-forgiveness: Effects of a laboratory-based exercise," *Self and Identity* 10 (2011): 101–26.

Chapter 5: Rumination

142 linked to a wide range of threats to our psychological and physical health: for a review see S. Nolen-Hoeksema, B. E. Wisco, and S. Lyubomirsky, "Rethinking rumination," *Perspectives on Psychological Science* 3 (2008) 400–424.

144 Scientists asked regular people on a regular day to reflect: Ibid.

146 researchers gave college students at risk for depression: G. J. Haeffel, "When self-help is no help: Traditional cognitive skills training does not prevent depressive symptoms in people who ruminate," *Behaviour Research and Therapy* 28 (2010): 152–57.

148 Angry feelings activate our stress responses and our cardiovascular systems: B. J. Bushman, A. M. Bonacci, W. C. Pederson, E. A. Vasquez, and M. Norman, "Chewing on it can chew you up: Effects of rumination on triggered displaced aggression," *Journal of Personality and Social Psychology* 88 (2005): 969–83.

149 one study put people through a frustrating experience: Ibid.

149 Rumination involves such intense brooding: S. Nolen-Hoeksema, B. E. Wisco, and S. Lyubomirsky, "Rethinking rumination," *Perspectives on Psychological Science* 3 (2008): 400–424.

150 For example, women with strong ruminative tendencies: S. Lyubomirsky, F. Kasri, O. Chang, and I. Chung, "Ruminative response styles and delay of seeking diagnosis for breast cancer symptoms," *Journal of Social and Clinical Psychology* 25 (2006): 276–304.

150 Other studies found that cancer and coronary patients with ruminative tendencies: P. Aymanns, S. H. Filipp, and T. Klauer, "Family support and coping with cancer: Some determinants and adaptive correlates," *British Journal of Social Psychology* 34 (1995): 107–24.

154 the visual perspective we use when going over painful experiences: O. Ayduk and E. Kross, "From a distance: Implications of spontaneous self-distancing for adaptive self-reflection," *Journal of Personality and Social Psychology* 98 (2010): 809–29.

155 In addition, their blood pressure was less reactive: E. Kross and O. Ayduk, "Facilitating adaptive emotional analysis: Distinguishing distanced-analysis of depressive experiences from immersed-analysis and distraction," *Personality and Social Psychology Bulletin* 34 (2008): 924–38.

158 In now-classic experiments: D. M. Wegner, D. J. Schneider, S. R. Carter III, and T. L. White, "Paradoxical effects of thought suppression," *Journal of Personality and Social Psychology* 53 (1987): 5–13.

158 distraction has proven to be a far more effective weapon: S. Nolen-Hoeksema, B. E. Wisco, and S. Lyubomirsky, "Rethinking rumination," *Perspectives on Psychological Science* 3 (2008): 400–424.

159 imagining the layout of our local supermarket: Ibid.

161 the verdict of all such studies has been virtually unanimous: B. J. Bushman, "Does venting anger feed or extinguish the flame? Ca-

tharsis, rumination, distraction, anger, and aggressive responding," *Personality and Social Psychology Bulletin* 28 (2002): 724–31.

162 The most effective strategy for regulating emotions such as anger: O. P. John and J. J. Gross, "Healthy and unhealthy emotion regulation: Personality processes, individual differences, and lifespan development," *Journal of Personality* 72 (2004): 1301–33.

165 A series of recent studies examined the power of prayer: R. H. Bremner, S. L. Koole, and B. J. Bushman, "Pray for those who mistreat you: Effects of prayer on anger and aggression," *Personality and Social Psychology Bulletin* 37 (2011): 830–37.

Chapter 6: Failure

174 Participants were asked to kick an American football: J. K. Witt and T. Dorsch, "Kicking to bigger uprights: Field goal kicking performance influences perceived size," *Perception* 38 (2009): 1328–40.

177 Another common New Year resolution error is goal bingeing: E. J. Masicampo and R. F. Baumeister, "Consider it done! Plan making can eliminate the cognitive effects of unfulfilled goals," *Journal of Personality and Social Psychology* 10 (2011): 667–83.

179 Failures sap our confidence, our motivation, and our hope: L. D. Young and J. M. Allin, "Persistence of learned helplessness in humans," *Journal of General Psychology* 113 (1986): 81–88.

181 Failure can also be very misleading: Ibid.

183 Test anxiety is especially problematic: R. Hembree, "Correlates, Causes, Effects, and Treatment of Test Anxiety," *Review of Educational Research* 58 (1988): 47–77.

183 consider what happens when girls take math tests: S. Spencer, C. M. Steele, and D. M. Quinn, "Stereotype threat and women's math performance," *Journal of Experimental Social Psychology* 35 (1999): 4–28.

186 Fear of failure makes many of us engage in all manner of self-handicapping behaviors: A. J. Martin, H. W. Marsh, and R. L. Debus, "Self-handicapping and defensive pessimism: A model of self-protection from a longitudinal perspective," *Contemporary Educational Psychology* 28 (2003): 1–36.

187 Fear of Failure in Families: A. J. Elliot and T. M. Thrash, "The intergenerational transmission of fear of failure," *Personality and Social Psychology Bulletin* 30 (2004): 957–71.

189 Choking is based on a similar dynamic: M. S. DeCaro, R. D. Thomas,

N. B. Albert, and S. L. Beilock, "Choking under pressure: Multiple routes to skill failure," *Journal of Experimental Psychology: General* 140 (2011): 390–406.

191 Further, providing social and emotional support alone: N. Bolger and D. Amarel, "Effects of social support visibility on adjustment to stress: Experimental evidence," *Journal of Personality and Social Psychology* 92 (2007): 458–75.

194 a surprising aspect about failure: K. M. Sheldon, N. Abad, Y. Ferguson, A. Gunz, L. Houser-Marko, C. P. Nichols, and S. Lyubomirsky, "Persistent pursuit of need-satisfying goals leads to increased happiness: A 6-month experimental longitudinal study," *Motivation and Emotion* 34 (2010): 39–48.

196 One study illustrated this point with a group of seniors: C. A. Sarkisian, B. Weiner, C. Davis, and T. R. Prohaska, "Pilot test of attributional retraining intervention to raise walking levels in sedentary older adults," *Journal of the American Geriatric Society* 55 (2007): 1842–46.

196 Since it is best to pursue one goal at a time: R. Koestner, N. Lekes, T. A. Powers, and E. Chicoine, "Attaining personal goals: Self-concordance plus implementation intentions equals success," *Journal of Personality and Social Psychology* 83 (2002): 231–44.

197 defining your goal in ways that are personally meaningful: R. M. Ryan, G. C. Williams, H. Patrick, and E. Deci, "Self-determination theory and physical activity: The dynamics of motivation in development and wellness," *Hellenic Journal of Psychology* 6 (2009): 107–24.

200 For example, asking women intending to get a breast cancer exam: S. Orbell, S. Hodgkins, and P. Sheeran, "Implementation intentions and the theory of planned behavior," *Personality and Social Psychology Bulletin* 23 (1997): 945–54.

206 In studies, seeing the humor: J. Stoeber and D. P. Janssen, "Perfectionism and coping with daily failures: Positive reframing helps achieve satisfaction at the end of the day," *Anxiety, Stress, and Coping* 24 (2011): 477–97.

207 Jim Short: http://www.jokes.com/funny/jim+short/jim-short--not-a-loser.

209 Whistle While You Choke: S. Beilock, *Choke: What the Secrets of the Brain Reveal about Success and Failure at Work and at Play* (New York: Free Press, 2010).

210 In a series of recent studies, four hundred seventh graders: G. L.

Cohen, J. Garcia, V. Purdie-Vaughns, N. Apfel, and P. Brzustoski, "Recursive processes in self-affirmation: Intervening to close the minority achievement gap," *Science* 324 (2009): 400–403.

211 college women taking physics: A. Miyake, L. E. Kost-Smith, N. D. Finkelstein, S. J. Pollock, G. L. Cohen, and T. A. Ito, "Reducing the gender achievement gap in college science: A classroom study of values affirmation," *Science* 330 (2010): 1234–37.

Chapter 7: Low Self-Esteem

213 the overwhelming majority of self-esteem programs simply don't work: W. B. Swann, C. Chang-Schneider, and K. L. McClarty, "Do people's self-views matter? Self-concept and self-esteem in everyday life," *American Psychologist* 62 (2007): 84–94.

213 Further, people with low self-esteem are often less happy: for a brief review see K. D. Neff, "Self-compassion, self-esteem, and well-being," *Social and Personality Psychology Compass* 5 (2011): 1–12.

214 Having very high self-esteem has its own set of pitfalls: Ibid.

214 there has been a general "grade inflation" in our collective self-esteem: N. Maxwell and J. Lopus, "The Lake Wobegon effect in student self-reported data," *American Economic Review Papers and Proceedings* 84 (1994): 201–5.

215 people with higher self-esteem believe they are more attractive: E. Diener, B. Wolsic, and F. Fujita, "Physical attractiveness and subjective well-being," *Journal of Personality and Social Psychology* 69 (1995): 120–29.

217 people with low self-esteem also rated their own groups negatively: J. Crocker, and I. Schwartz, "Prejudice and ingroup favoritism in a minimal intergroup situation: Effects of self-esteem and threat," *Journal of Personality and Social Psychology* 52 (1987): 907–16.

217 how we feel about ourselves in specific domains of our lives: M. Rosenberg, C. Schooler, C. Schoenbach, and F. Rosenberg, "Global self-esteem and specific self-esteem," *American Sociological Review* 60 (1995): 141–56.

219 having higher self-esteem . . . can make us more psychologically resilient: J. Greenberg, S. Solomon, T. Pyszczynski, A. Rosenblatt, J. Burling, D. Lyon, L. Simon, and E. Pinel, "Why do people need self-esteem? Converging evidence that self-esteem serves an anxiety-buffering function," *Journal of Personality and Social Psychology* 63 (1992): 913–22.

219 people with low self-esteem experience rejection as more painful: K. Onoda, Y. Okamoto, K. Nakashima, H. Nittono, S. Yoshimura, S. Yamawaki, and M. Ura, "Does low self-esteem enhance social pain? The relationship between trait self-esteem and anterior cingulate cortex activation induced by ostracism," *Social Cognitive and Affective Neuroscience* 5 (2010): 385–91.

219 We are also more vulnerable to failure when our self-esteem is low: J. D. Brown, "High self-esteem buffers negative feedback: Once more with feeling," *Cognition and Emotion* 24 (2010): 1389–1404.

220 We also respond to stress much less effectively: S. C. Lee-Flynn, G. Pomaki, A. DeLongis, J. C. Biesanz, and E. Puterman, "Daily cognitive appraisals, daily affect, and long-term depressive symptoms: The role of self-esteem and self-concept clarity in the stress process," *Personality and Social Psychology Bulletin* 37 (2011): 255–68.

221 Stress can substantially weaken our willpower: L. Schwabe, O. Höffken, M. Tegenthoff, and O. T. Wolf, "Preventing the stress-induced shift from goal-directed to habit action with a β-adrenergic antagonist," *Journal of Neuroscience* 31 (2011): 17317–25.

222 The good news is that manipulations to boost self-esteem: for a review see S. E. Taylor and A. L. Stanton, "Coping resources, coping processes, and mental health," *Annual Review of Clinical Psychology* 2 (2007): 377–401.

222 low self-esteem limits our ability to benefit from positive ones: R. A. Josephs, J. Bosson, and C. G. Jacobs, "Self-esteem maintenance processes: Why low self-esteem may be resistant to change," *Personality and Social Psychology Bulletin* 29 (2003): 920–33.

224 we believe the program helped us improve when it actually did not: A. R. Pratkanis, J. Eskenazie, and A. G. Greenwald, "What you expect is what you believe (but not necessarily what you get): A test of the effectiveness of subliminal self-help audiotapes," *Basic and Applied Social Psychology* 15 (2010): 251–76.

225 Recent research into the usefulness of positive affirmations: J. V. Wood, W. Q. E. Perunovie, and J. W. Lee, "Positive self-statements: Power for some, peril for others," *Psychological Science* 20 (2009): 860–66.

226 One study found that poorly performing college students: D. R. Forsyth, N. K. Lawrence, J. L. Burnette, and R. F. Baumeister, "Attempting to improve academic performance of struggling college students by bolstering their self-esteem: The intervention that backfired," *Journal of Social and Clinical Psychology* 26 (2007): 447–59.

226 Another found that when college students with low self-esteem had roommates: W. B. Swann and B. W. Pelham, "Who wants out when the going gets good?" *Journal of Self and Identity* 1 (2002): 219–33.

227 praising people with low self-esteem for being considerate boyfriends or girlfriends: S. L. Murray, J. G. Holmes, G. MacDonald, and P. C. Ellsworth, "Through the looking glass darkly? When self-doubts turn into relationship insecurities," *Journal of Personality and Social Psychology* 75 (1998): 1459–80.

228 people with low self-esteem tend to speak up less: R. F. Baumeister, J. D. Campbell, J. I. Krueger, and K. D. Vohs, "Does high self-esteem cause better performance, interpersonal success, happiness, or healthier lifestyles? *Psychological Science in the Public Interest* 4 (2003): 1–44.

234 self-compassion was found to buffer incoming college students: M. L. Terry, M. R. Leary, and S. Mehta, "Self-compassion as a buffer against homesickness, depression, and dissatisfaction in the transition to college," *Self and Identity*, in press (2012).

235 quicker emotional recoveries from separation and divorce: D. A. Sbarra, H. L. Smith, and M. R. Mehl, "When leaving your ex, love yourself: Observational ratings of self-compassion predict the course of emotional recovery following marital separation," *Psychological Sciences* 23 (2012): 261–69.

235 recovered more quickly from failure and rejection experiences: K. D. Neff, "Self-compassion, self-esteem, and well-being," *Social and Personality Psychology Compass* 5 (2011): 1–12.

237 Reminding ourselves that we have significant worth: C. R. Critcher, D. Dunning, and D. A. Armor, "When self-affirmations reduce defensiveness: Timing is key," *Personality and Social Psychology Bulletin* 36 (2010): 947–59.

240 we can bolster our "relationship self-esteem": D. A. Stinson, C. Logel, S. Shepherd, and M. P. Zanna, "Rewriting the self-fulfilling prophecy of social rejection: Self-affirmation improves relational security and social behavior up to 2 months later," *Psychological Science* 22 (2011): 1145–49.

242 feelings of personal empowerment must be supported by evidence: L. B. Cattanco and A. R. Chapman, "The process of empowerment: A model for use in research and practice," *American Psychologist* 65 (2010): 646–59.

248 self-control actually functions more like a muscle: R. F. Baumeister, K. D. Vohs, and D. M. Tice, "The strength model of self-control," *Current Directions in Psychological Science* 16 (2007): 351–55.

249 Scientists have investigated several such "willpower workouts": M. Muraven, "Building self-control strength: Practicing self-control leads to improved self-control performance," *Journal of Experimental Social Psychology* 46 (2010): 465–68.

251 Half of them received lemonade sweetened with sugar: M. T. Gailliot, R. F. Baumeister, C. N. DeWall, J. K. Maner, E. A. Plant, D. M. Tice, L. E. Brewer, and B. J. Schmeichel, "Self-control relies on glucose as a limited energy source: Willpower is more than a metaphor," *Journal of Personality and Social Psychology* 92 (2007): 325–36.

251 Sleep and rest also have a big impact on our willpower's ability to function: R. F. Baumeister, "Ego-depletion and self-control failure: An energy model of the self's executive function," *Self and Identity* 1 (2002): 129–36.

251 The average person spends three to four hours a day exerting some form of willpower: W. Hofmann, R. F. Baumeister, G. Förster, and K. D. Vohs, "Everyday temptations: An experience sampling study on desire, conflict, and self-control," *Journal of Personality and Social Psychology* 102 (2012): 1318–35.

252 The best way to manage temptations is not to overestimate our ability to manage them: G. Lowenstein, "Out of control: Visceral influences on behavior," *Organizational Behavior and Human Decision Processes* 65 (1996): 272–92; L. F. Nordgren, F. van Harreveld, and J. van der Pligt, "The restraint bias: How the illusion of self-restraint promotes impulsive behavior," *Psychological Science* 20 (2009): 1523–28.

253 researchers in one study gave moviegoers stale popcorn: D. T. Neal, W. Wood, M. Wu, and D. Kurlander, "The pull of the past: When do habits persist despite conflict with motives?" *Personality and Social Psychology Bulletin* 37 (2011): 1428–37.

Index